The

The NHL's Mistake by the Lake

A History of the Cleveland Barons

GARY WEBSTER

McFarland & Company, Inc., Publishers

Jefferson, North Carolina

ISBN (print) 978-1-4766-8584-7
ISBN (ebook) 978-1-4766-4400-4

LIBRARY OF CONGRESS AND BRITISH LIBRARY
CATALOGUING DATA ARE AVAILABLE

Library of Congress Control Number 2021042692

Front cover image: Barons goaltender Gilles Meloche is
congratulated by teammates Al MacAdam (25) and Walt McKechnie
after a rare victory at the Richfield Coliseum during the 1977-78 season.
(Michael Schwartz Library, Cleveland State University)

Printed in the United States of America

*McFarland & Company, Inc., Publishers
Box 611, Jefferson, North Carolina 28640
www.mcfarlandpub.com*

Table of Contents

Introduction

This was the way it was supposed to have been.

On a Saturday night in June of 2016, almost 20,000 fans rose to their feet in Cleveland's Quicken Loans Arena after Oliver Bjorkstrand poked the puck into the opposing team's net with less than two seconds to play in the first sudden death overtime period, giving the home team a thrilling 1–0 victory and a four-game sweep of the championship finals. The crowd was the second largest in American Hockey League history, which dates back to 1935. The victory in the cup finals was the first by a hockey team representing Cleveland in 52 years.

The bedlam in Quicken Loans Arena was precisely what Mel Swig had envisioned when he and his co-owners, George Gund III and Bud Levitas, hastily moved the Oakland-based California Golden Seals of the National Hockey League to Cleveland in the summer of 1976. But the cup hoisted by the players in 2016 wasn't the Stanley Cup. It was the Calder Cup, symbolic of the championship of the American Hockey League, the sport's highest minor league. And though the players hoisting the Calder Cup wore the same red, white and black colors, they weren't the Barons of Swig, Gund and Levitas. They were the Lake Erie Monsters, who took the place of the two minor league clubs that succeeded the Barons. Swig's team lasted just two seasons in the Richfield Coliseum, the sports palace halfway between Cleveland and Akron. Swig owned the team for only the first of those seasons. It never came close to filling the Coliseum even once, as the Monsters had done in Quicken Loans Arena the night they won the Calder Cup.

The Monsters' triumphant moment should never have happened, because the Barons should never have faltered as badly as they did after relocating to Cleveland, a city with a proud hockey tradition. The 2015–2016 season should have been the franchise's 39th in northeastern Ohio, and the cup they would have been competing for would have been Lord Stanley's, the oldest prize in professional sports. But the Barons, and the NHL, departed Cleveland after two miserable seasons, leaving the city without a hockey team for 14 years. The International Hockey League transferred its Muskegon, Michigan, franchise to Cleveland in 1992. When that league folded, the AHL, of which the original Barons had been a member from 1937 until 1973, returned.

Sports writers have long observed that otherwise smart and astute businesspeople often check their acumen at the door when they purchase a professional sports team. Such was the case with Swig and Gund when they decided that they couldn't keep the Golden Seals in Oakland one more minute. A gleaming new building in northeastern Ohio beckoned, and the decision to move the team there seems to have consisted of little more than Gund, a native Clevelander, suggesting to Swig that he transfer the Golden Seals to Cleveland and Swig, after considering the suggestion for all of 30 seconds, responding, "Sure, why not?" Had Swig and Gund run the businesses that made their families rich the same way they would run the renamed Golden Seals once they arrived in Cleveland, they'd never have had the money to invest in professional hockey in the first place. They'd have been fortunate to find the money to buy a ticket to watch someone else's team play.

The Cleveland Barons of the NHL are the last major league sports franchise in North America to fold. Their demise could almost have been foretold from the moment they arrived in July of 1976. Swig and, later and to a lesser extent, Gund and his brother Gordon seemed to think that the NHL brand alone would be more than enough to attract large crowds to the Coliseum to watch an inferior product. And northeastern Ohio's hockey fans, for some reason, seemed to resent the Barons rather than welcome them.

The decade of the 1970s was a tough one for Cleveland. Jokes about the city abounded in the national media, some of them well-deserved. The Cleveland Barons were one of those jokes. This book is for northeastern Ohio hockey fans who have the stomach to relive the city's mercifully brief flirtation with the National Hockey League. And for anyone who enjoys reading about a good disaster. Because there's no other way to describe Cleveland's experience with major league hockey between July of 1976 and June of 1978. And there's no other way of describing major league hockey's experience with its Oakland/Cleveland franchise between 1967 and 1978. It was an $11 million fiasco, the last 23 months of which are revisited in detail in the pages that follow.

1

This Town Ain't Big
Enough for Both of Us

Cleveland and the National Hockey League were never meant to be. The embarrassment ... to both the league and the city ... that was the ill-fated Cleveland Barons of 1976–1978 might have been avoided if Al Sutphin hadn't been so loyal to his fellow team owners in the American Hockey League following the 1941–42 season. Sutphin's Barons had dominated the AHL, both on the ice and at the box office, since joining the league for the season of 1937–38. During the season of 1940–41, the Barons, playing in the five-year-old Cleveland Arena on Euclid Avenue at East 36th Street, had averaged 8,267 spectators per home game. That exceeded the per-game averages of both of the NHL's New York clubs, the Rangers and Americans, plus the Detroit Red Wings and the fabled Montreal Canadiens. A few years earlier, it had been rumored that Montreal's other NHL team, the Maroons, was looking to relocate to Cleveland. Instead, the Maroons simply folded. By the spring of 1942, the NHL was casting covetous glances toward Cleveland, and the Barons were listening.

Less than six months after Pearl Harbor, the Second World War had begun to affect professional sports by siphoning off manpower for the armed forces. Able-bodied athletes were enlisting in large numbers, and those who didn't volunteer were being drafted in both the United States and Canada ... with the latter providing the vast majority of the players in the National and American hockey leagues. The New York Americans were faltering both on and off the ice and would soon leave the NHL. Owners were concerned about their ability to maintain fan interest with just half a dozen teams and looked to expand by adding the AHL's Cleveland and Buffalo clubs. The Barons were the AHL's gold standard. The Bisons were properly situated geographically, being close to Detroit and Toronto (and Cleveland), and would give the NHL an even number of clubs, ensuring no one would be idle on lucrative Friday and Saturday nights, thus missing out on precious ticket (and concession) revenue.

Sutphin gave the NHL's offer serious consideration. He was convinced, however, that the loss of the Barons, especially if it was coupled with the loss of the Bisons, would wreck the American Hockey League. The Barons led the AHL in attendance regularly and were the league's top draw on the road. Sutphin had also grown accustomed to being a big fish in a relatively small pond. He wanted to elevate the Barons to major league status, but with playing talent suddenly scarce and about to become even more so, he realized his club probably wouldn't be able to dominate an expanded National Hockey League as it was dominating the American Hockey League. And Sutphin enjoyed being king of the hill. Ultimately, however, it was his loyalty to the AHL (with, perhaps, just a bit of hubris) that led him to reject the NHL's offer. He was certain that without his Barons, the young AHL would collapse. And he didn't want to be responsible for that.

The owners of the six remaining NHL clubs were said to be alternately flabbergasted by, and furious with, Sutphin's decision to stay in hockey's minor league. They couldn't believe anyone would turn down such an opportunity to compete with the best the sport had to offer. And they wouldn't forget Sutphin's rejection.

Sutphin sold the Arena and the Barons to Jim Hendy in 1949. Hendy wasn't worried about how the AHL would fare without Cleveland and applied for admission to the NHL in May of 1952. The major league still had only its original six clubs (Detroit, New York, Montreal, Boston, Toronto and Chicago) at that point. Cleveland was one of the 10 largest cities in the United States, and the Barons played in a centrally-located facility. As recently as the 1945–46 season, the Barons had averaged a sellout for every home game, packing 10,146 fans per contest into a building with just 9,739 seats. Attendance had slacked off a bit in the following years but remained robust ... especially on Saturday nights. A non-sellout on a Saturday night was a rare occurrence in the Cleveland Arena.

So certain did the Barons' acceptance into the small fraternity known as the National Hockey League seem to be that the Cleveland *Press* announced it with an eight-column, front page headline shortly after Hendy made his pitch to the league's owners. On July 2, however, the NHL's six clubs voted 3–3 on the question of admitting Cleveland as the seventh franchise. Detroit, Chicago and New York voted no. A decade after the Barons had rejected the NHL, the NHL returned the favor. Cleveland stayed in the AHL.

The dissenting teams cited lack of operating capital as one reason for rejecting Hendy and the Barons. Although the Barons had $318,000 in the bank with which to run the team, the owners of the Rangers, Red Wings and Blackhawks noted that the money had been borrowed ... a fact Hendy readily admitted. The NHL insisted that borrowed funds didn't constitute "operating capital." Borrowing the money was the only way Hendy could raise the necessary cash. He wasn't permitted to sell stock in the club to the public.

Another problem was the Arena. Although just 15 years old, it was already well on its way to becoming obsolete. Each of the NHL's franchises played in buildings that seated at least 12,000 spectators by 1952. Hendy said he could overcome the potential gap in ticket revenue by raising prices, which he felt justified in doing since the Barons would be playing in the major league. Major league hockey should cost more than minor league hockey. The NHL didn't accept Hendy's reasoning, and didn't think Cleveland's hockey fans would, either. The owners backed up their argument by pointing out that attendance in hockey across the board had declined since the coming of television.

Lastly, some of the owners and executives who'd invited Cleveland to join the NHL in the spring of 1942 were still involved with the league in 1952. They hadn't forgotten the stinging rebuff they'd gotten from Sutphin. The NHL hadn't been good enough for Cleveland in 1942. Now, Cleveland wasn't good enough for the NHL. It would stay that way in spite of repeated attempts to coax the NHL to add Cleveland for the next 20 years. The NHL would resist all expansion until 1967, when it doubled in size to 12 clubs. Cleveland wasn't one of them.

Cleveland's last effort to join the NHL was made in 1972 by Nick Mileti, the dynamic sports entrepreneur who'd purchased the Arena and the Barons in 1968. Mileti was able to convince the National Basketball Association to add a team in Cleveland for the 1970–71 season, but his pleas to the NHL fell on deaf ears. The NHL continued to expand, but it wanted no part of Cleveland or its aging and crumbling Arena. Mileti had secured an NBA team partially due to a promise that the Cavaliers would have a state-of-the-art facility in which to play within five years, and he made good on that pledge. But that wasn't enough to satisfy the NHL.

Cleveland had another option in the spring of 1972. Promoter Gary Davidson had founded the World Hockey Association to compete directly with the NHL. Unlike the AHL, Davidson's WHA would be major league ... or, at least, it claimed to be. As all new sports leagues do, the WHA would lavish money on stars of its competing league to lure them to the new one. When Mileti was turned down by the NHL, he approached Davidson and the WHA. Although the new league was already bulging at the seams with 11 clubs, it added Cleveland to the fold. The prestige of having another large market in which to sell tickets would be good for the fledgling WHA.

For some reason, Mileti believed the Barons and Crusaders could profitably coexist, even though the Barons were minor league and the Crusaders were billed from day one as finally bringing "major league" hockey to Cleveland. To prove he meant business, Mileti stunned the NHL by signing star goaltender Gerry Cheevers, who'd led the Boston Bruins to the 1972 Stanley Cup championship. Cheevers agreed to a five-year contract worth $200,000 per season. Signing Cheevers gave the Crusaders instant credibility and bolstered their claim to being "major league." The Crusaders opened the WHA's inaugural season amid a great deal of fanfare. It was inevitable that the Barons would be lost in the shuffle, and they quickly were.

Despite the fact that their club was the last to be admitted to the

After his application for an NHL expansion franchise was rejected, sports entrepreneur Nick Mileti (right) turned to the fledgling World Hockey Association to bring "major league" hockey to Cleveland. Mileti and WHA founder Gary Davidson (left) announce the formation of the Cleveland Crusaders at the Cleveland Arena in the spring of 1972 (Michael Schwartz Library, Cleveland State University).

WHA, Mileti and head coach Bill Needham assembled a competitive team that battled for first place in the league's eastern division all season. The Crusaders, led by Cheevers, compiled 89 points, the third highest total in the WHA, and finished five points behind the New England Whalers, who would win the WHA's first championship. Cleveland was eliminated in the second round of the playoffs. Cleveland's hockey fans gave their support to the newcomers and forgot about the Barons.

Crowds of less than 1,000 attended most Barons games, and Mileti quickly realized he'd miscalculated Cleveland's ability, or desire, to support both of his teams. His attempt to move the Barons to Lewiston, Maine, was blocked by the NHL, all of whose clubs had working agreements with an AHL team and thus supplied the vast majority of the league's talent. Despite leaving Mileti with nowhere else to turn but the WHA after rejecting his application to join the NHL, the older league wasn't going to allow him to become one of the renegades without paying a stiff price ... especially after he'd stunned the Bruins by stealing Cheevers. Mileti was going to be forced to squirm for a while. The Barons struggled through January of 1973, playing all of their home games in virtual privacy, before Mileti worked out a deal to relocate the team to the unlikely locale of Jacksonville, Florida. The NHL made no effort to block that move. It was certain that hockey and sunshine wouldn't mix. The once-proud Barons, kings of minor league hockey during the Sutphin years of the late 1930s and 1940s, played their final game in the Cleveland Arena in early February. Only 435 fans came to say goodbye.

Jacksonville was hardly a hotbed of hockey interest. A large crowd turned out for the Barons' first game in their new home, but hockey languished in northern Florida, and the once regal Barons died an unmourned death after the 1973–1974 season.

Hockey, however, hadn't heard the last of the Cleveland Barons.

In the meantime, the Crusaders weren't making the NHL regret its decision to not admit Cleveland into its ranks. The Crusaders finished sixth in the WHA in attendance in 1972–73, averaging 5,287 fans per game, or about 54 percent of the Arena's capacity. New England led the league with an average of 6,981 fans per contest. At the other end of the spectrum, the Ottawa Nationals, with a playoff team and no competition from the NHL, finished last in attendance at just 3,226 per game. The WHA shared six of its cities with the NHL, and none of those clubs averaged even 7,000 fans per game.

The 1973–74 Crusaders slipped to third in the WHA's eastern division with 83 points and were eliminated from the playoffs in the first round. Attendance increased by almost a thousand fans per game, however, to an average of 6,212. It was the last season the Crusaders would

Part of the "crowd" of 435 fans at the final game played by the Cleveland Barons of the American Hockey League in February of 1973. Team owner Nick Mileti foolishly believed Cleveland would support the Barons of the AHL and the Crusaders of the World Hockey Association (Michael Schwartz Library, Cleveland State University).

call dingy old Cleveland Arena "home." In the fall of 1974, they'd move into the gleaming, new $35 million Coliseum at the Interstate 271 and Ohio route 303 interchange in the heretofore sleepy village of Richfield, some 25 miles from downtown Cleveland and 15 miles from downtown Akron. Mileti managed to build the state-of-the-art facility he'd promised the NBA without spending a penny of public money, and he had big plans for the building, his basketball and hockey teams, and the surrounding area. Mileti envisioned the Crusaders and Cavaliers becoming regional franchises, with fans coming from Cleveland, Akron and Youngstown to watch the games in the Coliseum. In the case of the Cavaliers, he hoped basketball fans from Pittsburgh, who didn't have an NBA team to follow, would become fans of his team and make the two-hour trek via the interstate to Richfield to watch it perform. Mileti also had grand visions of the presence of his hockey and basketball teams spurring economic growth. He was sure the Coliseum would quickly be surrounded by hotels, restaurants, shopping malls and office buildings as the Cleveland-Akron-Canton metroplex expanded. At the center of all the development would be the Coliseum. In theory, Mileti's vision made sense. But it never materialized.

The Richfield Coliseum may have been the finest indoor sports venue in the United States. It seated 18,544 for hockey, making it larger than any arena with an NHL club. It was the pride of the WHA. But it also may have contributed to the demise of the Crusaders ... and, later, the Barons.

The Crusaders' third season in the WHA and first in the Coliseum was an artistic failure. They endured their first losing season and accumulated just 73 points. Guided by head coach John Hanna, a former Crusader player, and then by Hanna's replacement, Jack Vivian, Cleveland finished second in the eastern division and was sent packing in the first round of the playoffs. Average attendance increased by about 700 per game, to 6,931. But that meant almost two-thirds of the Coliseum's seats were unoccupied for every Crusaders home game. That wasn't what Mileti had planned on.

The WHA's fourth season, 1975–76, was a chaotic one. Fourteen clubs started the season. A dozen of them finished, and it was almost fewer than that. The Denver Spurs moved to Ottawa on New Year's Eve. The WHA had failed once in the Canadian capital, and it quickly failed again. In an extremely embarrassing development for the league, the transplanted Ottawa Civics struggled through three weeks and disbanded. The Minnesota Fighting Saints finally lost their battle with the NHL's North Stars and folded on February 28.

In Cleveland, Mileti sold 51 percent interest in the Crusaders to

businessman Jay Moore, who paid $650,000 for the privilege of eventu-
ally losing every penny he'd invest in the WHA. That wasn't the outcome
the 49-year-old Moore expected when he closed the deal with Mileti on
March 4, 1975.

"This is not a toy," Moore said at the press conference introducing
him as the Crusaders' new majority owner. "This can be a very successful business enterprise. If I didn't think it would be financially successful,
there would be no sense getting involved. The World Hockey Association is improving every year. And the people will come out if the team is
successful and has a good place to play. The product can be sold. I hope
there is a way to do it." Selling the product wouldn't involve breaking the
bank for talent, however. Despite the infusion of cash, the new majority
owner wasn't giving general manager Vivian a blank check to build the
Crusaders into a champion. "There will be certain limitations, and there
has to be,"[1] he explained.

Moore knew something about successful business enterprises.
He was a multi-millionaire who was board chairman of Samuel Moore
Company. He was also president of two car dealerships in northeastern Ohio and was a partner in a new Sheraton hotel that would open
soon near the tourist meccas of Sea World and Geauga Lake Park. But
all of Moore's business acumen couldn't rescue the Crusaders, who were
five million dollars in debt when he purchased controlling interest. They
played in the finest building in the WHA, if not in all of hockey, but
they had a miserable lease. The Crusaders didn't receive a penny from
the sale of the Coliseum's loges, or from concessions, or from parking.
Their broadcasting revenue was minimal. Nick Mileti owned the radio
station that broadcast Crusaders games, so he'd been essentially paying himself for the rights to put hockey on the air. The Crusaders relied
almost solely on ticket revenue to make money. They needed to average
13,000 fans per game to break even. They weren't even averaging half
that number.

Buoyed by their enthusiastic new owner, the Crusaders finished
second in the east in 1974–75 but were eliminated in the first round of
the playoffs.

The 1975–76 season was a debacle. By the middle of December,
Moore found himself unable to pay his star player, Gerry Cheevers. By
the middle of January, he couldn't pay the rest of the team. The players didn't get their January 15 paychecks until January 27, and many of
those checks bounced. "There was nothing in the kitty to pay us,"[2] said
Cheevers, whose contract ran through the 1976–77 season. He negotiated a release from his contract and returned to the Boston Bruins in early February, giving Moore, the Crusaders and the WHA an

embarrassing black eye. Moore secured a loan from Cleveland Trust Bank to enable him to meet his payrolls for the rest of the season. The Crusaders survived but posted a second straight losing year, blowing a chance to win their division by losing the season's final game to the San Diego Mariners at the Coliseum. The Crusaders earned 75 points and finished second in the east, in which no team had a winning record. Led by head coach John Wilson, Cleveland was beaten in the first round of the playoffs for the third straight season. Attendance decreased to 6,356 per game.

The Crusaders were swept by their chief nemesis, the Whalers, three games to none, in the first playoff round. After a 5–3 loss on the road in the opener, the Crusaders returned to the Coliseum and were beaten twice, 6–1 and 3–2. The April 11 defeat that eliminated the Crusaders was the final game the team would ever play.

2

Go East,
Young Golden Seals

Jay Moore wanted major league hockey to succeed in Cleveland.

Moore purchased the Cleveland Crusaders from Nick Mileti in March of 1975 with the best of intentions. But Moore lacked the deep pockets needed to dig the Crusaders out of the mountain of debt they'd accumulated during their first three seasons in the struggling World Hockey Association. Despite the Richfield Coliseum's accessibility from all directions via the interstate highway system (the main reason Mileti had moved the Crusaders and Cavaliers from downtown Cleveland to a beautiful arena sportswriters nonetheless derisively termed "the big house on the prairie"), fans weren't flocking to the shiny new edifice to watch the Crusaders play. And while the Crusaders were putting forth a respectable product, their performance had declined slightly every season of their existence.

The franchise had dodged a bullet when it was 12 days late meeting its January 15, 1976, payroll. Only a loan from Cleveland Trust Bank kept the Crusaders from folding in mid-season, as the WHA's Denver Spurs/Ottawa Civics and Minnesota Fighting Saints did. The Spurs, an expansion team, left Denver for Ottawa after just three months, then disbanded after just three weeks in Canada's capital city. Even though he was broke, Moore signed two Spurs players, Gary MacGregor and Barry Legge, for the Crusaders, adding to a payroll he already couldn't meet. The Fighting Saints ceased operations on February 28.

Matters weren't a whole lot better in the NHL. After fielding six teams for a quarter of a century, from 1942–43 through the 1966–67 season, the league yielded to demands for expansion. It expanded much too quickly, adding six teams for the 1967–68 season, two more for 1970–71, and an additional two teams for 1972–73. As if that wasn't enough, the NHL expanded again in 1974–1975. It had increased in size by 150 percent in less than a decade and was suffering growing pains.

The NHL's clubs in Oakland and Kansas City were pitifully weak. The Oakland Seals joined in the first round of expansion in 1967–68, and the NHL soon learned there weren't many hockey fans in the San Francisco Bay area. The Seals won just 15 games and averaged less than 5,000 fans per game. Dramatic improvement on the ice the following year wasn't accompanied by dramatic improvement in attendance. The Seals almost doubled their victory total to 29, led by their new head coach, former Cleveland Barons legend Fred Glover. They earned a play-off spot but lost in the first round. Attendance actually declined slightly, to less than 4,600 per game.

Glover's Seals won just 22 games in 1969–70, but still made the playoffs. They lost again in the first round, but attendance increased to 6,200 per contest. In an effort to broaden the team's fan base, owner Charles O. Finley changed its name to the California Golden Seals for the 1970–71 campaign. It didn't help. The Golden Seals won only 20 games, finished in last place in the NHL's western division, and attendance slumped to just under 5,400 per game. Another non-playoff season followed in 1971–72, but attendance was up slightly to almost 6,100 per game. Still, the attendance figures paled in comparison to the rest of the league. Hockey just wasn't catching on in San Francisco/Oakland.

The Golden Seals continued to sputter in 1972–73, winning only 16 games and amassing just 48 points as they plummeted to last place in the western division. Glover, who'd been fired during the 1971–72 season, was brought back during the '72–73 campaign but couldn't keep the Seals from sinking. Attendance was a paltry 5,300 per game. The 1973–74 season was even worse. The Golden Seals won only 13 of their 78 games and racked up just 36 points. Attendance dropped correspondingly to 4,800 per game. Glover was fired again before the season ended.

The NHL increased its schedule to 80 games for the 1975–76 season and split into four divisions, whose members were not selected by geography. The Golden Seals were placed in the Adams Division, along with the Buffalo Sabres, Boston Bruins, and Toronto Maple Leafs, which made for plenty of lengthy road trips for everyone. The Golden Seals won 19 games, accumulated 51 points, missed the playoffs, but managed to draw 6,200 fans per game. The NHL had removed the Golden Seals from Finley's clutches after the 1971–72 season and operated them for the next three years. A trio of businessmen led by Mel Swig purchased the club from the league prior to the 1975–76 season. Plans were on the drawing board for a new arena in downtown San Francisco that would've solidified the Golden Seals' future in the Bay Area. Those plans fell apart, and Swig made it clear his team couldn't compete in its present location.

The NHL's other albatross was the Kansas City Scouts, a second-year franchise that served as the perfect example of what happens when a sports league expands much too rapidly. The Scouts were the 12th team the NHL had added in less than 10 years. There just weren't enough "major league" hockey players to fill the rosters of 18 NHL clubs and 14 more in the WHA. There had been only six major league hockey teams in 1967. In 1975, there were (allegedly) 32! The Scouts won just 15 games in their first season in the NHL. They regressed to 12 victories in 1975–76. The fans didn't storm the gates of Kemper Arena to watch such a wretched excuse for a major league hockey team, although attendance was significantly higher than that of the Golden Seals. The Scouts averaged less than 7,400 fans per game their first year, and just below 7,900 their second. Their owners soon found themselves a staggering five million dollars in debt.

Adding up the carnage of the disastrous 1975–76 major league hockey season, the WHA allowed two teams, Minnesota and Denver/Ottawa, to quietly expire before their schedules had been completed. The Crusaders would've joined them had Cleveland Trust not loaned Moore enough money to meet the team's payroll for the rest of the season. Cleveland Trust specialized in propping up the city's struggling sports teams. As of the summer of 1977, the bank had loaned the Cleveland Indians six million dollars when team president Ted Bonda knocked on the loan officer's door asking for more. The loan was reluctantly approved.

By May of 1976, the WHA appeared to be on the verge of dissolution. The NHL had serious problems in Kansas City and Oakland. Both clubs were likely to be elsewhere when the 1976–77 season started.

As the Crusaders fought for a playoff spot during the final months of 1975–76, the players were dismayed by reports that Moore was negotiating with the owners of the Scouts to buy that team and bring it, and thus the NHL, to Cleveland for the 1976–77 season. Crusaders general manager Jack Vivian said he saw the NHL as the only way to keep major league hockey in Cleveland. The Crusaders, in Vivian's opinion, were too far gone to be salvaged.

"We were going down the tubes," Vivian said of Cleveland's WHA franchise. "We were going down faster than I could borrow money. Payroll was almost impossible to meet. So I informed Jay Moore that I felt that the only way we could save things was to get into the National Hockey League. That was the only answer."[1] Moore and Vivian met with Scouts officials, and it appeared probable that a deal could be worked out and the club moved to Cleveland. As horrid as they were, the Scouts possessed something the Crusaders lacked: the NHL's brand name.

And the thought of the Canadiens, Bruins, Maple Leafs, Rangers, Red Wings and Blackhawks coming to Cleveland, even if they would've made mincemeat out of the Scouts, or whatever the team would've been called, may have been more enticing to potential investors than visits by the Cincinnati Stingers, Indianapolis Racers and Birmingham Bulls. Moore didn't have the money to run an NHL club himself. He needed investors, and an NHL team, even one as pathetic as the Scouts, may have tempted people with money to spend it on Moore's hockey team.

Cleveland's angry players responded to what they perceived to be a lack of respect from management by declaring their game against Cincinnati on March 10 to be "black armband night." They asked every fan to wear a black armband to protest Moore's attempt to replace them with an NHL club. The game drew 12,286 fans to the Coliseum, the largest crowd of the season. Many of them wore black armbands as the players asked, others went even further by dressing totally in black. Some carried signs telling Moore they wanted no part of the Kansas City Scouts. They'd rather have the Crusaders. Ultimately, the talks with the Scouts fell through.

A month and a half after the Crusaders had been eliminated from the WHA playoffs by the New England Whalers in a three-game sweep, with the second and third defeats being administered before small crowds at the Richfield Coliseum, Moore addressed the state of his team. "We want to do whatever is in the best interests of the players and everyone else," he said on May 25. That included doing what was best for the team's cash-strapped owner. "I'd say our chances of operating here next season at the present time are about 50–50." Moore acknowledged the strong possibility that he'd either fold the Crusaders or sell them to an out-of-town buyer. That would've made the Coliseum available for a new hockey tenant, and Moore said he expected Nick Mileti, the Coliseum's co-owner, to look for an NHL team, since there was at least one, and quite possibly two, available.

"I would assume everyone concerned, which would mean the Coliseum and Mileti, would attempt to get an NHL franchise,"[2] Moore said. Moore had been consulting with Mileti about the Crusaders' problems, in which he had a vested interest. Losing the hockey team would leave Mileti with 40 dates to fill at the Coliseum. An empty building meant no revenue was being generated. Moore said that Mileti had no interest in reinvesting in the Crusaders. He was relieved to have unloaded them on Moore 14 months earlier, although he'd retained 35 percent of the team's stock.

On the same day Moore said there was no better than a 50 percent chance the Crusaders would stay in Cleveland, the NHL announced that it planned to terminate the Kansas City franchise. However, the city would be given 10 days to find new ownership to keep the Scouts from folding. Even though his first round of negotiations with Scouts officials had ended in failure, Moore hadn't given up hope of moving Kansas City's franchise to Cleveland in the autumn of 1976.

If the Crusaders were going to remain in Cleveland, Moore would have to prove he had the means to withstand another significant financial loss during the 1976–77 season. So would all owners of WHA clubs. The league wanted no repeat of the debacle of 1975–76, when, for all intents and purposes, three franchises went broke. Said an unidentified WHA executive in late May of the Cleveland situation, "we weren't too thrilled with the near-strike [by the players in late February after the payroll had been missed], the late paychecks, refunding the team's performance bond [to help it meet its payroll], and the rest of the financial mess you had there last season."[3] The WHA had scheduled its summer meeting for June 14. At that meeting, each team would have to prove it had sufficient funding to operate at a substantial loss during the upcoming season. Teams that couldn't meet the standard set by the board of governors faced expulsion. That seemed to be a distinct possibility for the Crusaders.

Two days after giving the Crusaders a 50–50 chance of operating in Cleveland in 1976–77, Moore said he was deep into negotiations to sell the team to Bill Putnam, the former president of the Atlanta Flames of the NHL. The Flames joined the NHL in the expansion of 1972–73 and had become a playoff team by the 1975–76 season. If Putnam completed the purchase of the Crusaders, he'd relocate them to a new arena in Hollywood, Florida. The Barons had failed in their attempt to interest the residents of Jacksonville in the AHL in 1973, but Putnam was convinced hockey could succeed in the Sunshine State.

"If we get together on a few items, Bill will come up here ... to talk about completing a deal,"[4] Moore said. Added Putnam, "we're on the same wave length."[5] Moore held out a glimmer of hope that the Crusaders might stay in Cleveland, but said he was disappointed by the city's response to his financial problems. Moore said he needed to sell 5,000 season tickets in order to keep the Crusaders in town, and as of May 28, the telephones in the team's sales department weren't ringing off the hook.

"There has been some reaction to the latest stories, but nothing overwhelming,"[6] he said dejectedly. Hockey writer Bob Schlesinger of the city's evening newspaper, the Cleveland *Press*, claimed that neither Moore nor his sales staff were risking exhaustion trying to sell those 5,000 season tickets. According to Schlesinger, Moore's effort to keep the Crusaders in town consisted of having his salespeople sit at their desks waiting for their telephones to ring.

Before ownership of the Crusaders had been officially transferred from Moore to Putnam, Moore was talking like a man whose ultimate ambition was, and had always been, to bring the National Hockey League to Cleveland. "As soon as the loose ends are tied up with the WHA, I'll then start to work harder to see what can be done about an NHL franchise for Cleveland. The potential for getting a franchise here is good."[7] The city's ace in the hole was the Coliseum. The NHL wanted one of its clubs in that building. But that couldn't happen until the Crusaders had formally vacated it, and that would take some time. The transfer to Putnam wouldn't go as smoothly as either Moore or Putnam would've liked.

Among the prominent Clevelanders weighing in on the topic of bringing the NHL to town was Art Modell, the owner of the Cleveland Browns. Modell said he'd be glad to use whatever influence he had to lure the NHL, but he couldn't own the team because the National Football League's by-laws didn't allow its team owners to dabble in other sports.

If Moore, or anyone else, was to acquire the Golden Seals, it was going to be expensive. Mel Swig owned 60 percent of the club's stock. His partner, native Clevelander George Gund III, owned 38 percent. Bud Levitas owned the remaining two percent. Swig was asking for seven million dollars to sell the team. Swig had paid $6.5 million for the Golden Seals when he bought them from the league, and he felt he was entitled to a profit from his investment. He said on June 2 that he was talking with potential buyers who'd move the team to Denver, which had lost its WHA franchise six months earlier. "We've been talking very seriously with Denver, but nothing is definite yet," he said. Seattle and Edmonton, which had a WHA franchise, were reported to be preparing offers for the Golden Seals.

Swig said he'd welcome an offer from Cleveland for his team. "Certainly I would. But Cleveland would have to make a pretty good offer. We have set a price, and I think it is a fair price. It is higher than the expansion price, but that's because this team is better than an expansion team."[8] Considering the Golden Seals won just 19 games in 1975–76, Swig's assessment of his team as being better than an expansion club was open to debate. The asking price for the Scouts was lower, but the new owner would be expected to assume the club's massive debt. Moore had lost interest in buying the Scouts. He wanted the Golden Seals.

Since Mileti owned slightly more than a third of the Crusaders' stock, his approval of their sale to Putnam was necessary, and he gave the deal his blessing on June 3, removing one hurdle preventing their transfer to southern Florida. An unidentified NHL executive was quoted by the Cleveland *Plain Dealer* as saying his league regretted rejecting Mileti's bid for a franchise in 1972, choosing Kansas City and Washington instead. "They realize they made a mistake and probably should have taken Mileti. They have been badly burned,"[9] admitted the executive. Kansas City's team was on the verge of extinction after just two seasons. Washington, which joined the NHL for the 1974–75 season, won only eight games while losing a staggering 67 times during its rookie year. But the Capitals would survive and eventually thrive. The Scouts would not.

The Kansas City franchise, according to the *Press*, could be purchased for three million dollars ... less than half of what Swig was asking for the Golden Seals. In assessing the merits of the two NHL teams that Cleveland was eyeing, Schlesinger noted that the league's rapid expansion had come at a price. He said early in the process, potential investors lined up outside the league's headquarters, checkbooks in hand, thinking that owning an NHL club amounted to a license to print money. After ownerships in Pittsburgh, Oakland and Kansas City had gone bankrupt and were rescued by the league, that rosy outlook changed. Schlesinger sounded a note of caution in his column comparing the Golden Seals to the Scouts. Both teams were weak, but the Scouts were weaker and further from becoming competitive than the Golden Seals. Schlesinger pointed out Cleveland's well-deserved reputation for not supporting losers. The Cavaliers had averaged just 3,500 fans a game during their first season in the NBA. The Indians hadn't drawn 10,000 fans per game between 1969 and 1973. Even the Browns had played before empty seats at home during the 1975 season, when they'd lost 11 games. Whichever cities the Golden Seals and Scouts were transferred to, if the Scouts were moved rather than disbanded, would be expected to support them in grand style. Even though neither one would be a playoff contender in 1976–77, or for several years in the future.

Just days after saying Cleveland had a strong chance at luring an NHL club to the Coliseum, Moore said he didn't think it would happen for the 1976–77 season. Swig had set a deadline of July 1 to sell the Golden Seals. "It makes sense," he explained. "It gives you enough time to establish a season ticket sale and gives the league enough time to draw up a schedule." Swig said he hadn't spoken to anyone from Cleveland, and Moore said he didn't think there was sufficient time to put together a group of investors in time to meet Swig's self-imposed deadline.

"You're talking about three weeks," Moore said on June 5. "I'm not optimistic." On the bright side, Swig's discussions with investors from

Denver had broken off, leaving Cleveland still in the running. "I'll do anything to make it happen," Moore said, although he didn't want to be the team's majority owner. "If necessary, I would spearhead a movement to organize a group. But I won't be a majority stockholder."[10]

The National Hockey League wanted a decision on the fate of the Golden Seals by June 25, a week before Swig's personal deadline. When the Board of Governors met in Montreal on June 7, Swig reported there was still a possibility the team would remain in the 12,000 seat Oakland Coliseum for 1976–77. That was because he had a meeting scheduled with officials from San Jose on June 11. The purpose of the meeting was to discuss a proposed 16,000 seat arena to be built in that city, which would save the Golden Seals for the Bay Area. Swig had another meeting scheduled with Denver sportscaster Bud Palmer, who was trying to put a group together to buy the Golden Seals and move them to the Mile High City. A report in an Oakland newspaper said that George Gund III had expressed a willingness to sell his stock in the Golden Seals if it would facilitate a quicker sale of the team. And that would spell doom for Cleveland's chance of acquiring the Golden Seals.

Gund, whose family had deep roots in northeastern Ohio, was nudging Swig toward moving the Golden Seals to his hometown. Swig admitted that Gund had brought up the possibility in May. "We were just kicking around possible places. But we dismissed Cleveland because the Crusaders were there at the time."

Said Gund of rumors that he'd buy Swig's and Levitas' stock in the Golden Seals and transfer them to Cleveland, "I really can't comment at this point. Not with the Crusaders there. I don't know what the status of the Crusaders is at this point."[11] Neither did Moore. The WHA had scheduled a vote on the sale of the Crusaders to Putnam on June 7 but postponed it due to "legal entanglements." Moore said he hoped to have the problem cleared up within a week.

Swig's meeting with Palmer didn't go well. Palmer was depending on financial support from Carl Scheer, the president of the American Basketball Association's Denver Nuggets. Scheer was expected to put up 50 percent of the money to purchase an NHL franchise. Scheer, however, was watching the merger negotiations between the ABA and NBA and withdrew his offer to assist Palmer. Palmer then pulled out of the talks with Swig. "We'll just have to withdraw our offer for now and suspend it. We'll see what happens,"[12] Palmer said.

The "legal entanglements" holding up the sale of the Crusaders were revealed to be the status of no-trade clauses in the contracts of certain players. Apparently, some of the Crusaders with such clauses considered the transfer of the team to Hollywood to be the equivalent of a trade, which would require their consent. The players wanted to be compensated for giving that consent, and Putnam was balking. "If players who have those clauses do not report, I won't assume the financial responsibility," he said. "I am unwilling to take that risk."[13] Whether or not the "legal entanglements" would scuttle the deal remained to be seen, but for the moment, the Crusaders were stuck in Cleveland.

The sports empire Nick Mileti built in Cleveland was crumbling. Mileti had purchased the Barons and the Arena in 1968. He added the Cavaliers in 1970 and the Indians and Crusaders in 1972. He pulled off the astounding feat of constructing the Richfield Coliseum without asking for public funding. Without the Coliseum, the NBA could have forced the Cavaliers to leave Cleveland, as it would force the Braves to leave Buffalo after the 1979–80 season. Like the Cavaliers, the Braves had assured the NBA that they'd be playing in a state-of-the-art facility within five years of their admittance to the league. The NBA gave the Braves an additional five years to live up to that promise. When they couldn't, the team was moved to San Diego. It's now the Los Angeles Clippers.

Mileti's purchase of the Indians was probably the most startling. The Arena was an aging facility. The Barons were a minor league team. The NBA was still a second-tier attraction in the early 1970s, and the WHA may have been "major league" in name only. But the Indians were a Cleveland institution, dating back to the American League's founding in 1901. Mileti managed to buy the team from Vernon Stouffer in the spring of 1972, after Stouffer agreed to a plan that would've split the team's 81 home games each season between crumbling Municipal Stadium and the New Orleans Superdome. The "share the Tribe" plan would've started once the Superdome was completed in 1974. Mileti quashed the plan. Observers of Cleveland sports wondered where Mileti found the cash to purchase a major league baseball team, even one as down on its luck as the Indians. As it turned out, he didn't have the cash. Team president and general manager Gabe Paul, who bailed out soon after Mileti bought the Indians, said he'd paid Stouffer $9.75 million in "green stamps and promises."[14] The Indians continued to lose games and money. Mileti was ousted as chief operating officer in August of 1973, and as team president in 1975. By that time, he was nothing more than one of dozens of minority stockholders.

Mileti had been forced by financial problems to sell majority interest in the Crusaders to Moore in the spring of 1975, and in June of 1976, he sold his 45 percent interest in the Coliseum to real estate investor Sanford Greenberg of Washington, D.C. That gave Greenberg control of 90 percent of the stock in the Coliseum. The Kettering Foundation of

Dayton owned the remaining ten percent. It was reported that Greenberg paid Mileti $16,000,000 for his share of the building.

Greenberg's purchase of the Coliseum was hailed by Bob Schlesinger, who wrote that the reclusive multi-millionaire had a financial relationship with the NHL's Washington Capitals, plus a sizable financial stake in the building the team played in, the Cap Center in Landover, Maryland. Greenberg was also on good terms with Chase Manhattan Bank, which supplied the money to build the Coliseum. "You have as solid a footing as can be found anywhere," Schlesinger said of the Coliseum's new management. And that figured to bode well for the Coliseum's chance of soon hosting an NHL club.

At the conclusion of the NHL's Board of Governors meeting, league President Clarence Campbell said that the Scouts had been given until July 1 to secure new ownership or face liquidation. As for the Golden Seals, Campbell said "the Seals will operate someplace in 1976–77. Where, or under whose auspices, I can't say because I don't know."[15]

The Crusaders sold the contract of center iceman Richie Leduc to the Cincinnati Stingers on June 16 in a straight cash deal. Leduc had played for the Barons before moving up to the Boston Bruins. He then deserted the NHL for the Crusaders, who signed him to a three-year contract starting with the 1974–75 season. Leduc produced 58 points in 1975–76 on 36 goals and 22 assists. He was one of the few Crusaders who didn't have a no-trade clause. He'd be paid $85,000 by the Stingers in the final year of his contract.

"The trade doesn't say anything about Richie as a player," insisted Crusaders general manager John Wilson. It said volumes about the Crusaders, however. "He's a fine hockey player, but let's face it. Our payroll is so high that nobody can afford to operate the team." At least Putnam apparently couldn't. The deal had been made at Putnam's urging and, according to Wilson, "we'll have to get rid of three or four other guys, too."[16]

Two weeks had passed since the WHA's Board of Governors tabled the matter of the Crusaders' sale due to "legal entanglements." Moore said it would take only a week to get the situation straightened out, but the *Press* reported that the problems were more complicated than the no-trade clauses in player contracts that Putnam complained about. The Crusaders had several minority owners, and they wanted a bigger piece of the club's sale price than Moore wanted to give them. Lawyers were wrangling over the monetary issue, and the club's sale to Putnam was still on hold. And as long as the sale of the Crusaders was pending, so was the possible move of the Golden Seals to Cleveland.

"I can't talk to Cleveland as long as you have a team there,"[17] Swig said.

On June 22, the WHA's Board of Governors approved the transfer of the team from Moore to Putnam, even though the sale hadn't been completed. Putnam said he had an option to purchase all of the Crusaders' assets for roughly two million dollars. Moore's attorney, Bingham W. Zellmer, said Putnam expected to exercise that option within 30-days. The team, which was to be renamed the Florida Breakers, would play in a 15,000-seat facility called the Sportatorium, located 10 miles from Miami and 20 miles from Palm Beach. Putnam said the Crusaders would relocate to Hollywood even if he chose not to exercise his option to purchase all of their assets. He didn't say who would own the assets he declined to purchase. It didn't sound as if Moore wanted, or could afford, to retain any part of the Crusaders.

With the Crusaders apparently out of the picture, events involving the Golden Seals began moving rapidly. Less than 24 hours after the WHA approved Putnam's purchase of the Crusaders, the *Press* quoted "a reliable source" as saying a deal to move the Golden Seals was "in the bag, a 99% certainty. Only an unforeseeable catastrophe can prevent it."[18] Denver was no longer in the running for the club. The interest on the part of Seattle hadn't been serious. Seattle's arena, home of the NBA's Supersonics, was only slightly bigger than Oakland's, and much smaller than Cleveland's. Edmonton already had the Oilers of the WHA. Unlike the Crusaders, they weren't leaving town. Swig had decided he couldn't spend another year in the cramped Oakland Coliseum while continuing to haggle with officials in San Jose over an arena that was nothing more than a pipe dream at that point. That left Cleveland as his only option.

"I think Cleveland is a very good territory," he said, "but nothing can happen until you clean up your skirts." That was a reference to the nagging question of whether the Crusaders had officially abandoned Cleveland. "We hope to resolve everything by this weekend. I guess we have investors in Cleveland, but that is George Gund III's department."[19] The majority owner didn't know whether his partner had lined up new investors or not.

Swig's curious statement may explain why the Golden Seals ultimately fared even worse in Cleveland than they had in Oakland. The transfer of a major league sports franchise was serious business and needed to be treated as such. The transfer of the Golden Seals was done far too quickly, with neither Swig nor the NHL doing what would be called today their "due diligence." The generally savvy Sandy Greenberg also failed to do his homework on Swig's finances, and the miserable team he was shifting to Cleveland. Training camp would start in little more than two months; the season would begin in the first week of October. Proper preparation was cast aside in the interest of expediency. Returning to Oakland wasn't feasible, even though the Golden Seals' lease ran for two more seasons. The few hockey fans in the Bay Area knew Swig would leave as soon as he found a suitable home for his team; who would've attended the games under that circumstance? The financial loss would've been staggering. Giving Cleveland sufficient time to prepare for the team's arrival just wasn't possible. With the departure of the Crusaders, Greenberg suddenly had 40 dates to fill in the building he now owned 90 percent of. Soon after purchasing Mileti's share of the Coliseum, Greenberg said his goal was to have something going on every day of the year, and, once that was accomplished, he'd start doubling up on the events. He wasn't about to be patient. The Golden Seals needed a new residence come October of 1976, and Cleveland, ready or not (it wasn't), would be that place.

Swig and Gund toured the Richfield Coliseum on June 23. Swig had never visited Cleveland before. Gund grew up in northeastern Ohio. His father, George Gund II, had been a pillar of the Cleveland community, serving as president and board chairman of Cleveland Trust Bank. The family's Gund Foundation raised millions of dollars for civic and charitable causes. Gund the Third graduated from the exclusive University School and attended Western Reserve University. Although he no longer lived in northeastern Ohio, he'd followed in his illustrious father's footsteps by serving on the boards of Cleveland Trust, the Cleveland Zoo and the city's nationally renowned Health Museum. He spent a considerable amount of time in the city and kept an apartment in Cleveland.

"Cleveland is a marvelous city for hockey," said Gund, who'd attended many a Barons game at the Arena in the city's American Hockey League days and played the game himself. "It has tremendous potential. I've seen the interest in the past, and I think there is a future. Geographically, Cleveland is very advantageous. It is near Buffalo, Toronto and Boston in our division, and the old Barons had a great rivalry with the Buffalo Bisons."[20] That rivalry ended when Buffalo joined the NHL in 1970. The Sabres had quickly become a powerhouse, winning 37 games and accumulating 88 points in just their third season. Those totals increased to 46 wins and 105 points in 1975–76.

After getting his first look at northeastern Ohio, and its hockey arena, Swig spent six hours (along with Gund) discussing a lease with Tom Embrescia, the Cleveland attorney who represented Greenberg. Another example of the process moving much too quickly. "We did a lot of talking to see if [the Coliseum] will be satisfactory to us if the WHA opens the territory to us. Their attorneys wrote up a lease to see if we liked it. We haven't worked everything out yet. We are making pretty good progress,"[21] Swig said. It bears repeating that the 58-year-old Swig, who managed the swanky Fairmont Hotel on San Francisco's trendy Nob Hill, had never visited Cleveland until the day he and Gund toured the Coliseum. Knowing absolutely nothing about the area except what Gund told him, he made the decision to move his multi-million-dollar business there. No discussions took place with local government or business leaders. No research was done to gauge the interest in hockey on the part of Clevelanders who hadn't beaten a path to the Arena, and later to the Coliseum, to watch the Crusaders play. Most people would give more thought than that to purchasing a used car. Cleveland's new hockey team was being set up to fail. Spectacularly.

NHL President Clarence Campbell tried to slow down the runaway train that the Golden Seals had become, to no avail. He wasn't convinced that Cleveland was available to join the NHL, which was determined to avoid any city affiliated in any way with the WHA. "The Crusaders would have to be totally, unequivocally, and irrevocably out of the World Hockey Association. If that is verified, the city would become an open territory, and it would be available to anybody interested in it. I am only interested in it if the WHA is abandoning the Cleveland territory,"[22] he said.

Campbell had good reason to be concerned. Although the WHA had technically approved the sale of the Crusaders to Putnam, the sale hadn't been finalized. Moore was out of town, vacationing with his family in Hawaii. He wouldn't return to Cleveland until after the July 4 holiday. In the meantime, Putnam was acting like he was in charge. Wilson's sale of Richie Leduc to Cincinnati was done with Putnam's blessing, and that was only the beginning of the anticipated fire sale. Rumor had it Putnam was holding up the official consummation of the sale until the Crusaders' payroll, which had been the highest in the WHA, was drastically reduced. Putnam said he'd retain Wilson as his coach/GM, and Wilson's orders were to trade as many high-priced players as possible and negotiate new (and cheaper) contracts with those he couldn't get rid of. Putnam said his team would have to average 10,000 fans per game in the Hollywood Sportatorium to break even, and he'd charge eight dollars per ticket for every seat in the house. In order to achieve that, the payroll of the team soon to be the ex-Cleveland Crusaders had to be trimmed dramatically.

"What remains of the Crusaders will be a skeletal team in a league that is on the verge of dissolution," wrote columnist Dan Coughlin in the June 23 edition of the *Plain Dealer*. "What will rise from the ashes will be the most stable hockey franchise in Cleveland since the Barons reigned over the old American Hockey League." Coughlin was right about the Crusaders, but wrong about Cleveland's new NHL team. The city's sports media didn't look into Swig's hockey operation and how badly mismanaged it had been in Oakland. Cleveland's sportswriters and sportscasters were just happy to have a hockey team in the established major league.

Swig asked the NHL Board of Governors to place the transfer of his Golden Seals from Oakland to Cleveland on the agenda for its June 30 meeting. Campbell sounded as if he was resigned to the move, even though he still wasn't sure Cleveland was no longer a WHA city. "There is no question [Swig] is taking the team to Cleveland after nine years of threatened moves all over North America. The move would be the same for any group owning a club, so I guess we have no choice but to approve the move." Campbell said it would be costly for Swig to buy his way out of the Golden Seals' lease at the Oakland Coliseum, which ran through the 1977–78 season. He again expressed doubt that the Crusaders were going to be sold and moved from Cleveland.

"[The move] is still up in the air, even though it has been announced," the league president said. "We don't want to get tricked. There is a possibility of litigation."[23]

Another Campbell comment offers more evidence of how the transfer was hastily arranged without the necessary investigation of the pros and cons by everyone involved. The NHL was about to approve the transfer of a franchise without the league president personally inspecting the facility it would play in. And while there's little doubt Campbell would've been impressed by the Richfield Coliseum (everyone was), he knew enough about its location to sound a note of caution. "I don't doubt its quality. People who have seen the building say it is fantastic and maybe the best in America. But you still have to give some thought to where it is."[24] And where the Coliseum was, was some 25 miles from downtown Cleveland, and about 15 miles from downtown Akron. Essentially, the Coliseum was in the middle of nowhere. There was but one access road, that being Ohio route 303. Entering and exiting the parking lot was a nightmare. When crowds were large, as they were for Cavaliers basketball games during the Central Division championship season of 1975–76, cars trying to reach the Coliseum from the north or south were backed up for a mile or more along Interstate 271. The same problem existed for cars approaching from the east or west along route 303. Unfortunately for the NHL, that would never be a problem for the hockey team. But the bottom line was, the Richfield Coliseum was out in the boondocks, and roads were often icy, snowy and treacherous in northeastern Ohio during the hockey season. Most fans would decide it wasn't worth the hassle to go to the Coliseum and watch a lousy team lose another game. Even if it bore the NHL brand.

One day before the NHL's Board of Governors met in Chicago to discuss, among other business, the transfer of the Golden Seals to Cleveland, the *Plain Dealer* reported that Moore's lawyer, Bingham Zellmer, had received a telegram from Ben Hatskin, the chief executive officer of the WHA, stating categorically that Cleveland was no longer part of the league. John Ziegler, the chairman of the NHL's Board of Governors, wanted to see the telegram before deciding on Swig's request to relocate his team. "We are waiting for something definitive from the WHA," said Ziegler. "I've heard reports that Bill Putnam has purchased the Cleveland franchise. I have not personally seen any statement that the league has given approval of the transfer or move."[25]

Swig was to meet with the NHL Finance Committee the night before the board meeting. "I'll tell them my options, and we'll determine together what the best move is,"[26] he said.

Despite the uncertainty of Campbell and Ziegler, Cleveland's chance of joining the NHL looked good. "Cleveland is looked upon with great favor," said Charles Mulcahy, the Bruins' representative on the Board of Governors. "I think Cleveland is a great city and has a great building. It is one of the best places I have ever seen."[27]

Among those in attendance at the governors' meeting was Bud Palmer, the sportscaster who'd tried to lure the Golden Seals to Denver. Having failed at that, he still hoped to convince the Board of Governors to allow the Kansas City Scouts to move to Colorado. Palmer said Swig called him on June 21, two days before he visited Cleveland. "He said he was sorry we couldn't get together. I wished him good luck. That's when I knew we had lost the Seals to Cleveland."

Palmer said the sticking point in his negotiations with Swig was an inability to secure a lease at McNichols Arena, the home of the Denver Nuggets, who'd be joining the NBA for the 1976–77 season following its merger with the American Basketball Association. McNichols Arena was owned by the city of Denver. The Richfield Coliseum was owned by Sandy Greenberg. "A city won't bend half as much as a private building regarding a lease. If I owned a private building, I'd do anything in the world to get a franchise in that building."[28] Palmer would succeed in getting the Scouts to move to Denver, where they'd fail almost as badly as the Golden Seals would fail in Cleveland.

Shortly before the Board of Governors meeting began on June 30, Clarence Campbell said he'd seen a copy of the telegram from Hatskin to Zellmer. Campbell said he was satisfied that the WHA had officially and completely pulled out of Cleveland. That opened the door for the Golden Seals to move in.

Some of the club's employees were already in Cleveland. Most of the office staff had journeyed from Oakland to Cleveland and was ready to hit the ground running as soon as the transfer was formally and officially approved by the Board of Governors. That was supposed to be a mere formality, according to an unidentified NHL owner quoted by the *Press* on June 30.

"I don't see any possibility of any hang-ups," said the mogul. "Mel Swig had our approval to move to Cleveland a week ago, as long as the WHA left town, and that has been taken care of from the information that I have. As far as I know, there's just no opposition from anywhere I've heard of to Cleveland."[29]

But the decade of the 1970s wasn't kind to Cleveland. It was the decade both the Cuyahoga River and mayor Ralph J. Perk's hair caught on fire (not simultaneously). The infamous "Ten Cent Beer Night" riot of June 4, 1974, plunged Municipal Stadium into chaos during the ninth inning of a baseball game between the Indians and Texas Rangers. The Browns were in decline. So was the downtown area, which hadn't been aided by the flight of the city's basketball and hockey teams to the relative wilderness of Richfield. If anything could go wrong with the transfer of a National Hockey League team to Cleveland, it would.

And something did. Three things, to be precise.

The NHL's Board of Governors, wary after having been burned by failed ownerships in Pittsburgh, Kansas City and Oakland, tentatively approved the transfer of the Golden Seals to Cleveland on June 30. The governors were nervous, however, because Swig and his co-owners, Gund and Bud Levitas, hadn't yet negotiated a lease with Greenberg for use of the Coliseum. They also hadn't attracted any local investors and hadn't secured a bank loan to stabilize the team's finances. Unless and until they did, approval of the transfer would be withheld.

Swig wasn't fazed by the setback, which he viewed as temporary. "I have no doubt we'll get that accomplished," he said as he arrived at Cleveland's Hopkins International Airport following the meeting. "I think that bringing the National Hockey League here is a fait accompli."[30] Swig was scheduled to meet with potential investors, and bankers, at the airport.

Hockey fans are left to ponder how different the fate of the Golden Seals may have been had they been owned by Art Modell, the owner of the Browns. Modell wanted to buy the team, but couldn't, thanks to a rule he'd urged his fellow owners to adopt several years earlier. The rule prohibited dual ownership in the NFL. "League rules prohibit me from owning even one share, directly or indirectly," Modell lamented. "If I had been successful in getting the rule changed, I would have bought control, or at least taken a major financial position."[31] Modell may have been sincere about wanting to purchase the Golden Seals, or he may have been courting public favor, knowing he couldn't get involved with Cleveland's hockey team. At least not financially. Given the feud Modell would carry on with the Indians after becoming their landlord at Municipal Stadium, and the way he'd eventually run the Browns into the ground, leaving him with no choice but to abandon Cleveland for Baltimore in 1995, the Golden Seals may not have fared any better under his guidance than they did under Swig's, although they probably would've lasted longer.

While the NHL's Board of Governors was essentially putting the transfer of the Golden Seals on indefinite hold, the Board of Governors of the WHA took up the matter of the sale of the Crusaders to Bill Putnam on June 30 and approved it. With Jay Moore still in Hawaii, Nick Mileti represented the Crusaders during the meeting at which they officially became the Florida Breakers. Although Putnam had said he'd keep John Wilson as his general manager and head coach, his first official act as owner was to hire Glen Sonmor as general manager. Sonmor was well known to Cleveland hockey fans. He'd played for the Barons and had been general manager of the defunct Minnesota Fighting Saints of the WHA.

No one in Cleveland seemed concerned about the delay in the transfer of the Golden Seals. Swig met with reporters at a local restaurant on July 1 to introduce himself. His family made its fortune in real estate, including once owning some buildings on Cleveland's Public Square that it had since sold. The Swig family owned hotels in San Francisco, Atlanta, Dallas and New Orleans. "I run the real estate, my brother runs the hotels, and our father still runs both of us, and he is 83," Swig explained. No one asked him what his father thought of his investment in hockey, or his decision to move that investment to Cleveland.

"I grew up on skates in Boston and played hockey in college," Swig continued. He attended Brown University in Providence, Rhode Island. He moved to San Francisco after graduation and, finding no professional hockey in the Bay Area, became involved in the movement to obtain some. He was instrumental in securing a Western Hockey League club in San Francisco, which he ran by default. "My knowledge of hockey certainly was not great, but I was the only one there who knew anything about it,"[32] he confessed. When the NHL expanded to Oakland in 1967, Swig bowed out. He purchased the Golden Seals in 1975.

Swig said he and other team officials had already met, and would continue to meet, Cleveland's hockey fans, even though the transfer of the Golden Seals wasn't yet a done deal. "We've talked to some already, and we want to continue those discussions. We want to hear their gripes about how hockey was handled here in the past, and do everything possible to correct those situations. I think we owe it to the hard-core hockey fans who have shown their loyalty to the sport."[33] Swig, and then George Gund III and his brother, Gordon, would soon decide there just weren't enough hard-core hockey fans in northeastern Ohio to support an NHL team. But in early July of 1976, everything was sunshine and roses. Sports editor Bob August of the *Press* was impressed with Swig's lack of ego and wrote that "he seems to bring a touch of class."

What Swig didn't bring was enough cash to operate an NHL team at a substantial loss while it tried to establish itself in a new market.

Swig was busy for the next two weeks, taking care of the concerns the Board of Governors had expressed about the transfer of the Golden Seals to Cleveland. He solved two of the problems, and on July 14, the governors made it official. The California Golden Seals would relocate to Cleveland for the 1976–77 National Hockey League season. Swig blamed the delay on the hurried nature of the situation. Only six weeks had passed since Cleveland became the preferred destination for Swig's team. One month had elapsed since the WHA had deserted the city, making it available to the Golden Seals and the NHL.

"There was so little time before that first meeting that we had to go in and tell them 'maybe this, maybe that.' This time, we had a lease and the financing details all arranged," said Swig. "I'm really glad that the approval is out of the way. I know that things are going to work out just fine in Cleveland."[34]

The Board of Governors was pleased, too. "The league is happy things worked out because Cleveland has had an extremely successful history in hockey," said NHL vice president Don Ruck. "Albeit it has been in the minor leagues. It has a sound hockey base and a sound hockey audience. The Coliseum is a large and fine facility."[35]

It's reasonable to say that it was the presence of the Coliseum, and the aggressiveness of its new owner, Sandy Greenberg, that secured an NHL club for Cleveland. Greenberg had invested a great deal of money in the Coliseum and desperately needed another tenant to make it a profitable venture. He acquired that tenant in the Golden Seals. The other elements needed for a successful operation were naively expected by all parties involved to simply fall into place. That didn't happen.

Swig noted while talking to reporters amid the euphoria of the

Board of Governors' decision that he hadn't met one of their requirements. "I haven't lined up any local investors yet,"[36] he admitted. But he expected to. Soon.

Before a single puck had been dropped, a large crack in the foundation of what the NHL hoped would be a strong franchise in Cleveland was already showing.

3

Becoming the Barons

Cleveland's hockey fans learned quickly what kind of organization they'd inherited from Oakland. Amid the fanfare of the NHL's arrival, however, they may not have noticed.

Paul Shmyr was one of the most popular, and productive, of the Crusaders during their four-year existence. Shmyr had defected from the Golden Seals to the WHA for its inaugural season of 1972–73 and remained on the team's negotiating list as it moved to Cleveland. Shmyr thought he had an agreement with Bill Putnam to stay with the Crusaders after they became the Florida Breakers, but it fell through. Given that the Golden Seals would bring a team of total strangers to Cleveland, it was thought that adding a familiar face, such as Shmyr, would help boost attendance. But that wasn't likely to happen.

"No doubt that Paul can play on our club and help us," said general manager Bill McCreary. The woeful Golden Seals needed all the help they could get, and Shmyr had been the WHA's top defenseman in 1975–76. "But it would have to be at our price. I'd like to have him for his talent and because it would be a popular move with the fans here. But I can't pay him what he was getting in the WHA, which is out of line with what our other players make. It wouldn't be fair to the other guys, and would hurt team morale."[1] Putnam couldn't pay Shmyr what his contract with the Crusaders called for, either, so where he'd play in 1976–77 was up in the air. He wouldn't move to Florida with the Crusaders, and he wouldn't join the Golden Seals. McCreary was willing to part with Shmyr's negotiating rights if he could make a deal he believed to be favorable to his team. But he'd also told Cleveland's hockey fans, who'd be charged NHL prices for the team's tickets, that it didn't have the money to compete with the league's elite. If it did, Mel Swig wasn't willing to spend it.

The Golden Seals announced on July 16 that ticket prices would range from $4.50 to $10. The most expensive seat at a Crusaders game at the Coliseum had been $6.50. "The owners of the Seals are convinced they will offer a far superior product to the Crusaders and the World Hockey Association," wrote Bob August in the *Press*. "They must be. Raising the top tickets to nine dollars and $10 is a pretty stiff boost."[2]

McCreary didn't think so. He said the Golden Seals' ticket pricing scale "puts us roughly in the middle half of the league, probably in the lower half. We're not the highest by a longshot."[3]

Swig established a goal of 10,000 season tickets. "It's unrealistic, but that's what we're hoping for,"[4] he admitted. He said he'd be satisfied with 5,000 to 6,000 season tickets. Two days after the transfer of the Golden Seals to Cleveland had been formally approved, nearly 1,000 season tickets had been sold. However, 625 were purchased by the owners of the Coliseum's luxury loges, whose lease agreements required them to buy season tickets to hockey and basketball games. Still, McCreary was impressed that, within 48 hours of the transfer becoming official, 375 average fans purchased season tickets.

"We've sold probably 50 today, and we have only one phone,"[5] he said proudly. The club would have more telephones, plus a sales force of eight to 10 people on the streets of Cleveland within a week. Those people were being trained in the proper methods of selling hockey tickets even as McCreary spoke.

The Golden Seals signed their top draft pick, 20-year-old defenseman Bjorn Johansson of Sweden, on July 18. Before the WHA arrived, the NHL had ignored European talent. When the WHA, in desperate need of players to stock its teams, looked across the Atlantic Ocean to help fill its rosters, the NHL started to do the same. Johansson was the third overall selection of the NHL draft and explained why he signed with the Golden Seals rather than the Birmingham Bulls, who'd drafted him in the WHA.

Through his agent, who doubled as his interpreter, Johansson said, "I would like to play in the NHL. I like hockey very much."[6] Monetary terms of Johansson's contract weren't announced.

About 100 people attended what could have been termed a "Meet the Golden Seals" luncheon on July 22. The only Seals on hand were the head coach, Jack Evans, and three players: Wayne Merrick, Dave Gardner and Rick Hampton. The only reason Merrick, Gardner and Hampton were there was because they lived in the Toronto area, so the trip to Cleveland was relatively short and inexpensive. The club wasn't going to foot the bill to fly players into Cleveland from distant places just to make a good impression on the community that was expected to embrace the NHL with open arms. Merrick, Gardner and Hampton gave their stamp of approval to the team's new red, white and black uniforms, which were unveiled during the luncheon, as was the new logo and nickname: the Barons. No one was surprised.

"That's not just the nickname, that's the true name," said Bobby Carse, who played with the original Barons of the American Hockey League at the Cleveland Arena in the 1940s and 50s. "It has a great heritage. What the heck, the Barons really built the game of hockey here, and I'm pleased to see it continued."[7]

Carse's Barons teammate, Ed (Whitey) Prokop, agreed. "I talked to people on the street and on the golf course, and all they said was 'Barons, Barons, Barons.' There are an awful lot of people who never went to a Crusaders game who will come back now that the NHL and the Barons are here. Changing the name to Crusaders soured some people."[8]

Changing the name of the Golden Seals to Barons soured at least one ex-Baron. Bill Needham played for Cleveland from 1956–57 through 1970–71, appearing in a club-record 981 games. He was the first head coach of the Crusaders, posting an 80–64–12 record with two playoff appearances from 1972 to 1974. Needham wasn't so certain christening the NHL team with the old AHL team's nickname was a good idea. "A lot of AHL records will get lost in the shuffle. It might not mean much to some people, but it does to me. There's a sadness about it."[9]

But Needham was the only one attending the luncheon who felt any sadness as the NHL was officially welcomed to northeastern Ohio. Barons co-owner George Gund III reflected on the whirlwind events of the past two months. "It seems amazing now that it's really happening. Just a couple of months ago, with the Crusaders here and nothing we could do about that, this just wasn't going to happen."[10]

The Crusaders were no longer Cleveland's problem, but they were still Jay Moore and Nick Mileti's problem. As of July 29, the sale of the Crusaders to Putnam still hadn't been finalized, and there were strong indications that it never would be. "I wouldn't say the sale was falling apart," insisted Putnam. "There are normal business problems. I'm going to have a hockey team in Florida this fall with orange and turquoise blue colors. I expect a settlement with Jay within 10 days. We've had a number of problems with Cleveland lawyers. I expected a settlement with Jay Moore on June 1st. About the first week of June things started getting strung out and the original deal had been changed."[11]

Moore's attorney, Bingham Zellmer, responded. "That's not quite the story. [Putnam] had two different lawyers. The second one wanted to change the whole set up."[12] After months of negotiating, Moore and Putnam couldn't agree on a payment schedule. Putnam was to pay Moore and Mileti $1.4 million for the Crusaders. Moore wanted 40 percent

($560,000) in payments to be made on August 1 and August 15, with the remaining 60 percent ($840,000) to be paid incrementally over two years. Putnam said he couldn't raise $560,000 so quickly and asked that the schedule be altered so that the first payment would be due September 1, and the second on September 15 or 30. That was unacceptable to Moore.

"We can't wait until the middle or end of September and then find out the deal is no go,"[13] said Moore.

"I can't enter an agreement I can't live up to," said Putnam, adding that the odds of his finalizing the purchase of the Crusaders were only 50–50. He said he'd sold 800 season tickets, and the response to the arrival of a hockey team in south Florida had been "fantastic." He characterized his negotiations with Moore as "ridiculous,"[14] and said he was looking into purchasing the WHA's San Diego Mariners, who'd finished the 1975–76 season under the league's financial control. Moore, who still owned the Crusaders, said Mileti was exploring the possibility of selling the team to groups from either St. Paul or Ottawa. St. Paul had already lost one WHA club, and Ottawa had lost two.

Having stabilized (or so they thought) the Golden Seals by allowing them to move to Cleveland to become the Barons, the NHL's Board of Governors in the final days of July took care of the league's other problem child. The governors rejected a last-ditch effort by Kansas City to keep the Scouts in town and ordered the club's owners to sell the team to Bud Palmer's group from Denver. If they refused, the Scouts would be disbanded by the league. Under no circumstances would the Scouts return to Kansas City for the 1976–77 season. Palmer's determination to acquire an NHL team for Denver had paid off. The season would open in slightly more than two months; training camp was little more than a month away. Palmer had a lot of work to do.

"The next step is now to get the assets and uniforms transferred over here to Denver," he said. "We have to hire a staff, hire a general manager and coach and get the competition started to find a name for the team."[15] The California Golden Seals had become the Cleveland Barons. The Kansas City Scouts were about to be transformed into the Colorado Rockies. The NHL thought it had solved its two most pressing problems.

It hadn't. The Barons would fold after two miserable seasons in northeastern Ohio. The Rockies would struggle through six seasons in Denver before being moved to Brendan Byrne Arena in the New Jersey Meadowlands, across the river from New York. The Big Apple had essentially three teams for the 1982–83 season.

As July came to a close, Bill McCreary announced that the Barons had sold 2,000 season tickets and banked $60,000. The NHL had been in Cleveland just two weeks but appeared to be off to a promising start.

While the Barons settled into their new home, the Crusaders continued to search for one. During the first week of August, the vagabond hockey club was reported to be on its way to St. Paul, then on its way to Florida, and then on its way back to St. Paul, all within six days. The *Plain Dealer* reported on August 3 that the sale to Putnam had fallen through. Moore had lost $1.5 million in the slightly less than year-and-a-half he'd owned the Crusaders, and Mileti had opened negotiations with city officials and civic leaders in St. Paul, who needed a tenant for the 16,000 seat Civic Arena. The facility had been built specifically to house the Fighting Saints of the WHA, and without a hockey team had no primary tenant. Guarantors of the arena were being asked to purchase four times as many season tickets as they'd purchased from the Fighting Saints in order to lure the remnants of the Crusaders to St. Paul, and they weren't happy about the expenditure. They also, however, weren't happy about owning an empty arena. Mileti was trying to reach an agreement that wouldn't obligate Moore financially, but would entitle him to a portion of the profits if the Crusaders succeeded in St. Paul. Such an arrangement was proving difficult to achieve. Mileti and Moore were also trying to void the player transactions Putnam had made while he was running a team he didn't own.

"We have advised Florida Pro Sports the trades should be reversed because they had no authority to make them. The feedback from the league is that none of the trades will be approved,"[16] Moore said. But the feedback proved to be wrong.

Moore was allowing Mileti to handle the negotiations with anyone interested in buying the Crusaders. This was because Mileti was once again the team's majority owner. An odd clause in the agreement Moore signed when purchasing 51 percent of Mileti's stock in the team enabled Mileti to reassume majority ownership if Moore decided to move the Crusaders out of Cleveland. The Crusaders were leaving, so Mileti exercised the option to reclaim majority ownership.

While Mileti was talking to representatives of St. Paul, Moore was in Washington, D.C., testifying before the House Select Committee on Professional Sports, which was investigating the cost of owning and operating a major league sports franchise. "We were constantly fighting to prove we played a good brand of hockey in Cleveland," Moore told the committee. "We just couldn't overcome the stigma of not being thought of as a major league team as the other teams in Cleveland are."[17] Moore said he needed to sell 8,000 season tickets and average 12,000 fans per game in order for the Crusaders to have been profitable. The team never approached either figure. He said, given the fact that they carried the NHL brand, the Barons had a good chance of making hockey work in Cleveland, but Mel Swig had to be prepared to lose money during the 1976–77 season.

On August 4, WHA chief executive officer Ben Hatskin said the league definitely would have a club in Hollywood for 1976–77. And Bill Putnam definitely would own it. "He may purchase either the San Diego or Cleveland franchises, or we may have to hold an expansion draft,"[18] Hatskin said. The matter would be resolved at the WHA trustees meeting on August 10 in Toronto.

In St. Paul, it was reported that 4,000 season tickets had been sold for a team the city didn't have. Fans responded to a newspaper advertisement literally pleading with them to buy season tickets to entice Mileti to relocate the Crusaders to the city's vacant arena. Mileti and Moore were still leaning toward Florida.

"If Putnam calls and says he can close the deal, that will be it," said Mileti. "If not, the St. Paul thing may be ready to go ... if the people there can fulfill certain targets that have been established."[19] Estimates as to how many season tickets Florida Pro Sports had sold for a non-existent hockey team varied wildly. Late in the spring, Putnam said he'd sold 800 season tickets. By early in August, that estimate had either shrunk to a mere 300, or expanded to 1,000, depending on the source of the information.

By August 7, Putnam had come to the realization that he couldn't compete with billionaire Ray Kroc, the owner of the San Diego Padres, who had decided to save WHA hockey for the city, as he'd rescued major league baseball two years earlier. Kroc would buy the bankrupt Mariners, and Putnam turned his attention back to the Crusaders. Mileti got a call from Putnam, but not to say he could close the deal. He wanted to reopen negotiations. The sticking point was no longer the dates on which Putnam's payments would be received. "The dates are not the problem now," Moore said. "The problems are how the money is to be paid and what protection we have that we get it."[20] Moore disputed the report of 4,000 season tickets being sold in St. Paul and claimed the figure was closer to 2,700. Moore said he'd rather sell the Crusaders to Putnam because the $1.4 million price would allow him to recoup most of the money he'd lost operating the team since March of 1975. If the Crusaders moved to St. Paul, Mileti would be their owner, and Moore would be out of luck.

One day after it was reported that Putnam and Hollywood were back in the picture, the Associated Press broke the news that the Crusaders were bound for the frozen north. "We've got it!" said St. Paul mayor George Latimer. "I've just got off the phone with Mileti ... and the deal has been made. Of course, it's conditional, pending league approval, but right now I'm very, very excited and happy. I think this is a victory for the people of our city ... they literally made it happen with our enthusiasm over the past two weeks."[21] Latimer was happy to have "major league" hockey return to St. Paul, but he was happier to have a tenant for the city's arena. Mileti agreed to a three-year lease at a flat rate of $1,500 per game. He promised to put $50,000 in escrow to guarantee payment for the first year of the agreement. Moore wouldn't be recouping the money he'd lost trying to save WHA hockey for Cleveland.

"Nick will operate the club in St. Paul and I will get out of hockey," Moore explained. "He will be the only general partner. I will remove myself and he will take over. I am sorry to get out of hockey, but it just didn't work out."[22]

Said Mileti, "that's the deal. Jay gets off the spot and I get back on." Mileti said he was reluctantly returning to hockey in order to save the franchise for the players and see to it that the Clevelanders who'd invested in the Crusaders (particularly Moore) didn't lose every penny they'd put into the club. "The way the Hollywood thing was going, there would have been nothing for my partners. This way, we're hoping to see that they still get something for their investments."[23] The key word was "hoping." There was no guarantee anyone who sank money into WHA hockey in Cleveland wouldn't be saddled with a total loss.

The WHA approved the transfer of the Crusaders to St. Paul on August 10. However, the city would be getting an emaciated version of the club, as the league's trustees surprisingly decreed that the player transactions Putnam had ordered to slash the team's payroll would stand, even though Putnam didn't have the authority to make them. It's possible Mileti wanted those trades and sales to stand, since he wasn't exactly awash in cash himself, and was grateful to be out from under those financial obligations.

The WHA trustees also approved the sale of the Mariners to Kroc. As for Putnam and Hollywood, both were left holding the bag. There would be no expansion team. With the start of the 1976–77 season just two months away, there simply wasn't time to organize a team from scratch. Only an organization as slipshod as the WHA would even have considered such an outlandish idea.

Meanwhile, the Barons were going about the business of preparing for their first season in Cleveland. The NHL announced the team's schedule on August 11. As anticipated, the Barons would open at the Richfield Coliseum, but the opposition wouldn't be provided by the division rival Toronto Maple Leafs, as originally speculated. The Los

Angeles Kings would visit Cleveland on October 6 for the city's first NHL contest.

During the heyday of the original Barons, Saturday nights in the fall and winter were hockey nights. Al Sutphin owned the Cleveland Arena and the Barons, and he had the clout with the American Hockey League to make sure the bulk of his club's home games were scheduled for Friday and Saturday nights ... mostly Saturdays. Mel Swig and the new Barons didn't have that kind of pull with the NHL, or with Sandy Greenberg, their landlord at the Coliseum. Cleveland would play 16 of its 40 home games on Wednesdays, and that had to affect attendance. The Barons would skate on home ice on a Saturday night just four times. The Cavaliers, who had scheduling priority, would play at home 11 times on a Saturday during the 1976–77 NBA season. The Barons would benefit from 11 Friday night home contests.

Both of Cleveland's daily newspapers interviewed Barons head coach Jack Evans in mid–August. Evans was born in Wales in 1928, and his hockey career dated back to the 1947–48 season. He played 15 seasons in the NHL between 1948–49 and 1962–63, the first nine with the New York Rangers and the last six with the Chicago Blackhawks. Evans had a minimal familiarity with Cleveland, having served as the Buffalo Bisons' player-coach during the 1963–64 AHL season. His career continued for eight more years in the Western Hockey League, with the Los Angeles Blades, California Seals and San Diego Gulls. After retiring as a player, he coached the Gulls from 1972 to 1974, and then moved on to Salt Lake City, where his team won the 1974–75 Western Hockey League championship. That earned him the head coaching job in Oakland, and his Golden Seals improved by eight victories during the 1975–76 season. The Golden Seals were 27–42–11 in their final season on the coast and were out-scored by just 28 goals. Anticipated improvement by the team's young players figured to turn some of those close defeats into victories. Cleveland's two hockey writers, Rich Passan of the *Plain Dealer* and Bob Schlesinger of the *Press*, spouted the company line that Swig had brought an up-and-coming hockey club to Cleveland.

Evans seemed to have the proper attitude, or at least the necessary sense of humor, to coach a young team. "Somebody said that if you are a coach, every night you go to bed and sleep like a baby," he told Bob August of the *Press*. "Meaning you wake up and cry a lot."[24] Unfortunately, the Barons would give Evans plenty to cry about during the coming season.

Several Cleveland radio stations expressed an interest in broadcasting the Barons' games. Ownership wisely decided to steer clear of

WWWE, the 50,000-watt, clear channel station owned by Nick Mileti which already broadcast the Indians and Cavaliers games and had been the voice of the Crusaders during their brief existence. The contract was awarded to WJW, a station with a much weaker signal of just 5,000 watts. But the smaller coverage area would allow the station and the club to build a far-reaching network of stations throughout Ohio, and possibly neighboring states such as Indiana and Kentucky.

"There were other stations considered for our broadcasts, but WJW's guarantee of carrying all 80 of our games was a major factor in our decision,"[25] said Bill McCreary. Though there would have been prestige involved in having the Barons' games broadcast on the power-house WWWE, whose signal (so it claimed) could be heard in 38 states and half of Canada at night, the team needed exposure. On WWWE, the Barons would've taken a back seat to both the Indians and Cavaliers. Some of their games would've been either broadcast on tape delay, joined in progress, or bumped altogether due to conflicts with baseball and (mostly) basketball. The Barons needed to attract fans. They couldn't afford to have people tune in only to be informed that they wouldn't hear hockey because the Cavaliers were playing. The NHL season ended early enough that an April conflict with baseball was unlikely (unless the Barons made the playoffs). And the thought of a conflict with the Indians in October was laughable in 1976.

The Barons would open their first training camp in northeastern Ohio at Kent State University's ice rink on September 15. They'd play two exhibition games at the Richfield Coliseum, and hoped to add a third to be played at Kent State.

Shortly after arriving in Cleveland, McCreary had put a damper on the idea of former Golden Seal (and Crusader) Paul Shmyr returning to the club. Shmyr squashed it altogether on August 25. He was under contract to the team formerly known as the Crusaders and apparently headed for St. Paul for the 1976–77 season. "There's just no way I'm going to play in Cleveland,"[26] he said. And he said it emphatically rather than ruefully.

Aside from signing Bjorn Johansson, their top draft pick, the Barons had made no personnel moves since relocating to Cleveland. McCreary said he didn't expect to do any wheeling and dealing during two days of meetings with his fellow general managers in Toronto on August 26 and 27. "There's nothing very serious in the works right now," he said. "It's tough to make a trade at this time of the year, until the general managers get to training camp and are reminded about the weak spots in their rosters. But still, when we get face-to-face instead of talking over the phone, you never know what might happen."[27]

Aside from the significant signing of the Barons' top goaltender, Gilles Meloche, to a reported six-year contract worth $750,000, McCreary made no personnel moves. The general manager and his head coach were certain their club could move up in the NHL standings with the players on hand.

4

Where's the Red Carpet?

The task of molding the Cleveland Barons into a competitive team began on September 15, 1976, when 49 skaters reported to training camp at Kent State University.

"We've got three weeks of training camp and the six exhibition games. We should be in good shape by the time we hit the league opener," said head coach Jack Evans. "With travel to other pre-season games, the actual ice time at camp is limited, so we expect the players to be able to go into light scrimmages timing, passing and shooting from the start."[1] In order to help build a bond with their new fan base, the Barons opened the practices at Kent State's ice arena to the public.

There were supposed to be 51 players in camp in mid–September. Veteran defenseman Jim Neilson was experiencing immigration problems at the Canadian border and would report as soon as those annual routine matters were disposed of. Goaltender Gary Simmons figured to be much more difficult to lure into camp. While his teammates were familiarizing themselves with northeastern Ohio, Simmons was sitting at home in Hayward, California, demanding that his contract be renegotiated.

According to Simmons, he was merely exercising a clause in his deal that allowed him to renegotiate after two seasons. "Nobody has called me all summer," the netminder said. "Maybe they were too busy." Simmons' demand was simple. "All I want is more money, or a trade to a team that will give me the money."[2] Barons general manager Bill McCreary had a different view of the situation.

McCreary said Simmons' contract didn't contain a renegotiation clause. Instead, McCreary's predecessor as GM, Garry Young, had given Simmons a promise of renegotiation that he scribbled on a slip of paper. McCreary didn't consider Young's promise binding, even if it was, technically, in writing. Complicating matters was the six-year, $750,000 contract the Barons had given their other goalie, Gilles Meloche, weeks before. A team needed a pair of top-notch goaltenders to compete in the

NHL, but with the team paying a hefty salary to Meloche, how much was McCreary willing to pay Simmons? Not as much as Simmons wanted, which was a four-year contract worth half a million dollars.

"I have a good idea what I'm worth," he said. "I have the stats on my side."[3] And he did. Simmons and Meloche split the Golden Seals' goaltending duties evenly in 1975–76, with Meloche playing in 41 games and Simmons in 40. Simmons' goals against average was 3.33, with a pair of shutouts. Meloche's goals against was 3.44 with one shutout. Simmons stopped 88.6 percent of the shots he'd faced; Meloche turned back 89 percent. Simmons' record in goal was 15–19–5 to Meloche's 12–23–6. The significant difference between the two was in their ages: Simmons was 32, Meloche 26. McCreary had chosen to secure Meloche's services for the long term with a six-year, six-figure contract. Simmons, whose numbers were marginally better than Meloche's, was asking for fewer years and fewer dollars. McCreary wasn't inclined to pay big bucks to both.

"We tried to accommodate him with a trade, but you don't give away talent for nothing," said McCreary, who offered Simmons to the Vancouver Canucks for Gary Smith in an even-up exchange of goaltenders. The

Barons head coach Jack (Tex) Evans gives instructions to his players during the first practice of the 1976–77 season at the Kent State University ice arena (Michael Schwartz Library, Cleveland State University).

Canucks rejected the deal. "We're going to make every effort to work things out," the general manager vowed. "I don't think there are any hurdles you can't overcome. He's a battler, and we sure want him back on our roster."[4]

It was whispered that there was a second reason for Simmons' hold-out: he was balking at the idea of playing in Cleveland. He didn't want to move his family from California, so he was trying to force a trade. Simmons said it wasn't true. He reiterated that he was holding out for one reason. "I signed a very low contract two years ago. I had to because I had never played in the NHL before." Although he was six years older than Meloche, Simmons was entering only his third season in the NHL. Meloche was starting his sixth. "Now I believe I've proved that I'm a quality big league player and I'd like to get paid like one. The only way I don't want to play here is if they don't want to pay what I'm worth. In that case, I'd like to be traded to someone who will."[5]

After two days of scrimmaging, Evans noted that "some of the guys think they are in mid-season shape, and they are not. They have to work into shape gradually, the younger kids particularly. They think they are going to make the team and usually get carried away with their eagerness. I know what the players we had last year can do. The young people we have here look promising."[6]

The players quickly grew weary of scrimmaging. They'd been on the job a week when the first exhibition game arrived. "We're really eager to get at it," said center Dave Gardner. "Practicing against ourselves gets monotonous. Playing other teams gives us something to prove."[7] Coming off a season in which they'd failed to make the playoffs and lost 15 more games than they'd won, the Barons had plenty to prove.

Cleveland would host its first National Hockey League game on Wednesday, September 22, with the Detroit Red Wings providing the opposition. The head coach and the players may have been excited about the event, but the fans weren't. "It's more than an exhibition game to us," said Evans. "This is our first game in front of the home fans, and we want to give them a good impression."[8] As an added incentive to Clevelanders to attend the city's first NHL game, the *Press* designated the evening as "Helping Hand" night. A portion of the proceeds from each ticket sold would be given to the newspaper's "Helping Hand" fund.

The Red Wings opened the scoring with a first period goal by Dennis Hextall and closed the scoring with a third period goal by Dennis Polonich. In between, Al MacAdam scored for the Barons in the 2–1 defeat.

"They were eager and nervous," said Evans of his club's debut in its new home. "They can skate with anybody. They'll settle down."[9]

Veteran Red Wings goalie Eddie Giacomin was impressed with the Barons. "This is a good, young club. They're going to make a lot of noise this year."[10]

Noise was missing from the Coliseum on that Wednesday night. Although it was just an exhibition, the crowd of 2,238 had to be a huge disappointment, if not an outright shock, to Mel Swig and George Gund III. Apparently Clevelanders didn't care to contribute to the *Press'* "Helping Hand" fund while taking in the city's first NHL contest.

Bob August, the *Press'* sports editor, described the first game in the Coliseum as "a rather eerie atmosphere." While conceding that the game was just an exhibition, August hoped that Swig and Gund took notice of the empty seats. "The size of the crowd also furnished a warning. Cleveland is a sophisticated sports city, long accustomed to teams performing at the highest level of competition in everything but hockey. Because of this, the NHL is especially welcome, its arrival so long delayed. But just being an NHL team is not enough to ensure the success of the Barons. The franchise has a job to do selling itself, both on the ice and in a vigorous promotional effort."[11]

Part of what the Barons considered to be a sufficiently vigorous promotional effort was on display in the September 21 edition of the *Press*, in the form of a nearly half-page advertisement for individual game tickets to the Coliseum. All 40 Barons games were listed in chronological order, with plenty of space for fans to fill in which game or games they wanted to attend, how many tickets they wanted, and what price they wanted to pay. That may have been a decent start, but much more promotion would be needed.

Bob Schlesinger was on the same page as August, his boss. "The turnout of 2,238 showed that hanging out an NHL sign on the door is not enough to put people in the seats by itself, no surprise to anyone who hasn't been looking at the hockey picture through rose-colored glasses,"[12] he wrote. Cleveland's hockey picture had been chaotic since the Crusaders forced the AHL Barons out of town back in 1973, and the arrival of the NHL wouldn't bring much improvement.

Gary Simmons, on the advice of his agent, reported to Kent on September 23. He was, after all, under contract, and was facing a $500 fine for each day he was AWOL. As for the effort to renegotiate his deal, Simmons said McCreary was offering "too many bonuses and not enough base."[13] McCreary's position was that if Simmons was to get really big money, he'd have to earn it between the pipes through incentive bonuses.

The Barons' second and last home exhibition game was against the New York Rangers on Friday, September 24. Much was made by

Cleveland's newspapers of the fact the Rangers were coached by John Ferguson, who'd played for the Barons of the AHL in the early 1960s. He didn't enjoy his visit to his old stomping grounds as the Barons beat the Rangers, 4–1. Ralph Klassen started Cleveland's scoring with a first period goal. New York's Steve Vickers tied the game later in the same period. Charlie Simmer put the Barons ahead in the second stanza, and a pair of power play goals in the third period by Gary Holt and Greg Smith sealed the victory.

"The youngsters really came through for us,"[14] said Evans. Only 2,017 watched. It was far from the type of atmosphere Ferguson remembered while playing at the Cleveland Arena.

Just 4,255 fans had paid their way in to the Coliseum to watch the Barons' first two games in their new hometown. Again, in fairness to the fans, it must be remembered that these were *exhibitions*. Still, the players on both sides commented on the sparse crowd for Friday's game. "It was kind of lonely out there,"[15] understated Ken Hodge of the Rangers.

"It's disappointing," said Gilles Meloche. "We left California because no one came to see us. I expected more than this. I mean, we have an exciting team. The crowd can help us win five or six more games this season. It's such a beautiful place to play in, too."[16]

Twenty-two-year-old right wing Fred Ahern was just as downcast as Meloche. "I could understand about our first game with Detroit, being on a Wednesday night. But I thought there'd be more people tonight ... a Friday night and the Rangers and all. I even asked the policeman about it when I was in the penalty box, but he said it'd be all right once the season starts. Boy, I hope so. The fans will be a big part of our success. And we're eager to show them something."[17]

It hadn't taken Cleveland's hockey fans long to show the Barons something ... that they weren't impressed with the NHL or their new team.

Two days later, the Barons defeated the Red Wings in an exhibition rematch in Kalamazoo, Michigan, 6–4. Cleveland scored three times in the first period and cruised from there.

The Barons broke camp in Kent on September 28 and headed west for their remaining exhibitions. As far as the roster was concerned, Evans said he was "more confused than ever." Not because the Barons didn't have enough talented players, but because they had too many. Or so it appeared.

The Los Angeles Kings, the Barons' opening night opponent at the Coliseum, hosted them in an exhibition game on September 29 and skated to a 5–3 victory. Attendance was 8,316, or roughly four times more fans than had witnessed either of the exhibitions in Cleveland.

The next night in Salt Lake City, the Barons and Kings tied at two apiece. Cleveland's goals were scored by Wayne Merrick and Jim Moxey. The game was viewed by 2,522 fans. The Barons stayed in Salt Lake City to take on their Western Hockey League farm team on October 1. The two teams agreed to a unique swap of goaltenders. Barons goalie Gary Simmons played the entire game for Salt Lake City. The Eagles' three goalies, Ray Martiniuk, Jim Warden, and Larry Hendrick, each saw some action between the pipes for the Barons. Simmons made 19 saves against his teammates but was beaten twice by Dennis Maruk and once by Merrick and Bob Girard. Salt Lake City won, 6–4. A crowd of 3,480 watched. The Barons had two farm clubs in 1976–77: the Eagles and the Toledo Goaldiggers of the International Hockey League.

The Barons finished the exhibition season with a record of 1–3–1. They flew back to Cleveland to prepare for the opening of the regular season at the Coliseum on October 6. A considerably less than capacity crowd was expected, and Rich Passan wasn't surprised. The hockey writer for the *Plain Dealer* told his readers on October 3 that the Barons had their work cut out for them if they were to reignite interest in the sport in northeastern Ohio.

"Even though the fabled NHL has finally arrived in Cleveland, crowds will not flock to see the teams," Passan wrote. "And for a very good reason. The hockey fans in this area, for the most part, are turned off to the game. The World Hockey Association Crusaders took care of that." In Passan's opinion, the Crusaders' front office had been indifferent to the fans, and the product it put on the ice had been mediocre at best, underachieving at worst. Following the Crusaders' chaotic final season, the fans were fed up with hockey. Then Barons arrived in Cleveland with a team full of promising players, but players the local fans had never heard of. Star players on visiting teams wouldn't be enough to lure fans to the Coliseum while the Barons established themselves.

Passan concluded the column with this thought: "this is a good hockey town. A good hockey team will prove that, but it will take time. Hopefully, the Barons will give it that time." Unfortunately for Passan and northeastern Ohio, the Barons wouldn't.

The Kings brought some star power to the Coliseum on opening night. Center Marcel Dionne was starting his second season with Los Angeles. Dionne scored 132 goals and 366 points in four years with Detroit before signing a million-dollar contract with the Kings in 1975. In his first season in Los Angeles, Dionne scored 40 goals and assisted on 54 others. The Kings' record declined, however, from 42–17–21 without Dionne in 1974–75 to 38–33–9 with him in 1975–76. To add a little muscle, the Kings sent a pair of draft choices to the Philadelphia Flyers for defenseman/enforcer Dave Schultz just a week before they arrived in Cleveland to help the Barons start their first season in their new home.

Fred Ahern spoke for most of his teammates when he admitted to being nervous about the first game that would count in the standings. "I'm anxious to get started. I'm anxious to see what kind of crowd we get."[18] Added Dave Gardner, "I hope we can come up with a good performance. It seems funny, but we have to impress the people in our first couple of games. But I don't think the guys are worried. We know we have a good enough team."

The almost non-existent crowds at the Barons' two home exhibition games left an impression on Gardner and his teammates. "When we played in California, we had to play for ourselves at times. Here, we want to play for the community as a whole, and make them proud of us."[19] The vast majority of Cleveland's hockey fans adopted a "wait-and-see" attitude regarding the city's new team.

National Hockey League president Clarence Campbell chose to skip the luncheon introducing Cleveland to the league and the league to Cleveland on October 5. He also chose to skip the Barons' first regular season game in the Coliseum. The NHL was represented by executive director Brian O'Neill. The opening night festivities included the introduction of 13 former members of the American Hockey League Barons, plus speeches by Mel Swig and George Gund III. Then Cleveland mayor Ralph J. Perk dropped the ceremonial first puck.

There were 8,899 fans in the Coliseum seats to witness the pre-game hoopla, and the action on the ice that followed. It took the Barons until the third period to score their first NHL goal, with Ahern's tally tying the score at 1–1. Less than three minutes later, Dennis Maruk put Cleveland in front, 2–1. Two minutes after that, the Kings' Mike Murphy rifled the puck past Gilles Meloche and ended the scoring. The game wound up in an unsatisfying 2–2 deadlock. Meloche stopped 26 Los Angeles shots. Rogatien Vachon stopped 27 of Cleveland's shots. It didn't take long for the fans to voice their displeasure with their new team. A smattering of boos was heard in the third period when the Barons failed to score in spite of holding a two-man advantage. The fans were new to the NHL, but not to hockey. Clevelanders had been watching hockey since the 1920s. They knew what a team was supposed to do with a 5-on-3 power play.

"For a first game, it was very well played by both teams," was Jack Evans' assessment. Evans was asked why he'd put the team's top draft pick, 20-year-old Bjorn Johansson, in the contest in the first period. "I might as well see now what he'll do," the coach responded. "I've got to show him I've got confidence in him."[20] Johansson was on the ice in the third period when Maruk scored the goal that put the Barons ahead briefly.

In between games and practices, the players spent their time getting accustomed to northeastern Ohio. Gary Simmons had purchased a home in the nearby city of Hudson and admitted there'd been some truth to the rumor that his reluctance to report to Cleveland was prompted by more than a salary disagreement with management. Said Simmons, who owned a pizzeria in California that he didn't want to leave behind, "it took me a while to get over my original thoughts of Cleveland. I don't like snow. I hate it. I've played without it for seven years. My [seven-year-old] daughter, the cat and the dog haven't seen it yet. The dog will hate it."[21] Simmons worked on a sheet of ice. He wasn't keen about having to deal with ice and snow in order to get to work, as he knew he'd often have to do when the Barons played at home.

With the Cleveland Cavaliers not having started their NBA season yet, the Barons were scheduled for a rare Saturday night home game on October 10, with the opposition to be provided by the woeful Washington Capitals. The third-year franchise had been the worst expansion team of all time (in the NHL or any sport) during its inaugural season of 1974–75, winning just eight games and losing a staggering 67. Five games ended in ties. The Capitals improved slightly to 19 victories in 1975–76. Sounding like a typical coach, Evans insisted that "we're not taking Washington lightly. We'd be insane to do that. We can't take any team in this league lightly. We're a building team and on the way up. We're not like Montreal, Philadelphia and Boston, teams that can beat a team like Washington at will."[22] But the Barons were good enough to hand the Capitals a 6–3 loss before a disappointing crowd of 5,209. The term "disappointing crowd" can be used to describe all but a handful of the gatherings that attended the Barons' 80-home games during their two seasons in Cleveland.

The Barons grabbed a 1–0 lead in the first period on Charlie Simmer's goal. Washington took a short-lived one-goal lead in the second period on scores by Guy Charron and Ace Bailey. Maruk and Bob Murdoch retaliated to put the Barons up, 3–2, at the second break. After the Caps' Hartland Monahan tied it early in the final period, Merrick, Moxey and Johansson lit the lamp for the comfortable victory. Johansson also assisted on Moxey's goal, giving him his first points as a professional. Simmons turned away 20 Washington shots on goal.

"I get so excited watching them sometimes that I find myself cheering on the bench,"[23] said the generally unemotional Evans in one of his few happy moments as Barons coach. The next day's game in Boston would bring an end to his joyful mood.

Making the Barons' 4–3 loss in the Boston Garden harder to swallow was the fact that Bruins goalie Gerry Cheevers was named "Star of the Game." The same Gerry Cheevers who'd been chased out of Cleveland by the Crusaders the season before, when Jay Moore wasn't able to pay his $200,000 salary. In an effort to save face, the Crusaders, after reaching a financial settlement with Cheevers, hinted that the team would be better off without him and that his performance had declined during his three and a half seasons in Cleveland, where he often single-handedly kept the Crusaders respectable. Cheevers had no hard feelings toward the city or its fans. His beef had been with Moore and general manager Jack Vivian. If he felt vindicated by his strong showing against Cleveland's new team, he hid it.

"Maybe I'm lucky that the Barons haven't seen me too often," said the man often called "Cheesy" by the fans. "They're not used to my style on breakaways. That probably helped me." Cheevers said he liked what he'd seen of the Golden Seals/Barons since returning to the NHL in February of 1976. "I'll tell you, Cleveland's got one heck of a hockey team. I was impressed with them last season and again tonight. They really skate and work and move that puck. The fans in Cleveland really ought to appreciate the way those guys play."[24]

Cheevers stopped 32 shots in the victory, which was achieved when Wayne Cashman slipped the puck past Meloche at 8:31 of the third period, breaking a 3-all tie. Cheevers kept the Barons at bay the rest of the way, and Cleveland had its first loss of the young season.

Boston's veteran goalie wasn't the only Bruin impressed by the Barons. Don Cherry, the reigning NHL "Coach of the Year," praised the visitors, who shared the same division with the Bruins. "Cleveland could move right up to second place, and possibly take first,"[25] Cherry said.

In what may have been a case of a self-fulfilling prophecy, Bob Schlesinger posed the question of how the Barons would draw on weekdays before the Atlanta Flames visited the Coliseum on a Wednesday night. The Flames were a strong team but had no star player who might entice fans to head for Richfield in the middle of the week. Why the uncertainty as to how the Barons would fare at the box office on weeknights? The bottom line was, during the heyday of the original Barons of the AHL, in the 1940s through the late 1960s, Saturday was hockey night in Cleveland. In the 1940s, Al Sutphin not only owned the hockey team, but he also owned the Cleveland Arena. Thus, he made sure his team got favorable playing dates. It was common for the Barons to play half of their home games on Saturday nights. Most of the others were played on Fridays. Weekday games were unusual. After Sutphin sold the Arena and the Barons in the early 1950s, the hockey team remained the building's only tenant and had dibs on Saturday nights until the Cavaliers were born in 1970. In contrast, the new Barons would play 16 of their 40 home games on Wednesday ... a night when adults had to get up for work the next morning, and kids had to get up for school. For established teams with loyal followings, weekday games were no problem. An entire hockey season, however, couldn't be squeezed into Friday nights, Saturday nights, and Sunday afternoons. Not in the NHL. For the Barons, weekday games gave the fans another excuse to stay home and listen on the radio. Or to ignore the games altogether.

The Barons were stymied by an old nemesis in their 4–2 loss to the Flames on October 13. During the 1975–76 season, Atlanta goalie Phil Myre faced the Golden Seals three times and allowed just two goals, shutting them out once. Myre was sharp again as the Flames handed the Barons their second straight loss. "I don't know what it is. I don't have any special feeling of confidence against the Barons, but I just seem to do well against them,"[26] said Myre, who stopped 26 of Cleveland's 28 shots. The one bright spot for the Barons was Dennis Maruk's third goal in four games. The attendance was a dismal 3,812.

The red flags were already flying above the Coliseum.

"It seems when we go flat, the whole team does it,"[27] said McCreary of the loss to the Flames. Part of the problem was the failure to capitalize on power plays. Through their first four games, the Barons had a man advantage 22 times, but had converted those chances into just four goals. They had been eighth in the NHL on power plays in 1975–76. "We've got to make our power play produce,"[28] McCreary said.

Right winger Mike Fidler, who impressed no one in training camp, and center Rick Shinske were playing well at Salt Lake City in the early going of the Western Hockey League season. McCreary said Fidler appeared to be the type who practiced poorly but performed well in games. "Now we know we have depth if we need it. Some guys have to get going soon. We can't wait much longer,"[29] McCreary said. The season was less than two weeks old at that point.

Advance ticket sales for the visit by the Chicago Blackhawks on October 19 were reported to be brisk. So were sales of tickets to the game against the two-time Stanley Cup champion Philadelphia Flyers on the fifth of November.

The Flyers had been dethroned as Stanley Cup winners by the Montreal Canadiens in 1975–76. If the Canadiens didn't win the Cup again in 1976–77, Evans thought he knew who would. "They're going to be the next Stanley Cup champions," he said of the New York Islanders while the Barons practiced at the Nassau County Coliseum on October 15. "They have good size, a lot of talent and are just a good, solid team."[30]

The Islanders were coached by Al Arbour, who'd been a teammate of Evans with the Blackhawks from 1958 to 1961.

Arbour's Islanders dominated Evans' Barons but came away with only a 4–4 tie. Cleveland led, 4–2, heading into the third period, but surrendered the tying goals amid a flurry of shots on goaltender Simmons, who spent the final 20 minutes of the game under siege. The Islanders fired 19 shots at Simmons in the third period and snuck two of them past him. Simmons was up to the task when the Islanders played the game's last two minutes with a 5-on-3 advantage as the nearly 15,000 fans screamed and pleaded with them to score the winning goal. The Barons, in the third period, managed just two shots against Islanders goalie Glenn (Chico) Resch. He stopped both. For the game, the Islanders out-shot the Barons, 40–21.

Considering his team had been out-shot by a 2–1 margin, Evans was satisfied with the tie. "I'd like to think the club is just rising to its capabilities," he said after the contest. "We're playing so well, so consistently, it has to be that. Some of the situations under which they have been playing have been real pressure spots." Such as killing a two-man power play by the Islanders in the final 120 seconds of the game.

"That was a confidence builder," said Evans of the deadlock. "For us to play the way we did against them and control the game until the late stages, definitely has to give the guys considerable confidence."[31]

Said Islanders general manager Bill Torrey of the Barons, "this is a very good team and should win a lot of games."[32]

Until the fans got to know the Barons, the front office was counting on the opportunity to watch in action superstars they'd previously only heard about to attract paying customers to the Coliseum. One of those superstars was Bobby Orr, who'd revolutionized hockey while playing defense for the Bruins. Orr was the game's first defenseman who was also a scoring threat, and he led the Bruins to the Stanley Cup title in 1971–72. Orr had undergone five knee surgeries by the time he signed a five-year, three-million-dollar contract with the Blackhawks prior to the 1976–77 season. Any time either of his knees experienced even the slightest twinge of pain, he was shut down until the pain subsided. Orr felt such a twinge before the Blackhawks visited Cleveland, so he didn't play. The fans were disappointed, but the Barons weren't.

Without Orr, the Blackhawks couldn't sustain any offense and fell to the Barons, 3–0. Former Blackhawk Jim Pappin scored the game's first goal. Pappin said he wasn't out for revenge against the team that traded him away. "I've played against them three times and have three goals. I've always wanted to beat them, but I've been away now for two years, and it's not like it was last year."[33]

Meloche stopped 31 Chicago shots en route to his ninth career shutout. "I wanted the win first. I didn't think about the shutout until the last five or six minutes."[34] Maruk and Greg Smith scored the other goals in the first shutout in Barons history. In spite of published reports that tickets had been selling well, the attendance was only 5,653.

Two days later, the Barons polished off the St. Louis Blues at the Coliseum, 6–2. Maruk was too much for the Blues to handle, scoring twice and assisting on two other goals. Blues head coach Emile Francis wasn't particularly impressed with the Barons and laid blame for the defeat squarely at the skates of his players. "They got too many goals without having to work for them," Francis moaned. "We dug a hole early for ourselves. When you get behind 3–0, you're asking for trouble, and that's what we got. From our standpoint, we gave them the game. From theirs, they capitalized on those mistakes. We just gave them three bad goals. We did the work and they got the scoring chances."[35] Simmons turned away 26 St. Louis shots in the easy victory. The Thursday night game was witnessed by just 3,453 fans.

The next night, the Cleveland Cavaliers opened their NBA season and drew a crowd of 19,783 to Richfield.

Evans said he was pleased with what he'd seen of his young Barons after seven games. "The big difference up here is the consistency and the caliber of the teams in the league. I always expect consistency, because I ask for it. It's not always there, though."[36]

The schedule-maker gave the Barons a five-day break between the game against St. Louis and the visit by the New York Rangers on October 26. "We'll either come back like gangbusters or stink the joint out," said Evans. "There is no in between. It's almost like the first game of the season. The players are unsure of how they will play and are scared until they get confidence in themselves."[37]

Brothers competed against each other when the Barons hosted the Rangers. Twenty-three-year-old Bob Murdoch played for Cleveland. His 20-year-old brother Don played for New York. Bob described his relationship with Don as being more like best buddies than brothers. Before the season started, the Murdochs made a $1,000 bet as to who would score the most goals in 1976–77. "If I win, the money goes to my dad," explained Bob. "If Donny wins, the money goes to my mom. My dad isn't too happy."[38] That was because, entering the October 27 game, Don had scored nine goals, including a five-goal explosion against the Minnesota North Stars. Bob had been sidelined by a pulled muscle and scored just twice.

Don Murdoch added two goals at the Barons' expense as the Rangers triumphed, 5–2. Evans had been right about his team stinking out the joint but didn't want to blame the performance on the long lay-off. "I don't want to use that as an excuse. We just didn't play a good game. That's what it amounted to. The team apparently was not sharp. That's my responsibility, and I'll take the blame for it."[39]

Rangers center Phil Esposito, who was in the twilight of a Hall of Fame career, was generous toward the vanquished Barons. "I don't think they played as well as they can," he said. "This is a helluva team. We didn't let them get untracked tonight."[40] Another Wednesday night game attracted a pitiful crowd of 4,716. Schlesinger looked at the gathering through the rose-colored glasses he'd alluded to in an earlier column and mentioned a crowd of "almost 5,000" in his game summary.

Evans was asked about the meager crowds during a luncheon the day after the loss to the Rangers. He said the silence in the big building had no effect on his players. "Once the game gets started, you lose awareness of how many people are in the building. But it would be nice to play to big crowds."[41]

Assistant general manager Harry Howell had an explanation for the small crowds. "I think people are taking a 'wait-and-see' attitude. We're the new kid on the block and they are waiting a little longer to see how we'll do."[42] Evans and Howell said the right things for public consumption, but everyone involved with the Barons, from ownership down to the players, had to be stunned by the apathy that greeted their arrival in northeastern Ohio.

The late transfers of the Golden Seals to Cleveland and the Scouts to Denver played havoc with the NHL's 1976–77 schedule. Both clubs logged a lot of air miles, particularly the Barons. A brief two-game west coast swing saw them visit Vancouver on October 28 and Los Angeles on October 30. The Canucks beat Cleveland, 3–1.

"We did not play well, but we still could have won because we got chances," said right wing Al MacAdam of the loss in Vancouver. "We played better than we did against the Rangers, but not as well as we can."[43]

The chances MacAdam referred to were snuffed out by Canucks goalie Cesare Maniago. "Maniago was the difference," said Evans. "We should have had three or four more goals."[44]

Before the Barons moved down the coast to Los Angeles to meet the Kings, Schlesinger devoted his column in the *Press* to the team's attendance woes and what Mel Swig planned to do about them. He also sounded an ominous note in the form of a quote from NHL president Clarence Campbell, when asked about the lack of enthusiasm Cleveland had shown for his league so far.

"The transfer of Oakland to Cleveland should help," Campbell said, "although there's still a question about the strength of the ownership there."[45]

In an earlier column, Schlesinger complained that the Barons ticket prices were too high and suggested they be reduced by two to three dollars. He also griped that promotions had been non-existent. He gave Swig a forum to respond to those criticisms. "We're obviously unhappy about the attendance so far," the Barons' majority owner admitted. "But this may merely indicate that we've made some early sacrifices for the good of the long-range program. Actually, things are improving in terms of advance sales and group sales.

"I think it should be pointed out that we haven't had any giveaways or 2-for-1 deals. That means our crowd of 6,000 or 8,000 may be equivalent to 10,000 or 12,000 fans in a heavily discounted house." Unfortunately, since drawing almost 9,000 fans on opening night, the Barons hadn't enjoyed a crowd of 6,000 or 8,000. They'd come relatively close once, drawing 5,653 against Chicago.

Swig dismissed Schlesinger's contention that ticket prices were too expensive for average Clevelanders. "I think it's important to realize our ticket prices are on the low or low-middle side in comparison to other teams in the National Hockey League. And in some cases, clubs with higher prices don't have as good a club as we do." He also shot down Schlesinger's complaint of a lack of promotion. "Sure, maybe we could fill the Coliseum with cut-rate customers. But it would be cheapening our product and it wouldn't be fair to the season ticket holders, who have paid full price."

Swig was confident the Barons would weather the storm. "I think part of the problem, right now, beyond the fact that we've had rotten luck with the schedule in terms of being up against the presidential debate and the World Series, is that our players are not well known yet. When the fans get to know and appreciate a Dennis Maruk, a Gilles Meloche, or an Al MacAdam, for example, it's going to make a huge difference. It wouldn't be honest to say we've been thrilled by the response so far. But I haven't cooled at all on the idea that Cleveland's a good hockey market. We'll get there. It just takes some time."[46]

On what evidence did Swig base his faith in Cleveland as a market for hockey? There's no reason to believe he had anything more than George Gund's reminiscences of Saturday nights at the Cleveland Arena in the 1960s, and those days were long gone. The transfer of the Golden Seals had been hasty, to say the least. The move was put together in a matter of weeks because Swig's team needed a larger building to play in, and Cleveland had one. No consideration was given to the fact that the Barons gave Cleveland a fourth major league team to support ... or not support, as was turning out to be the case. Cleveland had a beautiful building for hockey, but a decreasing population and an industrially based economy that was in a steady decline. Fans whose disposable income was getting smaller now had another option for spending that income. Could the city's sports dollar be split four ways? Sports marketing wasn't nearly as sophisticated in 1976 as it is today. Had it been, many more questions would've been asked about northeastern Ohio's ability to support the NHL before a decision would have been reached as to whether it was the right place to relocate the Golden Seals. In short, Cleveland had a sparkling arena for Swig's team to play in, and a large, if not necessarily thriving, population base for it to draw from. That seemed to be enough.

As for the concern Campbell expressed about the solvency of the Barons' ownership, it was significant that Swig's effort to attract local partners to join him and Gund had produced nothing. No Clevelanders with money seemed interested in investing in the National Hockey League. Apparently those who lived in the community weren't as confident in its ability to support major league hockey as Swig was. The club's absentee ownership wasn't helping. Swig and Gund were monitoring Cleveland's response to its new sports franchise from 2,500 miles away. Swig wasn't a Clevelander, and Clevelanders didn't care to have their sports teams owned by out-of-towners. As far as the fans were concerned, it didn't feel as if the Barons belonged to Cleveland. As far as the players were concerned, Cleveland didn't feel like home.

The Barons wrapped up their first month in the NHL with a 4–3 loss to the Kings on the night before Halloween. They returned to Cleveland, and a four-game home stand, with a record of 3–5–2 and three straight defeats.

5

Hockey for the Holidays

The Barons returned home from their brief journey to the west coast in search of their power play. It was becoming a familiar refrain.

"Our power play has fallen off to the point where it's embarrassing," said coach Jack Evans. How embarrassing was Cleveland's power play? Playing with a man advantage, the Barons had scored just once in their last five games, and not at all in either Vancouver or Los Angeles. "It's a combination of things. We have the same people working on it. They are the same people who made it go last year. A good power play can win games for you." Since the same people who gave the Golden Seals the eighth most productive power play in the NHL in 1975–76 weren't getting the same results for the Barons, Evans considered changing some faces. Ultimately, however, he was resigned to the fact that rearranging personnel probably wasn't the answer. The players who'd produced for him the previous season would have to produce in 1976–77, and the coach was confident they eventually would.

"Sometimes these things go in spurts," Evans said. "We'll come out of it."[1] And they did, in a 6–3 loss to their Adams Division rivals, the Toronto Maple Leafs, at the Coliseum on November 1, opening a four-game home stand. Two of Cleveland's three goals were scored when Toronto had a man in the penalty box. But that was all the Barons did right. Only 3,488 watched them fall three points behind the Maple Leafs in the division.

Toronto head coach Red Kelly was benevolent toward the Barons. "I thought the Barons might be flat in the first period," he said. "That often happens to a team that played out west in a different time zone two nights earlier. They were flat, and we were able to take advantage of it."[2]

"Every time we come up against Toronto in a big game, we foul it up," Evans moaned. "We seem to fall apart."[3] In an effort to add some power to the Barons' power play, and to the offense in general, the club recalled right wing Mike Fidler from Salt Lake City. Fidler had accumulated 18 points in 10 games for the Eagles with a dozen goals and a half

56

dozen assists. The game against Toronto was Fidler's first in the NHL, and he didn't score.

Evans said it was important for him to remain calm during the Barons' losing streak, which reached four with the loss to the Maple Leafs. "If there is panic on the coaching level, the players might also panic. We have to work through this and apply ourselves more than we have."[4] Evans' hockey career had begun almost 30 years earlier, and he'd seen plenty of losing streaks ... many of them much longer than a mere four straight games. While it was important to be patient, especially since he was coaching the youngest squad in the NHL, Evans also had to make it clear that the performance of those youngsters at the moment wasn't acceptable.

"We can't play like this and win hockey games," he said after supervising a 90-minute practice the day after the Toronto game. The session concentrated on puck movement, which the coach felt was lacking the evening before. "We're making mistakes we normally don't make. It's very frustrating after playing so well in the previous five games. This is a better team than it has showed and has to bounce back. I can't jump on them when they're down like this. I have to get them back on the right track."[5]

The Kings handed Cleveland its fifth consecutive loss on November 3, scoring two goals in the game's closing seconds to break a 2–2 tie. Defenseman Dave Hutchinson slammed a 25-foot slap shot past Gary Simmons with 1:09 to play. Evans then pulled Simmons for a sixth attacker, and the Kings' Tommy Williams rammed the puck into the Barons' unguarded net with six seconds to go. Only 3,157 were on hand to watch the Barons lose again.

The sparse crowd dropped the Barons' per-game average to about 4,800 ... considerably less than the 7,100 the Crusaders had averaged at the Coliseum through eight home games during the 1975–76 season. That figure included a huge throng that descended on Richfield the night the Crusaders gave team jackets away. The promotion was a fiasco. The club ran out of jackets and had to issue vouchers to the fans who showed up after the supply had been exhausted. Among the many headaches Jay Moore had to deal with during his final days as the Crusaders' owner was trying to satisfy angry patrons who were still waiting for their jackets from a promotion that had taken place eight months before. It was another reason many fans rejected the Crusaders' claim of being a major league team. Major league teams rarely made those kinds of mistakes, and when they did, they corrected them quickly.

The attendance figures proved, in Schlesinger's opinion, that the Barons' ownership had underestimated the task of marketing the team

to northeastern Ohio and overestimated the power of the NHL to draw
fans to the Coliseum. Advertisements for future games in the city's
two daily newspapers didn't urge Clevelanders to cheer for their Barons. Instead, they encouraged fans to watch NHL hockey. Mel Swig and
George Gund (or the team's promotions department) remained stub-
bornly convinced that the NHL brand was enough to convince Clevelanders to beat a path to Richfield. And that approach wasn't working.

After two scoreless games getting acclimated to the big league,
Fidler showed the Barons the form that had almost forced them to promote him from Salt Lake City. And he did it against one of the best
teams in the NHL, the two-time Stanley Cup champion Philadelphia
Flyers. Fidler scored twice and assisted on a third goal. Bob Murdoch
added a pair of goals as the Barons surprised the Flyers, and a crowd of
10,297 at the Coliseum, with a 6–4 victory on November 5.

"I felt better than I did in my first game," Fidler admitted. "I was in a
daze that night [against Toronto]. But now I'm relaxed. I felt more confident, especially after the first goal. It was a good feeling." Fidler undoubtedly spoke for his teammates when he added "I was pretty charged up by
the crowd."[6]

Evans praised Murdoch for fighting through an injury, which limited his effectiveness. "Imagine, there I was giving Bobby hell after every
game and practice, and he never said a word. It turned out that he had
a badly pulled groin muscle since training camp, and he didn't tell me
because he wanted to stay in the lineup."[7]

The victory was a good feeling for the entire team, coming against
a quality opponent in front of the biggest home crowd of the young season. "It's very satisfying when you win one like that and bounce back,"
said Evans. "It's very frustrating to see them work hard in practice and
then the puck bounces wrong for them during the game. This game will
do a lot for our kids. This should help us get on track just in time for our
trip."[8]

Before that six-game journey which would take the Barons to both
the west and east coasts and a few cities in between, the Pittsburgh Penguins came to town ... without their star player, center Pierre LaRouche,
who had been suspended for insubordination. LaRouche had skipped a
practice and then argued with the front office and was left at home when
the Penguins made the short trip northwest on the interstate to take
on the Barons. His absence left a gaping hole in Pittsburgh's offense as
LaRouche had scored 53 goals and assisted on 58 others in 1975–76. But
the Barons couldn't take advantage of their short-handed visitors.

Simmons was almost hot enough to melt the ice beneath him after
Pittsburgh's Jean Pronovost scored a second period goal to give his

team a 2–1 lead. Simmons insisted Pronovost had swatted the puck into the net with his glove. He protested to referee Bruce Hood, but got no satisfaction.

"Hood didn't have a clue!" snarled Simmons after the game. "I'm telling you he definitely batted it in with his glove. If I'm lying, I'm dying!"[9]

"I don't know why they were arguing," smirked Pronovost, like the proverbial cat who swallowed the canary. "It hit the shaft of my stick and went in."[10]

Fortunately for the Barons, the missed call by Hood didn't cost them the game. Dennis Maruk snapped out of a scoring slump with a third period goal that tied the game at two, and Simmons made 11 saves to be sure it stayed that way. Apparently not many fans in the solid crowd that watched the game against the Flyers stopped by the Coliseum's box office on their way out to buy tickets for the Penguins game. Attendance was only 4,617.

A disturbing pattern by the Barons was on display again in the tie with Pittsburgh. They had dominated the game until Pronovost's phantom goal, after which they went into a shell for the rest of the period. They emerged in the third and salvaged a tie, but Evans wasn't pleased with the 10 sluggish minutes his team played after it fell behind. "They seem to get rattled each time a goal is scored against them, and they shouldn't,"[11] he fumed.

Evans was asked if his players' inspired performance versus Philadelphia was due to the sizable crowd. "I know the players responded in the Philadelphia game, and it's possible that could have had an effect. But I don't want the players to use the size of the crowds as an out. I want them to play their best regardless."[12]

Although everyone involved with the Barons tried to downplay the situation, there was concern in the front office that a young team which could've benefited from large, loud crowds at their home games was affected by the small, quiet gatherings at the Coliseum. Particularly since the players had been promised they'd be playing in a beautiful building packed with enthusiastic fans when the team moved to northeastern Ohio. General manager Bill McCreary talked to the team about the sparse attendance at its games before it departed for the first extended road trip of the season on November 9.

"When they come back off the road … against the Montreal Canadiens, we expect a crowd of between 12,000 and 14,000. I told them not to be concerned with the attendance now because they will eventually get the fan support from the community."[13] But the fact McCreary was addressing the team about the subject indicated he was worried about their frame of mind after a month of playing before small crowds in their home arena.

The Barons' six-game trip would take them to Denver, Atlanta, Washington, Los Angeles, Minnesota and Detroit. Evans looked forward to hitting the road, noting that his club had played its best hockey so far away from the Coliseum. He said he felt confident about the journey and thought earning six points on the trip was a reasonable goal, although, of course, he hoped for more.

McCreary agreed that it would be good for the Barons to get away from the Coliseum for a while, too. "Some of the guys might be feeling a little pressure at home. On the road, they don't have to put on a show, just win hockey games."[14]

Cleveland picked up two of the six points Evans hoped for in its first game, a 2–1 victory over the Colorado Rockies in Denver. Goals by Fred Ahern and Greg Smith were enough for Gilles Meloche, who picked up a game misconduct penalty for trying to break up a fight between his teammate, Mike Christie, and Colorado's Phil Roberto in the closing seconds. Simmons had to put on the goalie pads and protect the Cleveland net for the game's final three seconds. The Rockies were struggling to attract fans to McNichols Arena just as the Barons were struggling to attract them to the Coliseum. Attendance was 6,447. Bigger than most crowds in Cleveland, but still not very good. Considerably smaller, in fact, than the team had averaged in Kansas City the season before. The Rockies were coached by former Crusaders coach John Wilson.

Stating the obvious, Evans said, "it's always good to win the first game of a long trip."[15]

Two nights later, on November 12, the Barons tied the Flames in Atlanta, 3–3. Rick Hampton scored the tying goal for the visitors with 6:19 to play in the third period, and Simmons kept the Flames off the board from there. The next stop was Washington, where goals by Christie, Wayne Merrick and Al MacAdam and stingy goaltending by Meloche gave the Barons a 3–2 victory. Christie's goal was the game-winner.

"It was great to get a goal," said the defenseman. "Particularly a game-winner. I don't get too many of them."[16]

Evans was pleased with the victory, but not with his team's habit of losing its aggressiveness after being scored on. It happened again in the game against the Capitals. "Our guys let [Washington's] first goal get them down and didn't get back in the game for a while. It's the kind of thing that has hurt us from time to time. We have to get over it."[17]

While the Barons were on the road, management announced a minor reduction in ticket prices. Starting with the November 24 visit by Montreal, high school and college students with valid identification cards could save two dollars on seats in the five-dollar section of the Coliseum.

With half of the six-game journey still ahead of them, the Barons had already picked up five of the six points Evans set as a goal. Given the strong start to the trip, the coach readily admitted he wanted more. "Everyone is in the frame of mind now where they think they can win the remaining games of this trip," he said after beating the Capitals. "That Philadelphia game must have done something to us. We stopped having weird goals scored against us. The puck is bouncing our way now."[18]

Added left wing Rick Hampton, "the way we're going right now, we're all looking forward to the next game. We all want to play hockey because we know we can play well. When we went through that five-game losing streak, the guys were down. We weren't looking forward to playing the next game."[19]

Cleveland's next game was against the Kings in Los Angeles, and it ended in a 0–0 tie. Simmons stopped 37 shots and was the star of the game in the opinion of Kings center Butch Goring, who spent a long and frustrating evening trying to slip a puck past him. "Simmons just played super," praised Goring. "He had a brick wall up there. It's the kind of game where we could have thrown aspirins and he would have stopped them."[20] But Simmons' teammates couldn't score, and his first shutout of the season earned the team just one point.

The next night in Minneapolis, the Barons rallied from an early 3–0 deficit to achieve a 3–3 deadlock with the North Stars. Goals by Dave Gardner and Mike Fidler closed the gap to 3–2 in the second period, and Mike Christie tied the game with six minutes to play. Meloche recorded 25 saves. The Barons' eight-game unbeaten streak was the longest in the brief history of the Oakland/Cleveland franchise, and the team's 6–7–6 start was its best ever.

The franchise-record unbeaten streak ended on November 19 in Detroit, where a successful road trip concluded on a sour note. A weary bunch of Barons lost to the Red Wings, 5–2. "We didn't play well. We looked tired," said Evans. "Ten days of travel has to catch up to you sometime. We played in flashes. I'd have to say it was fatigue. We were passing wrong and turning wrong. This is a strenuous game, and they were bound to get tired."[21] The Wings got off 46 shots on goal against Cleveland's tired defense. Simmons stopped 41.

The Barons finished an odyssey that took them from the Rocky Mountains to the southeast to the nation's capital to southern California to the Midwest with two victories, one defeat, and three ties. "I think we did well," asserted Dennis Maruk. "We could have won tonight. I think we did exceptionally well on the road."[22] Defensively, the Barons had been outstanding, surrendering just 14 goals in the six contests, with five of them coming in the final game, when the players were worn out. But they'd scored an anemic 13 goals.

General manager Bill McCreary said he'd been exploring trade possibilities to improve the Barons' offense but didn't want to pull the trigger on a deal too quickly. "If we don't score more at home, I'll be more aggressive," he said. "If we could get another good center man, we could move one of our other centers to left wing."[23] Evans thought the needed improvement on offense could come from the talent already on the roster.

"It's just a lack of finishing off their plays," explained the coach. "They are creating the chances. Either they don't have the finesse to finish them off, or the goaltenders are coming up with the big saves. I just want them to keep shooting and thinking about scoring goals. You can't win in the league by scoring three goals a game."[24]

Evans was asked how he was preparing his players for the visit by the defending Stanley Cup champion Montreal Canadiens to the Coliseum on the night before Thanksgiving. "I'm telling them to go to church, pray a lot, and help little old ladies across the street," he cracked. Evans said the champs were "a dream hockey club, and a delight to watch. I hope we don't stand around and watch them."[25]

Evans had to stand behind the Barons' bench and watch the Canadiens for about three hours on November 24, and he didn't like what he saw. Neither did the 11,774 fans who started their Thanksgiving holiday with a hockey game. The Canadiens toyed with the young Barons and skated to an easy 8–1 victory. The Canadiens fired 45 shots at Meloche. The Barons managed just 23 shots. Bob Murdoch's fifth goal of the season was the only shot that found the inside of the net.

"That's the best they ever played against us, and we didn't play nearly as well as we're capable of,"[26] was Evans' analysis of the drubbing. The Barons weren't the only team to have been embarrassed by the Canadiens during the first two months of the 1976–77 season. The defending champs had defeated the Pittsburgh Penguins by 10–1 and 9–1 scores. They'd clobbered the Chicago Blackhawks, 11–3; the St. Louis Blues, 8–1; and the Philadelphia Flyers, 7–1. So the Barons had some company in their misery.

Thanksgiving was no holiday for the Barons. Evans wasn't satisfied with their effort in the previous two games, and he put them through a practice just hours after they'd been demolished by Montreal. The emphasis of the session was on checking. "We have given up 13 goals in our last two games. We have to get back to preventing the score. We have a much better chance of winning," he understated. He also said he expected his players to bounce back the following night when the Penguins came to the Coliseum.

"When you get beat badly, you are determined to play better the next game,"[27] he said, possibly intending to send a message to his players via the newspapers. Before hosting the Penguins, the Barons sent three players to Salt Lake City: wingers Jim Moxey and Bob Girard and defenseman Bjorn Johansson, their first pick in the 1976 draft. That reduced their roster to 21 skaters.

The Barons gave a better effort against Pittsburgh on the night after Thanksgiving, but not enough to win. The offense was again absent, and the Penguins posted a 3–1 victory before a crowd of 6,374. The confidence and optimism of the recent eight-game unbeaten streak had vanished.

"Everybody is tight," said Simmons, who suffered the loss to Pittsburgh. "Even when we were winning, we were having trouble scoring. The way the league is now, you don't generally win when you score one, two or three goals."[28]

Evans was satisfied with the Barons' effort, which produced 46 shots on goal to the Penguins' 27. Only defenseman Glenn Patrick managed to put the puck in the Pittsburgh net, and it was the rookie's first NHL goal. "I can't knock them for effort," Evans said. "They tried hard throughout the game. They seemed to be fighting the puck. They didn't have a natural rhythm. The passing was terrible."[29] The Barons had produced just 17 goals in their past nine games.

The Barons finished the month of November with a game against Adams Division rival Toronto in Maple Leaf Gardens. Evans emphasized the importance of intra-division games to his players. "Every time we meet Toronto, it is THE GAME for us. We certainly have put forth every effort against Toronto because we have scratched and clawed to get where we are." Then Evans made the mistake of predicting the game's outcome. "We should not come out of there with anything less than a tie."[30]

The Barons scratched and clawed their way to a lifeless 5–1 loss to the Maple Leafs. The defense allowed the Leafs 40 shots against Meloche, who stopped 35 of them. The offense mustered only 20 shots on goal. Dave Gardner had the only tally. Cleveland had scored a meager 18 goals in its last 10 games. The dull defeat got the attention of McCreary.

"I'm very disappointed the way the team is playing, and we're going to have a session tonight to find out why," said the general manager. After the session, he had more to say. "I think they are playing below their capabilities. Merrick is way behind what he was doing at this time last year. MacAdam is not way behind, but he's not doing what he did last year at this time. We have to have a certain amount of patience with certain people, but we can do it just so long. We're not going to live with this situation much longer."[31]

In addition to Wayne Merrick and Al MacAdam, whose production was down from 1975–76, Dennis Maruk had slumped after a blazing start. Maruk scored seven goals and assisted on seven more in the Barons' first seven games. In the 16 games since, he'd managed just eight points on four goals and four assists.

As December began, the NHL's Adams Division standings looked like this:

TEAM	W	L	T	PTS	GF	GA
Boston	18	5	1	37	96	70
Buffalo	13	6	3	29	76	54
Toronto	11	9	4	26	90	81
Barons	6	11	6	18	61	77

The Barons started the month with a visit to Denver, where they'd beaten the Rockies earlier in the season, 2–1. Colorado was winless in its last six games. That changed by the time the Barons left town. Cleveland skated to a quick 2–0 lead it couldn't hold. The Barons benefited from four power play chances but converted only one of them: a goal by Rick Hampton. Cleveland enjoyed a man advantage for 13 of the second period's 20 minutes but had only Hampton's goal to show for it, thanks to the work of Colorado's back-up goaltender, Michel Plasse.

"He was marvelous. He was stupendous. What else can you say about the guy? He made breakaway save after breakaway save,"[32] raved Rockies coach John Wilson.

Evans agreed Plasse's goaltending was the difference in the game, keeping the Barons from breaking the contest open in the second period when they had several breakaways they failed to convert.

Aside from Hampton's goal, the other tallies came off the sticks of MacAdam and Gary Sabourin. The final score was 5–3. The NHL wasn't faring any better in Denver than in Cleveland. Only 3,373 fans went to McNichols Arena to watch, so the Barons should have felt right at home.

After the loss, McCreary repeated his earlier belief that the Barons weren't playing up to their potential ... or, at least, what McCreary and Evans perceived their potential to be. "Eventually, they will settle down," McCreary insisted. "The big difference in our power play is that we are 22 or 23 goals behind our pace of last year. Maybe there's too much youth on the team. When things don't work, they seem to wish it upon themselves not to work. Then they'll skate like mad fools and take off again. It will take a big effort to come out of this. It's not a case of letting down, but some of them are not playing as well as they can."[33]

Evans agreed with McCreary and offered the opinion that his team was snake-bit. "Everything the other team shoots goes into the net. We are hitting the post, or the other goaltenders. We are a better team than this."[34] Making matters worse, center Charlie Simmer and left wing Ralph Klassen were injured in the loss to the Rockies and would miss a few games.

The brief road trip was followed by an even shorter home stand. The Barons tied St. Louis, 2–2, on December 3, stretching their winless streak to eight in a row. Maruk scored both goals, and the second tied the game with five minutes remaining. "I told our guys before the game that we had to concentrate on stopping that little bugger," said Blues coach Emile Francis. "He was the one who killed us the last time we were here."[35] Cleveland's defense limited the Blues to 19 shots on Gilles Meloche, who turned away 17 of them.

"The goalies in this league are not that good!" said a frustrated Evans afterward. "Goals have been tough to come by, but it has to turn our way." The Barons had lit the lamp just 23 times in their last 12 games.

"All I can say is that it is going to change," Evans continued. "Al MacAdam is a prolific goal scorer. Wayne Merrick, Bob Murdoch and Gary Sabourin are all behind in their production. And Jim Pappin is a goal scorer. I'm confident ... no, I know ... we'll score more goals than we have."[36]

Francis blamed the fact that his club didn't win on the officiating. "They got away with more hooking and holding than they usually get away with,"[37] he barked. Apparently, not many fans knew the Barons had a home game sandwiched between visits to Denver and Philadelphia. Either that, or no one cared. Attendance was a slim 3,344.

With the Flyers and Canadiens coming up, the last thing the Barons needed were more injuries. But that was what they got in the physical game with St. Louis. Wingers Fidler and Sabourin each sustained knee injuries. Fidler suffered a bruised kneecap and Sabourin strained ligaments. With Gardner, Simmer and Klassen also hurt and unavailable, Cleveland needed reinforcements. Wingers Jim Moxey and Bob Girard were summoned from Salt Lake City. Moxey had scored six goals since being shipped to the Western Hockey League, and Girard racked up nine points in only four games. Those stats proved there was a big difference between the WHL and the NHL.

Evans wasn't looking forward to the Barons' first visit to Philadelphia. The Flyers were 10–1 on home ice and were still trying to figure out how they'd lost to the Barons in Cleveland a month before. "They should be frothing at the mouth waiting for us,"[38] Evans said, trying to muster a smile. The Flyers were ready, and easily beat Cleveland, 6–2, on December 5. The Barons had a power play for five minutes over the end of the second period and beginning of the third but couldn't score. Pappin was added to the club's injury list. He suffered a sprained wrist and wouldn't get off the bench the next day in Montreal.

The Barons suited up only 16 players against the mighty Canadiens, and two of them were hurt during the game. Defenseman Len Frig was injured in the first period and didn't return, and center Fred Ahern was carried off the ice on a stretcher in the second. What was originally described as an arm injury turned out to be a broken arm. The Barons finished the game with just 14 available players, but those 14 held the Canadiens to a single goal, by Guy Lafleur in the first period. The Barons, however, were held to nothing by the Canadiens. Meloche rejected 31 of the 32 shots he faced. Montreal's Ken Dryden was perfect on 23 save opportunities. The winless streak had reached 10, and the Barons had managed only 24 goals in their last 15 games.

NHL president Clarence Campbell visited the Barons' dressing room in Montreal's Forum after the contest. He thanked them "for making tonight's game the best one I've seen played all season."[39] The kind words were appreciated, but it was still a loss.

Evans got some good news when the team returned to Cleveland. Fidler, Simmer, Sabourin and Gardner were cleared by the Barons' medical staff to play when division rival Buffalo visited the Coliseum on December 8. The bad news was Ahern's broken arm would sideline him for two months, and Frig's pulled thigh muscle would keep him out of action indefinitely.

Cleveland's 5–1 loss to the Sabres was low-lighted by a lack of fan support (just 3,960 on another Wednesday night) and disagreements between Jim Neilson, Gilles Meloche, and referee Alf Lejeune. Meloche was assessed a pair of unsportsmanlike conduct penalties, and Neilson received a game misconduct. "It's a crying shame what happened out there tonight," he moaned in the quiet Barons dressing room. "We're going bad enough as it is. We don't have to get shafted. But this guy is a joke. He sees something, but hasn't got the guts to call it. We're trying to get out of a slump and meet a jerk like this."[40]

McCreary absolved Lejeune of any blame for the Barons' defeat but called the referee's performance "total incompetence. That's what it is. How can you have a man like that destroy the game of hockey? That type of official does not belong in the game if those are his capabilities."[41] McCreary said he'd call NHL supervisor of officials Scotty Morrison to complain about Lejeune the next day. The complaint was likely to be ignored, since the Barons weren't in the league's good graces at the moment.

Of the listless loss, Evans said, "I keep telling myself it will end. The only way I can go now is to shock them out of it with harder work. I'm going to try every avenue."[42] The avenue Evans tried the day after the defeat was to put his players through a 45-minute workout without pucks. The winless streak had reached 11, four short of tying the franchise record. The Barons had scored 25 goals in their last 16 games.

Fortunately for Evans and his beleaguered players, the NHL schedule maker had the cure for what ailed them: a home-and-home series with the pitiful Washington Capitals. Cleveland took out 11 games worth of frustration on the hapless visitors with a 7–1 victory on December 10. Even though it was a Friday night, only 3,774 ventured to Richfield to watch. For the first time in a long time, Evans could crack a smile and a joke after the game. "I thought I had the Montreal Canadiens out there,"[43] he said of his team.

Neilson, in a much better mood than he'd been two nights earlier after being ejected from the loss to the Sabres, said the visitors didn't put up much of a fight. "They didn't play all that well. They didn't look like they were motoring, and that gave us a chance to motor."[44]

Sounding much like Evans and McCreary, Sabourin said, "we're a lot better team that we've shown the last 11 games. We're a completely different team when we win. When we're not winning, the guys are crabby. It means everybody is not doing their job."[45] Before the game, the Barons decided Charlie Simmer and Rick Shinske hadn't been doing their jobs and sent them to Salt Lake City.

Capitals coach Tommy McVie was asked how his team could allow the offensively challenged Barons to explode for seven goals. "If I could tell you why things like that happen, it certainly wouldn't have happened to my club tonight,"[46] he responded.

The next day in Washington, the Barons finished the sweep with a 4–2 victory. "There is nothing like winning and seeing the guys score," said Evans of the twin victories by a cumulative score of 11–3. "That released the tension and pressure under which they have played. They are beginning to enjoy playing the game again. They are relaxed, and it shows by their play. They are more confident, doing things they know they can do."[47]

In the absence of a network TV contract, the NHL put together a network of its own. Starting on Monday, January 3, the league would broadcast a "game of the week" for the next 13 weeks. Each NHL city would receive the broadcasts ... except Cleveland. The games weren't going to preempt network programs on the city's NBC, CBS and ABC affiliates. Cleveland's independent UHF station, WUAB/43, had been offered the games but declined. "They asked us if we want to carry it," said station manager Jack Moffitt, an enthusiastic hockey fan. Nonetheless, "we cannot economically justify it. We cannot find any [sponsor] interest."[48] Moffitt's sales staff was having trouble selling advertising on the four remaining Barons games WUAB was under contract to televise during the 1976–77 season. The first game, versus the Bruins in Boston on October 10, had been viewed in only 25,000 homes in the greater Cleveland area. The broadcast faced competition from a major league baseball playoff game, but the numbers were still embarrassingly low. Crusaders games on WUAB the previous season had averaged 60,000 homes per broadcast. It's little wonder sponsors weren't lining up outside Moffitt's door waving checkbooks and begging to sponsor the remaining four Barons games. Clevelanders weren't attending NHL games in person, and, on the one opportunity they'd had to watch the Barons on television, they didn't. It was another example of the lack of research done by the Golden Seals and the NHL into the Cleveland market before rushing into a decision to transfer a franchise there.

It was a decision the NHL was already beginning to regret.

On December 13, the Barons recalled right wing Frank Spring from Salt Lake City. Spring had scored three goals for the Golden Seals during the 1974–75 season and led the Central Hockey League with 44 goals in 1975–76. He'd scored eight goals and assisted on 10 when he was told to report to Cleveland. The Barons would need another right wing sooner than they thought.

Thirty-seven-year-old veteran Jim Pappin informed Bill McCreary that he was retiring on December 14. "I just lost it," he said. "I couldn't get myself motivated enough to help the team. I started thinking that when the shots stopped going in, it would be time. You don't make the kind of money I make being a defensive specialist."[49] Pappin had contributed 10 points on two goals and eight assists. McCreary didn't ask him to reconsider.

"When a player makes up his mind he is no longer motivated by the game, I think he's made the right decision," said the general manager. "Jim is one high-quality individual. Naturally, this comes as a surprise to us and places an additional burden on the right side of our team."[50] To ease that burden, the Barons recalled right wing Ken Kuzyk from Salt Lake City. Kuzyk had been Mike Fidler's line mate at Boston University.

Pappin's unexpected retirement may have created a burden on the Barons on the ice, but it slightly eased the burden of meeting the payroll off the ice. The burden on Mel Swig to meet the Barons' payroll was growing greater each first and 15th of the month.

Meanwhile, the WHA team that had abandoned Cleveland, allowing the Barons to move in, was having problems of its own. The Minnesota Fighting Saints, formerly known as the Cleveland Crusaders, filed a $6.5 million lawsuit against the city of St. Paul and its Chamber of Commerce in the middle of December. The suit accused city officials of deception in the form of promises that hadn't been kept (specifically regarding season tickets) to lure the Crusaders to town.

The Barons stretched their winning streak to three with a 7–3 pounding of the Red Wings at the Coliseum on December 15. Cleveland peppered Detroit goalie Eddie Giacomin with five goals in the first period, and the visitors, who were in the midst of a miserable season, couldn't catch up. Bob Murdoch chalked up a hat trick and Frank Spring scored his first NHL goal. Only 3,220 watched.

The slim crowds the Barons were attracting didn't escape the notice of an Oakland resident who missed his Golden Seals. The fan wrote a letter to Hal Lebovitz, the sports editor of the *Plain Dealer*, mildly chastising Cleveland's hockey fans for not supporting the team and claiming the city had gotten a team that was going to win the Stanley Cup within three years. Lebovitz commented on the Barons' poor attendance and said surely ownership and the NHL came to town with the understanding that it would take more than one season for the club to catch on in northeastern Ohio. Lebovitz said the Barons had a five-year lease at the Coliseum, and predicted they'd be drawing sell-out crowds to every home game long before it was time to negotiate an extension to that lease.

Pittsburgh ended Cleveland's brief winning streak with a 5–4 victory in the Civic Arena on December 16. The two teams traded goals until Jean Pronovost scored the game-winner with nine minutes to play. The Barons weren't able to answer.

Mileti dropped his lawsuit against St. Paul after mayor George Latimer, who'd been ecstatic in August when it was announced the Crusaders were moving to the city, said that enough money had been found to keep the Fighting Saints in business through December 31, giving Mileti time to search for local ownership. The St. Paul Chamber of Commerce would finance a $200,000 trust fund, to be administered by Latimer's office. Of that money, $123,000 was earmarked for player salaries and lease payments. Latimer would appoint a three-member committee to find a local buyer for the Fighting Saints. He said the final two weeks of 1976 "will test in a professional way whether St. Paul wants hockey." He said of the $200,000 the Chamber of Commerce had put up to fund the team through New Year's Eve, "I believe we have gone as far as we can go."[51]

Mileti was reported to be asking $850,000 for the Fighting Saints, substantially less than the $1.4 million Jay Moore thought he'd get from Bill Putnam for the Crusaders. The Fighting Saints were averaging about 4,000 fans per game in their 17,000-seat arena.

A big crowd had been expected at the Coliseum on Friday, December 18 when the Boston Bruins visited. It didn't materialize, although the crowd was sizable by Cleveland's standards, and the 7,222 fans watched the Barons catch the Bruins napping in the first period, slipping the puck past goalie Gilles Gilbert four times. The Bruins snapped out of their lethargy in the game's remaining 40-minutes, but the Barons held on for a 6–4 victory, their fourth in the last five games.

Cleveland managed only 11 shots on goal in the second and third periods, while the Bruins used Meloche for target practice. He stopped 39 enemy shots. Dave Gardner, Rick Hampton, Dennis Maruk and Murdoch scored once for the Barons, and Spring contributed a pair of goals.

The next day in Madison Square Garden, the Barons lost to the New York Rangers, 3–2. They also lost Gary Sabourin for at least two months. At first, Sabourin's injury was thought to be torn ligaments. It turned out to be cartilage damage, and surgery was scheduled for later in the week. To replace Sabourin, the Barons signed former Colorado right wing Phil Roberto. Roberto had a goal and five assists with the Rockies before being released. In his most productive season, he'd scored 20 goals for St. Louis in 1972–73.

"He's a big, tough kid nobody pushes around,"[52] said McCreary of the 27-year-old Roberto. In another personnel move, the Barons promoted defenseman Brent Meeke from Salt Lake City.

Jack Moffitt announced on December 22 that his TV station would carry the first of the NHL network's Monday "games of the week" on January 3. Clevelanders would be able to watch the Flyers take on the Canadiens, and Moffitt would have a chance to gauge the audience's interest in hockey. "I think we owe it to the Barons to back this to a degree that we give the fans a chance to see what the NHL is like,"[53] he said. Sales representatives from WUAB would make 500 random telephone calls and tally up the number of households that were watching the game. Moffitt said WUAB would definitely carry the telecast of the NHL All-Star game on January 28, and a late February Barons game against the Blues in St. Louis.

The Barons beat the Minnesota North Stars, 4–3, at the Coliseum on December 22. It was their last game before a three-day Christmas break. Jack Evans started his break early. He was given permission to leave before the game ended to catch a flight to his home in San Diego, where he'd spend Christmas with his family. Assistant general manager Harry Howell was behind the Barons' bench in Evans' absence in the third period, and afterward, laughingly claimed credit for "one-third of the victory. They played a helluva third period,"[54] he joked. Murdoch tied an Oakland/Cleveland franchise record with a goal in his seventh consecutive game as the Barons extended Minnesota's winless streak to 11. The crowd was a scant 4,496.

The victory was Cleveland's fifth in seven games, and Murdoch talked about the team's improved frame of mind. "When we had that bad streak, we weren't scoring. We had to dig deep and play that much harder. It's much nicer when you're winning because you go out and feel good right off the bat."[55]

Although the Barons had been playing better hockey at home in December, the lack of support still bothered the players. "I personally would like to see more fans at the games," said Dennis Maruk, the club's leading scorer with 15 goals. "I expected to see a lot more. No less than 8,000 to 10,000. They wanted the NHL here. They waited a long time to get it. Now they should come out and help us. We play better before good crowds, but we still try our best before 2,000 to 3,000."[56] Cleveland had waited a long time for the NHL. But the city's response to the Barons raised the question of how badly it actually wanted major league hockey.

A couple of days after having cartilage surgically removed from his left knee, Sabourin relaxed in his home and spoke to the *Plain Dealer* of his concerns about the state of hockey in Cleveland. "Everybody is thinking the same thing. We have to prove we are a good product to draw crowds. You play better before bigger crowds. Even me, an old pro (age 33), is disappointed to skate in front of 3,000 to 4,000 people."

Sabourin then revealed that there was worry in the team's clubhouse about the future of the Barons. The players had been told Cleveland would be the land of milk and honey. The move from an old building in Oakland to a sparkling new building in a market hungry for the NHL was supposed to cure all of the franchise's problems. That hadn't been the case, at least not as of late December. "We all hope our ownership is stabilized," he said, echoing a concern expressed by NHL president Clarence Campbell a few weeks earlier. "We worry about this, especially the older fellows. We sort of have been told we will be here for at least three years. That helps, but you can only pour so much into the team before somebody has to be hurting."[57] Barons majority owner Mel Swig was hurting, but no one (except, based on Sabourin's comments, at least some of the players) knew just how much. Everyone would find out by the end of January how dire the club's financial condition was.

When the Barons had beaten Boston at the Coliseum, they jumped on the visitors early, scoring four first period goals. In the rematch at the Boston Garden on the day after Christmas, the Bruins returned the favor, scorching Meloche for four goals within a 10-minute span of the opening period. That was more than enough for Gerry Cheevers, who faced 23 shots and stopped 20 in a 6–3 victory. The following day in Montreal, the Canadiens beat Cleveland, 4–2.

The Barons returned home for a "four-point game" against division rival Toronto. The winner, assuming the game didn't end in a tie, would earn two points and would keep its division opponent from picking up two points. The Maple Leafs arrived in Cleveland for the December 29 contest leading the Barons by nine points in the race for third place in the Adams Division. Veteran defenseman Jim Neilson explained the importance of the game. "If they win to push it out to 11, win a couple and we lose a couple, bingo. Then it's out to 15. The other way and the gap is closed."[58]

Evans looked at the game's playoff implications. "We have to catch that Toronto team to get a playoff spot, and we've only lost three more games than they have. So we've still got a good chance with more than half a season to go."[59]

The Barons didn't close the gap between themselves and the Maple Leafs, and after losing 6–2 in front of a gathering of 5,464 they'd lost four more games than Toronto. In three meetings so far, Toronto had out-scored Cleveland, 17–6. Evans was fuming after the loss. "Not even Montreal or Philadelphia do that to us, and the Leafs certainly aren't better than those two teams," he said. But they were obviously better than the Barons. So were the other two Adams Division teams, Boston and Buffalo. In 1975–76, the Golden Seals were 2–13–3 against their division rivals. So far in 1976–77, the Barons were 1–6.

The 1976 portion of the 1976–77 season ended for the Barons with a visit to Detroit on New Year's Eve, where they were out-muscled by the Red Wings, 4–2. Gary Simmons was in goal for the first time since December 5 and stopped 39 shots. Cleveland's goals were tallied by Greg Smith and Merrick.

The Adams Division standings as the new year dawned:

Buffalo	24–8–3	51	123–82
Boston	23–11–3	49	146–114
Toronto	17–15–6	40	142–126
Barons	11–21–7	29	112–137

The Barons were 11 points behind the Maple Leafs in their quest for third place in the division and a playoff spot. They'd soon find themselves with more pressing problems than making the post-season.

As in making it to the end of the season at all.

6

Buddy, Can You
Spare a Payroll?

The Barons started the 1977 portion of the 1976–77 season by hosting the Philadelphia Flyers at the Coliseum on January 1. The Flyers' first visit to Cleveland in early November produced the first 10,000-plus crowd the Barons had drawn and had inspired the players to upset the 1974–75 Stanley Cup champions. The Flyers' second visit was one of only four Saturday night home games the Barons were scheduled for. Most Clevelanders, however, decided to cap off their New Year's Day celebration by staying home and watching the Ohio State Buckeyes defeat Colorado, 27–10, in the Orange Bowl.

A crowd of 5,331 watched the Flyers toy with the Barons while extending their unbeaten streak to 20 games with an easy 7–2 victory. After riding the bench for nearly a month, Gary Simmons played his second game in 24 hours. He stopped 32 shots. The Barons were limited to goals by Glenn Patrick and Bob Girard.

Rich Passan was so discouraged by the lopsided loss that he confided to his readers in the *Plain Dealer* that Cleveland's hockey fans may have been sold a bill of goods by the Barons' front office, which insisted it brought a talented young team on the rise to northeastern Ohio. The club's record indicated otherwise. The loss to the Flyers was Cleveland's fifth straight. "The Barons aren't really that good," Passan wrote in his first column of 1977. "There are times when they will rise up and smite one of the big boys, but don't let that fool you." Judging by the size of the crowds at the Coliseum, the fans weren't fooled. They knew an inferior product when they saw one.

Barons head coach Jack Evans was more discouraged than the writers or the fans. After the drubbing by Philadelphia, he said the time had come "to pick up the pieces and start at the beginning. What can I say? I'm a little discouraged, but I have to look at it realistically. With the exception of Detroit, we played some of the top teams in the National

Hockey League. We were going along well until then. We'll just have to recover."

Before the losing streak began, the Barons had won five of seven games. "Morale was so high before this streak," Evans said. "It hurts the morale when you lose five games in a row, no matter how good the team you lose to is." The coach warned that he'd crack the whip when the players reported to their practice facility on January 3. "They won't quit. They didn't quit on me last year when we hit some rough spots. Trying is not one of their problems. It's a lack of talent in certain areas, and a lack of toughness."[1]

WUAB-TV had carried the Montreal-Philadelphia telecast on Monday night, January 3, and the audience response was encouraging. Station general manager Jack Moffitt said 11 percent of northeastern Ohio's households watched the game. He wouldn't commit to airing the 12 remaining games of the NHL's Monday night TV package, however. "I can commit myself on a game to game basis, providing the interest remains there. That's what I really want to do."[2] Moffitt would shortly go out on a limb and commit the station to carrying all the January games. WUAB also added a game to the Barons' television schedule. The station would telecast Cleveland's game against the Flyers from Philadelphia on March 10. The Barons had purchased two advertisements during the Canadiens-Flyers match and announced on January 6 that the remaining Friday night games on the schedule would be "Family Hockey Nights." Children age 16 and under, when accompanied by an adult paying full price for their ticket, could buy a ticket for half price.

The Barons fell to another division rival on January 5, losing to Boston at the Coliseum, 3–2. Bruins goalie Gerry Cheevers was again effusive in his praise of the Barons ... after vanquishing them. "When they find out how good they really are, they are going to be awfully tough to play against very soon. They have all the ingredients,"[3] insisted Cheevers, who was beaten for goals by Frank Spring and Jim Moxey. Gilles Meloche was almost as good as Cheevers, stopping 28 of the Bruins' 31 shots. A Wednesday night crowd of 4,136 watched Cleveland's losing streak reach six in a row. In addition to losing a game, the Barons lost right wing Bob Murdoch to torn knee cartilage. Surgery would be needed, and Murdoch would miss at least two months of action.

The prognosis for center Fred Ahern was worse. Ahern suffered a broken arm in the loss to Montreal in late December, and it was determined that he'd likely have to sit out the rest of the season.

January 7 was the first "Family Hockey Night" at the Coliseum, and those who took advantage of the promotion were treated to plenty of offense as the Barons and Vancouver Canucks combined for 86 shots on goal. Cleveland snapped its losing streak with an 8–4 victory, led by wing Phil Roberto, who scored twice and should've had a hat trick. Roberto somehow missed an open Vancouver net in the game's closing seconds. Roberto said he'd been approached by a few teams after being released by Colorado in November. "I've been kicked around in Denver. I played the first eight games and then sat on the bench. When I got here, I hadn't played in two months."

Roberto said he signed with the Barons because "they were hurting on the right wing. I'm pleased with the amount of ice time I'm getting. I just want to play hockey. It doesn't matter where I play."[4] With the Barons struggling with injuries, Roberto figured to get a lot of ice time.

Roberto was joined by Len Frig, Moxey, Dave Gardner, Ralph Klassen, Merrick and Mike Fidler as Cleveland enjoyed its biggest offensive output of the season. It appeared "Family Hockey Night" would take some time to catch on. The Friday night crowd was just 5,368. And the lack of support for the Barons had just about exhausted Mel Swig's patience.

Another game against a division rival meant another defeat on January 9. The Barons traveled to Buffalo and lost, 7–4. It was Cleveland's 20th road game of the season, and it had won just three. The Barons had scored 47 goals away from the Coliseum and allowed 72.

The Barons' plight reached the point that Swig could no longer sit in his San Francisco office and monitor the situation. He visited Cleveland during the second week in January to investigate why northeastern Ohio was ignoring his hockey team. He laid it on the line in interviews with the hockey writers of Cleveland's two daily newspapers.

"If we can't survive here, then Cleveland will lose hockey and I'm afraid that is a possibility. If nobody makes it here, Cleveland will lose hockey forevermore or for a long time because people will be afraid to come in here," Swig warned. "If the fans want hockey, they should be giving us a little help. I can't put my finger on why they aren't coming out. I don't understand the whys of it." That was the reason for Swig's trip to frozen northeastern Ohio. He hoped to learn what was keeping Clevelanders away from the Coliseum when the Barons were playing.

"There has got to be a reason," he said. "Granted, we've suffered from adversity. But the hockey people are watching is good hockey. It is infinitely better than they ever saw before. You're talking about some of the greatest players on ice. Everywhere the Montreal Canadiens go, there are turnaway crowds." Everywhere except at the Coliseum, where the Canadiens had drawn the largest crowd of the season. But Swig wasn't satisfied with the gathering of 11,774 that watched Montreal crush the Barons in November.

"That was peanuts compared to what it should have been," the owner growled. He said he wasn't warning the hockey fans of Cleveland that they were in danger of losing the NHL, then promptly warned them that they were in danger of losing the NHL. "No, it's not a warning. It's a beseeching more than anything else. It's a warning insofar as how much any one person can sustain [in terms of financial losses] and still stick around. We had very high hopes Cleveland would be an excellent hockey city. We didn't expect to sell out the building, but we expected to turn out a reasonable number of people."

"When you look at cities like Washington, Detroit, Colorado and Minnesota, who have teams no better than us and are drawing 4,000 to 5,000 more than us, something is wrong. If there was a reason we deserved it, such as thumbing our nose at the community or not trying to please the fans, then that would be different. But we are doing everything we can to gain the confidence of the community. Outside of a few games, we haven't loused up the joint. Cleveland should be more supportive. We are doing everything to accommodate the people short of giving away the joint."[5] Many fans, and media members, would've gladly debated Swig as to how hard the Barons had tried to please the fans and become a part of the Cleveland community.

Swig said he expected the Barons to average at least 8,000 fans per game, and he entered the team's first year in its new home prepared to drop between one million and $1.25 million. He said unless attendance improved dramatically during the last three and a half months of the season, the loss would be substantially larger. Word from NHL headquarters in Toronto was that the Barons were headed for a two-million-dollar loss, and Swig didn't question that analysis. He intimated that the team might not survive to see a second season in Cleveland.

"We're looking beyond this year. We are not quitting. But we would like to see some response to our work. I think there will be a club here next year. We have to have some evidence of fan support. I wish someone would give me an answer on what we could do to change this thing."[6] Cleveland's fans would shortly respond to Swig's plea with plenty of answers to that question.

Swig's comments didn't help boost morale in the Barons' dressing room. Gary Sabourin had mentioned several weeks earlier that at least some of the players were aware of the club's dire financial problem. Swig's admission that "I think there will be a club here next year" lifted no one's spirits. For those who'd worn a Golden Seals uniform the year before, it was a case of déjà vu.

"Here we go again," sighed wing Al MacAdam. "But that's understandable. I don't see how a man can operate with 5,000 or 6,000 people a game. What else can the man say? I sympathize with him. I thought it would be different. I was excited about coming here. This is supposed to be hockey country. I figured the people would be knowledgeable and support the team. Now I don't know. They are probably as knowledgeable as I thought they'd be, but the support is not there. I know if I were a fan, I'd be coming to see the Montreals and the Islanders. Time is of the essence. I guess Mr. Swig doesn't have it. Time costs money in his world. Maybe if Mr. Gund had taken over from Mr. Swig, he could have afforded to wait a couple of years. You have to think in terms of the team folding because there is a lot of money. But I'm not worried about it at all. If the team folds up and nobody picks me up, I'll go home."[7]

Said Evans, "I am disappointed in the attendance. I thought people would come out of curiosity to see what the National Hockey League was like."[8]

"Getting the big crowds here is up to us," said Merrick. "We're the guys who have to do it. We have to have a winning team."[9]

"We like to be appreciated," added Gardner. "We're like performers that we don't like to give a bad performance because we want the people to come back."[10]

At least one member of the Barons, Dennis Maruk, had studied the history of Cleveland sports and was able to put the situation into its proper perspective. "Look, it took the Cavaliers a few years to get a following. It took them four years [actually five] before they got going. I don't know if it will take us four years. From what I hear, we need the good crowds now. We're not stupid. We know we're in trouble. We were in trouble last year, too. We had hoped those troubles would disappear here. It was hard on the guys to move here from Oakland, and it would be hard to move from here."[11]

Maruk had more to say when he was guest speaker at a meeting of the Blueliners Club. "You try to put [rumors that the club would move or fold] out of your mind and go ahead and do your job, just like we try to ignore the empty seats at the Coliseum. But this isn't just a game, it's our job, the way we earn a living. It's bound to bother our guys when they hear that we might not have our jobs any longer."[12]

Maruk's comments about the Cavaliers were spot on. Cleveland's basketball team had been virtually ignored during its first season in the NBA, averaging 3,500 fans per game. The 1970–71 Cavaliers won just 15 games, and Clevelanders weren't going to flock to the Arena to watch the star players on visiting teams ... which the NHL and the Barons were expecting hockey fans to do at the Coliseum. Attendance grew slowly but steadily as the team improved, but it wasn't until the Cavaliers won a division title and earned a playoff berth that fans began beating down the Coliseum doors to watch them. Attendance was declining slightly in 1976–77, as the team struggled, and the excitement of the previous season's playoff run began to fade. Cleveland had a long and well-deserved reputation of not supporting a loser. Even the Browns had played to thousands of empty seats in Municipal Stadium when the team lost 10 games in 1974 and 11 in 1975.

Indications are that Swig moved his hockey team to Cleveland largely on the recommendation of his minority partner, George Gund III. Gund then essentially disappeared, drawing harsh criticism from the Cleveland media for his reclusive behavior. Passan in the *Plain Dealer* told his readers that he'd tried in vain for weeks to contact Gund. He was never in his office when Passan called, and Passan's messages were ignored. Doug Clarke was equally critical of Gund in a column in the *Press* in mid–January. Swig said he thought he'd made a deal with Gund to have the Cleveland native assume majority ownership of the Barons. At the time, Swig owned 60 percent of the team. Gund owned 38 percent. Bud Levitas owned the remaining two percent. The deal called for Swig and Gund to flip-flop their ownership percentages, with Gund taking Swig's 60 percent and Swig taking Gund's 38 percent. Swig said the paperwork had been drawn up, then Gund went into hiding.

"I really don't know what happened," said a perplexed Swig. "I haven't seen George in some weeks. But in plain words, he loused it up. He's really a nice guy, very nice, and I think he'll come back. But I don't know. I think he got frightened. Why, I don't know."

Swig said he'd invested $50,000 to advertise the Barons for the rest of the season. Each home game for the remainder of the year would feature a promotion of some sort. The enticements started with the January 7 game against Vancouver, when children 14 and under received Barons snow caps. "I'm confident we'll be here next year," Swig said. "If you want to put a figure on it, make it that I'm at least 90% sure. We do have a lease at the Coliseum that runs for four more years, and I intend to talk to Sandy Greenberg about some help, perhaps financial. We can't personally continue to handle these large losses for four years. Nobody can. We may try to get some investors from the community at a later date. But right now, fans are what we need."[13]

Swig said he'd try to arrange a meeting with Cleveland mayor Ralph Perk and other civic leaders. Such a meeting should've been arranged before he made his decision to move the Golden Seals. If such a meeting took place, Swig said he'd lay it on the line with the elected officials. He wanted to keep the Barons in Cleveland, but "if it seems we're just pouring money down a rat hole, then we'll have to sell or fold the franchise."[14] There would've been no objections to Swig selling the team, as long as he sold it to Clevelanders. Absentee ownership was a new concept in Cleveland, and it wasn't being embraced. But no Clevelanders were interested.

Bob Schlesinger laid most of the blame for the Barons' problems at Swig's door. He noted that Cleveland had never supported a sports team that had lost twice as many games as it won (as the Barons had as of mid–January), and the Barons wouldn't be an exception even though they'd brought the novelty of major league hockey to town. Schlesinger noted that Barons general manager Bill McCreary, undoubtedly on orders from ownership, had passed on a few opportunities to potentially improve the team by adding some available, big-name players. Notably, former Boston Bruins superstar Derek Sanderson, who'd recently been released by his current employer, the St. Louis Blues. While admitting that Sanderson was on the downside of his career, Schlesinger was certain he would've looked good in a Barons uniform, and his former notoriety might have lured some paying customers to the Coliseum. But McCreary said taking on Sanderson's three-year, $175,000 contract would've upset the Barons' salary structure and might have caused dissension among the players. He'd given the same reason for not pursuing former Cleveland Crusader Paul Shmyr during the summer of 1976.

Schlesinger said Swig's apparent blind faith that Cleveland would support the Barons with little or no effort on his part to promote the team wasn't entirely unjustified. He said when the club arrived in July of 1976, its makeshift office was deluged with phone calls from "civic leaders and just plain folks" welcoming the Barons and promising unqualified support. Swig had ample reason to be optimistic that all he had to do was open the doors to the Coliseum and watch the fans stream in. But when the doors opened, the promises of support dried up.

Cleveland's sports writers didn't appreciate Swig's comment about pouring money down a rat hole. And the fans took issue with his claim the Barons had done everything possible to accommodate the fans and become part of the community. Swig's plea that someone tell him how to make the club's situation better may have been made rhetorically, but it got a response. Schlesinger wrote on January 12 that the Barons' office, and the *Press'* sports department, received a number of calls from fans with suggestions as to how Swig should've been running his hockey team.

According to Schlesinger, fans were avoiding the Barons because the team antagonized them by failing to sign popular former Crusaders like Shmyr and Jim Harrison when both players were available; the Barons were a lousy team; tickets were too expensive; there weren't enough special promotions; the radio station broadcasting the games had a weak signal and was hard to hear outside Cleveland; the Barons and the NHL had a smug attitude; the Barons were dull and didn't score enough, and the Barons were cheap and wouldn't spend money to get better players. Swig vowed to take the fans' comments and complaints seriously and take corrective steps immediately. Among those steps was an announcement that, for the rest of the season, all youth college age and below could buy five-dollar tickets (the cheapest seats in the house) for just three dollars.

Another corrective step was the hiring of public relations director Eddie Coen. Schlesinger, who described Coen as the best PR man in the business, had a suggestion for him. The Barons needed to stop promoting the NHL and start promoting themselves. The mere attraction of the NHL wasn't bringing fans to the Coliseum. And it wouldn't. That belief, on the part of the team and the league, was part of the "smug attitude" the fans were complaining about.

Amid the chaos off the ice, the Barons played a game on January 12 and beat the Red Wings, 3–1. Only 3,249 fans witnessed the chippy contest, during which 26 penalties were called. "The last two games we played in Detroit, they ran the heck out of us," said defenseman Len Frig. "We had to get some respect back. They would've begun to laugh at us if we hadn't. We couldn't stand back and take it much longer."[15] Merrick scored twice for the Barons, and Mike Fidler added a goal. Meloche made 36 saves.

The victory over Detroit was Bill McCreary's last game as general manager of the Barons. He was fired the next day. Swig said he thought McCreary's responsibilities handling the club's business and personnel operations had overwhelmed him. "He was hired to do a job maybe more than he was capable of doing. The business side of the job was probably more than he could handle. Maybe it was my fault for putting him in that position."[16] Swig said he didn't blame McCreary for the Barons' failure to draw fans to the Coliseum.

McCreary was replaced, on an interim basis, by his assistant general manager, Harry Howell. "It's difficult for me to make sense now," Howell said. "This doesn't hurt anybody more than it hurts me. I've known Bill longer and better than anybody."[17] Howell and McCreary had been friends for 25 years.

Swig elaborated on his reasons for firing McCreary on January 14. "It's just a combination of things I'd rather not discuss. We're going to have to come up with a plan that makes some sense and more clearly defines everybody's duties."[18] For the moment, Howell would be in charge of the Barons' player personnel, and Swig would handle the business operations. The idea of Swig actually having a plan was greeted with skepticism from Cleveland's sports writers. The firing of McCreary may have been justified, but the timing was poor. It added to the perception of Swig as the befuddled captain of a sinking ship.

While the Barons, who were expected to be the picture of stability, were staggering, the remnants of the Cleveland Crusaders were doing even worse in Minnesota. Nick Mileti had been able to meet the Minnesota Fighting Saints' January 1 payroll, leading team president Bob Brown to say that "we were encouraged by local interests to keep it going. We're encouraged that there will eventually be local ownership, either in equity positions or control. We think hockey can work here."[19] The Fighting Saints were averaging 6,200 fans per game as they competed with the NHL's North Stars. The Fighting Saints had drawn five crowds of better than 9,000 to the St. Paul Civic Center. But as the January 15 payroll approached, the optimism evaporated.

The Fighting Saints all but collapsed on January 14. Following a 9–5 victory over the Indianapolis Racers, Brown announced that the team had sold seven players to the Edmonton Oilers. The Fighting Saints would not show up for their scheduled road games at Quebec on January 15 and at Hartford on the January 16. If local ownership couldn't be found by January 20, the team would fold. Adding to Mileti's woes, two former Crusaders, Bob Whidden and Ray Clearwater, were suing him for breach of contract.

McCreary shared his thoughts about his firing with Passan on January 16. He said he and Swig had been friends "for a thousand years." The relationship soured quickly after Swig's attempt to sell majority ownership of the Barons to Gund fell apart in early December. McCreary said he'd been "instrumental in Gund being involved in the game." According to McCreary, on December 12 he got a phone call from a friend in San Francisco informing him of a local radio report that Swig planned to dismiss him as Barons GM and replace him with Bud Poile, a friend of the owner who was president of the Central Hockey League. At the team Christmas party that night, McCreary asked Swig about the report. "He appeared unhappy and unsettled. He assured me the radio account was untrue. He said he would deny it if asked. That satisfied me."

Two weeks later, on the day after Christmas, McCreary learned that Swig had talked to Poile. "At that point," he told Passan, "I could see maybe there was some substance to the radio report." He said he knew the day before he was fired that he'd be dismissed because "the new ticket prices were put into effect. I had not recommended it." Swig was no longer listening to his general manager on matters of business policy. The next day, McCreary was no longer his general manager.

McCreary admitted the Barons had been seriously under-promoted. "There were many requests for dollars that never came through. We had $17,000 in the bank account, and it is difficult to start programs that under-capitalized. One mistake we made was not allocating more money to newspaper, television and radio advertising. We opened the season strictly on season ticket money. There was no capital infusion. There should have been."[20] McCreary claimed the Colorado Rockies had spent a quarter of a million dollars to promote the team after its relocation from Kansas City. The Barons had spent less than 10 percent of that amount.

The Barons made a quick and enjoyable trip to Vancouver on January 15. They knocked off the Canucks, 4–2, behind goals by Maruk, Fidler, Christie and Hampton. Meloche, who was now clearly established as the team's number one goaltender, stopped 25 Vancouver shots.

Evans said his players had been briefly startled by McCreary's dismissal, but had shaken it off. "The spirit of the team is very good," he insisted, refuting reports of a quiet, depressed dressing room. "The morale is surprisingly good, with all that has been in the newspapers. In this sport, it is the accepted thing when you lose your job. It is expected to happen at some time. Coaches get fired and managers get fired. You learn to live with it."[21]

According to the *Plain Dealer*, McCreary may have greased the skids for his departure as far back as November 9, when he met with the players following a practice at the Hudson Ice Barn. They were about to leave on a six-game road trip, and McCreary wanted to keep them appraised of the latest off-ice developments. He told the Barons Gund and his brother, Gordon, would assume ownership of the team and invest four million dollars in it to keep it solvent and in Cleveland for three years. Each of the Gunds would sink $1.5 million of their own money into the team, and they'd negotiate a million-dollar bank loan. When Swig learned of the unauthorized meeting, he confronted McCreary, who denied it. In mid–January, several players confirmed that it took place.

With McCreary gone, Swig spoke to the team and assured the players they had nothing to worry about as far as its finances were concerned. He said the team would play in Cleveland again in 1977–78. With Gund also apparently out of the picture, Swig planned to get more involved in the Barons' day-to-day operations, and in the Cleveland community. He was said to be looking for an apartment in northeastern Ohio. "We will do everything to entice fans into this building to watch hockey. We will be promoting, advertising, and making moves we believe will make this a better club,"[22] he said.

Montreal Canadiens head coach Scotty Bowman would coach the Prince of Wales Conference squad in the NHL's All-Star Game in late January. He added Barons wing Al MacAdam to the team on January 18. It was a curious choice, since Dennis Maruk had scored 18 goals to MacAdam's 11. MacAdam was grateful to be selected but knew his place among the game's elite. "I think I was chosen to fill out the team," he said modestly. "I would prefer to go in as an All-Star [rather] than filling in, but this is fair enough."[23] MacAdam had represented the Golden Seals in the game the previous year and contributed a goal and an assist.

The World Hockey Association held its All-Star Game on January 19. At a Board of Governors meeting prior to the contest, Nick Mileti was given until 10:00 p.m. on January 20 to sell the Minnesota Fighting Saints. If he couldn't meet the deadline, the franchise would be termi-nated. He couldn't, and it was. The remnants of the Cleveland Crusaders folded two hours before midnight on January 20, 1977. The new Fight-ing Saints became the second WHA club in St. Paul to disband within a year.

Bob Brown, Mileti's right-hand man who served as president of the Fighting Saints in their brief second incarnation, reflected on the tumul-tuous four and a half months the former Crusaders spent in Minnesota. "Today, I even feel relieved. I'm just glad that it's all over. It was obvi-ous it would fail. We came in here with high hopes, but in the end we couldn't even give it away. I don't have any bottom line on the debts. Let's just say Nick and Jay Moore lost a ton."[24] Mileti had been ousted as managing general partner of the Cleveland Indians in 1975, and, despite the success of the Cleveland Cavaliers in 1975–76, had been embroiled in a lengthy and bitter feud with his head coach and general manager, Bill Fitch. Now what was left of the Crusaders had been flushed down the toilet. The original Barons were just a memory, having folded after playing the 1973–74 season in Jacksonville. Brown said he thought Mileti was through with sports.

The new Barons had two home games remaining before the NHL All-Star break. They rallied from a two-goal deficit to tie the Rangers, 3–3, on January 19. Maruk and Frank Spring scored in an 84-second span of the third period to achieve the tie. "The spirit is good," Spring said. "We are starting to believe we can win now. It's been there for a while, and I don't know what the reasons are."[25] Meloche turned away 28 Rangers shots in the game, witnessed by another poor Wednesday night gathering of 4,848 at the Coliseum. Some of those people had the unex-pected pleasure of meeting Swig in person. The Barons owner spent the night walking around the Coliseum, introducing himself to some of the patrons and soliciting their advice as to how their hockey experience could be improved.

That Meloche had emerged as the Barons' top goalie was the result of a meeting between himself, Gary Simmons, and Evans after the team's 1–0 loss in Montreal in early December. Evans had alternated goaltenders during the 1975–76 season, with Meloche playing in 41 games and Simmons in 40. He continued the practice early in the 1976–77 season. Meloche and Simmons suggested that Evans settle on one goalie and put him in the net consistently. The coach agreed, and Meloche was his choice. "We told Tex [Evans' nickname] it would be best to go with one goaltender instead of rotating, and I think we were right in what we did,"[26] said Simmons. He wouldn't be Meloche's back-up much longer.

A game against an Adams Division opponent almost always meant a loss for the Barons, and it did on January 21 when the Bruins came to Cleveland. The visitors barely broke a sweat in posting a 5–2 victory before a Friday night crowd of 6,371. After the game, acting general manager Harry Howell announced that Simmons and Jim Moxey had been traded to Los Angeles for goalie Gary Edwards and center Juha (Whitey) Widing.

"Widing should be able to put some spark into our attack," Howell said. "He has very good goal scoring potential."[27] Widing had scored 138 goals in his NHL career, but only three (with eight assists) in 46 games for the Kings in 1976–77. Edwards was unhappy about his lack of playing time with the Kings, a situation that didn't figure to improve with the Barons, with Meloche having been established as the team's starting goalie. Edwards played in just eight games with Los Angeles, with a record of 0–6–2. Both new Barons were 29 years old.

A smiling Simmons made the rounds in the Barons' dressing room, shaking hands with his now former teammates. More than a few of them envied him and Moxey for being paroled from Cleveland. "Los Angeles is my kind of place," chortled Simmons. "LA was the spot I wanted."[28] Simmons said he hadn't asked for a trade but made no secret of the fact he loved California and hated the cold and snow of northeastern Ohio, which just happened to be in the midst of the coldest January on record. The average daily high temperature for the month was a frigid 11 degrees.

Passan wasn't impressed by the deal. He wrote that former general manager McCreary had said he wouldn't make a trade just for the sake of exchanging players and getting some new faces in the dressing room. He claimed that was exactly what Howell had done by getting rid of Simmons and Moxey and adding Edwards and Widing.

With one game left before the break, Evans wasted no time getting a look at Cleveland's two new players. He installed Edwards in goal against the Sabres in Buffalo, and the result was a rare Barons victory against a division foe. Maruk scored twice, the second time into an empty net as the clock wound down, and Fidler tallied once as the Barons brushed aside the Sabres, 3–0. Edwards' Cleveland debut was impressive as he recorded 26 saves and picked up his first victory of the season.

"That's a great way to start," said Edwards of his first game as a Baron. "The circumstances were more than gratifying. I hadn't won a game all year, and it was my first game with a new team."[29] Evans put the shutout in perspective, noting that the Sabres had been scuffling recently. The loss to the Barons was Buffalo's third straight.

The Barons reached the unofficial halfway point of the season with a record of 15–25–8. They were in last place in the Adams Division, 14 points behind third-place Toronto. Nobody was talking playoffs in Cleveland. But the next day, everybody (who cared about hockey) was talking about whether the Barons would survive until the end of the season.

The depth of the disaster that was the Cleveland Barons was revealed during the All-Star break. Swig's assurance to the players that the team would remain in Cleveland for the 1977–78 season hadn't been an assurance at all. "I told them I haven't let them down yet, and I hope not to let them down now,"[30] was what the owner had actually said to players worried about their team's future ... and their own. The term "hope" seemed to be exactly what the Barons had been built on following the team's move from Oakland. Swig *hoped* the relocation to northeastern Ohio would solve all of his problems. He *hoped* fans would flock to the Coliseum to watch their new team. He *hoped* the National Hockey League brand would be enough to entice paying customers to swarm the Coliseum. He *hoped* his young team would be a playoff contender. He *hoped* all these things would happen automatically, without spending much money on promotion and marketing, or acquiring better players.

While the Barons embarked on their mid-season break (except for MacAdam), their owner was in Vancouver, where the NHL's Board of Governors was scheduled to meet prior to the All-Star game. Swig first met with board chairman John Ziegler and told him the Barons couldn't survive the season without a fast infusion of cash. He reportedly needed a million dollars, and Ziegler told him to ask the governors for the money.

"This is the first time I've gone to the league," Swig said before making his pitch. "I'm not saying I'm banking on it, because I don't know the mood of the governors."[31] Harold Baldwin, the owner of the Toronto Maple Leafs, was one of the governors, and he was in no mood to bail out the league's failing Cleveland franchise.

"I'm sick and tired of handing out money because, after they get through with that money, they come back for more!"[32] Baldwin snorted. It may have been the first time Swig had asked the governors for a hand-out, but it wasn't the first such request from the Oakland/Cleveland franchise. And the Barons weren't the only team with money problems. The Atlanta Flames, Colorado Rockies, Minnesota North Stars and Pittsburgh Penguins were scheduled to meet with the Board of Governors during the break to ask for financial aid. It was little wonder Baldwin was in a surly mood.

Swig absolved himself of any blame for the Barons' dire straits and laid it at the feet of his partner, George Gund III. Gund's sudden decision not to assume 60 percent ownership of the Barons left Swig as the team's majority owner, and he wasn't prepared to handle that responsibility. "During the time George decided he wanted to take over, I did nothing. I invested no capital. Then when we broke off, we were left in a position of trying to pull things back together, and we weren't prepared to do it. The situation was tenuous, to say the least. He intended to obligate himself to raise $400,000 in working capital and elected not to do it. If he had come through, I wouldn't be here at all."

Swig said he and Gund had signed the papers giving majority ownership to Gund on December 6. Gund backed out of the deal four days later, reportedly because Swig had insisted on adding a number of "little clauses" to the agreement that Gund objected to. Swig said the truth was precisely the opposite. "He was the one who wanted the little things in the agreement,"[33] Swig claimed. Gund wasn't talking, but his confidants denied Swig's version of the events.

The latest rumor floating around Vancouver was that the Barons would move to nearby Seattle, possibly as soon as after the All-Star game. Swig said he hadn't heard the rumor and denied it. "I don't know anything about it. I haven't considered a move from Cleveland. I think Cleveland has the potential to be a very good hockey town. But it will take time to develop. It's no different than any other city. This problem is not unique to Cleveland."[34]

Attorney and player agent Alan Eagleson, who represented seven members of the Barons, was also the president of the NHL Players Association. He said there was a strong possibility the team would fold, at the end of the season if not before. "I would be surprised if there are 18 teams in the NHL next season," Eagleson said. "If I were guessing, I would say the NHL would have 16. Cleveland is an obvious choice not to make it." Keeping the Barons going through the remainder of the season would require a financial sacrifice on the part of both the NHL and the team's players. "It would be in the best interest of the NHL and the NHLPA for Cleveland to limp through the season. I'm hoping the players will be responsive to the owner's plight."[35]

The Board of Governors agreed with Eagleson, if for no other reason than to tweak the rival WHA, which had just lost its Minnesota franchise. The Fighting Saints had been the third WHA club to fold during a season in the past two years. The NHL didn't need that kind of embarrassment, even if it cost the established league some money. A tentative plan to save the Barons, at least for the rest of the year, was announced on January 25. The governors would allow Swig to pay his $250,000 franchise assessment in installments, without interest, as long as full payment was received by June. If that deadline wasn't met, the money would have to be paid with interest. Swig agreed to dip into his own personal fortune for $400,000 to operate the Barons for the rest of the season. That was the same amount Gund was to have provided but didn't.

"I did not ask for a specific amount," Swig said of his plea to the governors. "I told them what our problems were. When I was through, they believed it was totally adequate to support us with the proper funding for the rest of the year."[36] Wire service reports indicated Swig asked the governors for a loan of half a million dollars and was turned down.

The agreement to keep the Barons afloat through season's end would require the cooperation of the players. In all probability, they'd have to consent to either forfeit some of their salaries or accept deferred payments. Eagleson hoped the players would be reasonable. Ninety to 95 percent of their salaries (or full salaries if deferred payments were negotiated) was preferable to nothing, which was what the players would get if the Barons folded. On the other hand, players such as Maruk and Meloche, as well as several of their teammates, would undoubtedly be signed by other teams ... teams with more money which might give them more lucrative deals. Rather than ranting about the ineptitude of Cleveland's management (and the short-sightedness of the NHL in allowing the Golden Seals to move there without fully investigating the situation), Eagleson was the voice of moderation.

"We will try to embark on a structure to get the club through the rest of the season," he explained. "We are hopeful we can persuade the players to review the plight of the club in a reasonable fashion. The players will then have the option of accepting or rejecting my recommendation. This is all in the best interests of finishing the season. There may be four or five members who will say 'to hell with the recommendation,

I want my money.' I hope they are not as short-sighted as that. There's no way I can oblige them to take anything less than their required pay." Eagleson said the players might be asked to swallow pay cuts of five percent. Other, less optimistic projections set the figure at 10 percent. Eagleson said he thought the chances of the Barons playing out the rest of their schedule were at best "60–40."[37]

Veteran defenseman Bob Stewart was the Barons' player representative. It was his sixth season with the Oakland/Cleveland franchise, so he'd seen plenty of trials and tribulations. He wouldn't venture a guess as to whether his teammates would make the sacrifice necessary to keep the Barons going, and he didn't think they should've been asked to. "The team is in trouble, real trouble, and I don't know if the players helping out would solve it," Stewart said. "It is going to take a lot of serious thought after Eagleson tells them. Everyone is going to have a different idea. Some may even want to become free agents." It was understandable that the players wouldn't be interested in saving a team few people in Cleveland cared about. Stewart said he didn't think there would be hockey in Cleveland in 1977–78.

"It would be different if we knew the team would be here next year," he said. "We are not going to have a sudden rush of 10,000 people coming out."[38] As reasonable as that statement was, based on the reception the Barons had received up to that point, it turned out to be incorrect.

"I'd say the big thing is to get through the season," said Frank Spring. "I'm not ready to go home yet. We still have 32 games to go. This is a rough way to play hockey. But that's what happens when the fans don't come out. I thought they would."[39] If Spring's teammates shared his sentiments, a means to keep the Barons going through the end of the season could be achieved.

"This has us worried,"[40] under-stated defenseman Rick Hampton.

Swig was asked if, now that he planned to reside in Cleveland at least part of the time, he'd make the rounds of the city's business leaders, hat-in-hand. "Now would be a rough time to do that. We should show signs of growth first,"[41] he said. Before there could be signs of growth, it had to be determined whether the Barons would even continue to exist.

Swig's pleas of poverty weren't swaying NHL president Clarence Campbell. The man whose input had been minimal at best into the decision to move Oakland's team to Cleveland wasn't convinced Swig was desperate for money. "I don't think the problem is the availability of the resources to do what's necessary. It's a question of [Swig's] willingness to do it."[42] Campbell said he had no idea if the Barons would make it until the end of the season. "I can't say that. If the owner isn't that confident, I don't see how I can be."[43] Campbell left the impression that he was fed up with the constant headache that the Oakland/Cleveland franchise had been since it was founded in 1967, and he didn't seem to care what happened to it either way. Campbell said moving the Barons to Seattle, or anywhere, hadn't been discussed.

Amid the fussing, fighting and fretting about the future of hockey in Cleveland, the NHL managed to squeeze in an All-Star game. Al Mac-Adam represented the Barons and spent most of the game, including the entire third period, on the Prince of Wales Conference's bench. He didn't score. The Wales Conference stars beat the Campbell Conference stars, 4–3.

Evans spent the All-Star break scouting the Barons' Salt Lake City farm club, which was in the midst of a seven-game winning streak. Howell ran the Barons' practices during their coach's absence and bemoaned the fact the team had been beset by injuries. He couldn't help but ponder what his team's record might have been had so many players not spent so much time on the bench in street clothes.

Evans returned from Salt Lake City, and the Barons returned to the ice, on Friday, January 29. They lost to the Red Wings, 4–2, in Detroit. It was the Wings' first victory of 1977. Detroit had been 0–9–2 in its previous 11 games in January. From Detroit, the Barons made the short trip to Chicago and were pummeled by the Blackhawks, 9–3. The home team blew open a one-goal game with a late flurry in the second period. Three goals within 77 seconds turned a 4–3 Chicago lead into a 7–3 lead. All of the goals came at the expense of Gary Edwards, who was mercifully replaced by Meloche for the game's final 20 minutes. Meloche surrendered a pair of goals. Evans explained how his team came unglued in the late stages of the second period.

"It was a good game when it was 4–3," he said. "Then they got a power play goal, the puck took a couple of crazy bounces, they picked them up and got breakaways, and it was just one of those nights."[44] Evans' players could have been excused if they had other matters on their minds. The game was played on January 30, which was supposed to be payday. But Swig's ability to meet the team's payroll had come into question. When asked if he had the funds to pay the players, his answer was "no comment."

Swig was still in the process of negotiating with John Ziegler, who represented the Board of Governors. The preliminary agreement the two men had reached during the All-Star break had to be amended in order to satisfy both parties. "I'll probably have to go back to the league and negotiate some more," Swig confessed. "We have to get things done on a technical basis to make things more palatable."[45] Palatable to which side, Swig didn't say. It was revealed during the course of the negotiations with Ziegler that part of the reason Swig was short of cash was because he was still making payments to Charlie Finley, from whom the league purchased the Golden Seals in 1972. When Swig bought the Seals from the league, he assumed the $2.7 million debt it owed Finley. Earlier in the 1976–77 season, Swig made his scheduled $900,000 payment to Finley. He owed Finley two additional payments, for the same amount.

The Adams Division standings at the close of action on January 31:

Boston	30–16–5	65	193–157
Buffalo	28–15–6	62	174–133
Toronto	24–20–7	55	182–167
Barons	15–27–8	38	149–182

February opened with the short-handed Barons recalling defensemen Tom Price and Bjorn Johansson and right winger Lyle Bradley from Salt Lake City. Cleveland's most productive players through the first four months of the season were Dennis Maruk (20 goals, 27 assists, 47 points); Wayne Merrick (13 goals, 26 assists, 39 points); Al MacAdam (12 goals, 24 assists, 36 points); and Mike Fidler (15 goals, 16 assists, 31 points). Gilles Meloche had allowed 122 goals in 35 games (2,060 minutes) for a 3.55 goals-against average.

Swig withheld the players' paychecks, which were to have been distributed on January 30. He said he took the drastic step because he'd studied the Barons' books and found their financial woes to be much worse than he'd realized. He said he was disappointed that Cleveland's hockey fans and business leaders hadn't rushed in to support the club. Bob Stewart said it was his understanding that the checks had been drawn by the team's comptroller, who was then instructed to hold on to them. "Apparently, there is no money in the bank,"[46] Stewart said. Swig denied it.

"We are not short of money," the beleaguered majority owner insisted. "We have the funds, but we're holding back so something can be negotiated with the league."[47] The night before Swig's meeting with Eagleson, the Barons took the ice against the mighty Canadiens at the Coliseum. Despite not having been paid, Stewart said there'd been no talk in the locker room of a strike by the players. Montreal won easily, 7–3. Only 5,227 fans ventured to Richfield on a cold, snowy evening to watch the Barons battle the reigning Stanley Cup champions.

An aggravated Mike Christie sounded off after the game. "This is getting to be frustrating. It's like playing with a gun over your head. We get only 5,000 people for a Montreal game? You think we'll be here next year? I have serious doubts."[48]

Said MacAdam of the next day's meeting between Swig and Eagleson, "I don't know the circumstances yet, but I know it's upsetting everyone here."[49]

Swig said he'd talked to Sandy Greenberg, the owner of the Coliseum, and reported him to be disappointed and upset. He said he hadn't asked Greenberg to reduce, or waive altogether, the Barons' rent for the rest of the season. "We haven't discussed it. I'm going to talk to him. All I've done is ask him for any ideas."[50] Greenberg's mortgage on the Coliseum reportedly required that a National Hockey League team play there.

Eagleson reiterated that he expected Swig to ask the players to accept temporary pay cuts. The cuts would be returned to them on a deferred basis within 45 days of the end of the season. For the Barons, that would be April 3. He reconfirmed that he'd advise the players to slash their salaries in order to keep the team afloat through season's end. He acknowledged that several players might prefer to refuse the cuts and opt for free agency, but he warned that they needed to think of the teammates who'd be out of work if the Barons folded.

"There are some who simply won't get employment," Eagleson said. "So for the team's sake, the league's sake, and I think hockey's sake, I'd be happy just to see Cleveland survive until the end of the season, then determine if the franchise can be located in another city." He said the decision "has to happen as a team, and it has to be unanimous."[51]

Swig said a breakthrough in his negotiations with Eagleson wouldn't end the team's suffering. "Whatever we agree to will be only part way to solving our problems. There's a reasonable chance for optimism ... for the balance of the year, at least."[52]

On February 2, Swig told Eagleson what it would require to save his hockey team: the players would have to agree to a 27 percent pay cut, retroactive to January 1. The cuts would save Swig $250,000 and would be restored in deferred payments by May 15. Salt Lake City's players would have their salaries slashed by an even bigger amount, which hadn't yet been determined. Swig would demand that the Board of Governors defer Swig's $250,000 league assessment until May 15, without interest. If those terms were met, Swig would put up half a million dollars to see the Barons through until the end of the season. If Swig failed to reimburse the players by May 15, they'd become free agents.

Swig asked Eagleson for $333,000 in salary concessions from the players but settled for $250,000. He said $2.2 million had been spent on the Barons since the season started, and $1,540,000 of that amount had been his. The rest had been provided by Gund, who was reported to be fishing off the coast of Chile while the fate of the hockey team he'd lured to Cleveland and of which he was still president was being decided on a bone-chilling day in northeastern Ohio.

"I don't have a bottomless pit to manufacture the money," Swig said tersely. "If the players do their part, we'll do our part. Their choice is take it or the franchise folds."[53] Folding the franchise would've been just fine with many of the players, who would've been happy to be free of Swig and out of Cleveland.

One player who asked not to be identified told the *Plain Dealer*, "it doesn't look good. There is no guarantee the deferred payments will be made. If this was an established team, the guys wouldn't think twice about it."[54]

If the players agreed to Swig's ultimatum, as Eagleson advised them to do, the Barons wouldn't necessarily be saved. The NHL Board of Governors would still have to sign off on the agreement at a league meeting scheduled for Friday, February 11. And that wasn't a sure thing.

In presenting Swig's plan to the players, Eagleson was walking into a lion's den. He didn't waver from his belief that it was in everyone's best interests to do whatever Swig demanded to keep the Barons going through the end of the season in early April, preparatory to either disbanding the team, or moving it. He saw no hope for NHL hockey in Cleveland. "In the interval [between the players' vote and the league meeting] I have advised the players to honor their contracts. The players are obligated to play to the best of their abilities, which would be difficult under the circumstances."[55]

After meeting with Eagleson, Swig flew to Washington for a meeting with Sandy Greenberg, who had a strong interest in keeping the Barons going. Without them, he'd have an empty Coliseum on many nights in February and March, to say nothing of 40 nights in 1977–78. Greenberg was laid low by the flu, but Swig managed to meet with his representatives and returned to Cleveland with an alternate plan to save the Barons. He summoned Stewart to his private loge in the Coliseum between periods of the Barons-Penguins game on February 3 to explain the plan.

"He wouldn't go into depth, but he said it's possible something could be arranged where the team would be paid in full and kept intact the rest of the season," said the Barons' defenseman and player representative. "I'm definitely more optimistic, but I want to wait and see what he has to say. He said he would have to get the league to agree, and we would get paid if the NHL agrees to it."[56]

On the ice, the Barons and Penguins fought to a scoreless tie. Gary

Edwards, making his third start for Cleveland, registered his second shutout. He stopped 22 shots. Swig might have been pleased by the plan he'd worked out with Greenberg, but he couldn't have been happy as he looked over the Coliseum's 18,000 seats from his loge. Only 4,129 of them were occupied.

Swig revealed no more details of his new plan to the media than he had to Stewart. He said only that he'd been working on it for a long time, and it involved money from local investors. "If we can bring in these new people, then there is reason for optimism,"[57] he said. Swig said he'd discussed the plan with John Ziegler, but not in detail.

Cleveland *Press* sports editor Bob August described Swig as bringing "a touch of class" to the city's sports scene during the summer of 1976, when all was sweetness and light. August had changed in his February 4 column, although he stopped short of laying all of the blame for the mess in Richfield at the doorstep of the owner. He called the December agreement Gund had reneged on "booby-trapped, threatening calamitous possibilities from previous indiscretions." August accused the NHL of grossly misrepresenting the franchise it transferred from Oakland to Cleveland. The NHL promised that the former Golden Seals had been totally reorganized and were completely stable ... a promise August called "the second biggest snow job Cleveland was subjected to this brutal winter." Instead, "the corner bum of the National Hockey League" had been foisted on the community, and its hockey fans had been expected to embrace it. August accepted some responsibility on behalf of the media for simply being glad to have an NHL franchise and not investigating its background, or its majority owner's background, more thoroughly.

The *Press* also reported unconfirmed rumors that employees of Swig's real estate operation had been quietly dispatched to a number of cities seeking an NHL club. The purpose of the visits was to determine if any of those cities was prepared to have the Barons relocate there ... immediately.

The Barons beat the Blackhawks, 3–2, in the Coliseum on February 5. Before the game, Evans told his players point-blank that Chicago wasn't a very good team, and he expected a victory. The players responded, peppering Blackhawks goalie Tony Esposito with 52 shots, 49 of which he turned aside. The Saturday night crowd was a meager 5,236. So far, the Barons' cut-rate ticket promotions weren't having any effect on attendance.

One Baron, who wisely asked that his name be withheld, joked that beating Chicago may not have been such a good idea. "Maybe that wasn't so smart," the player cracked. "If Mel Swig sees that we played so well without pay, maybe he'll figure the way to win a championship is to never pay us again."[58]

On a serious note, Christie said the players never considered giving less than their best effort. "It was really a matter of pride," said the defenseman who'd been vocal in his criticism of the Barons' management and their fans. "Nobody's happy with the situation, but we're pros, and you know you don't go out there and just lay down. Our guys just aren't made like that."[59]

The topic of conversation in the dressing room, at the prodding of Passan and Schlesinger, turned to the pay cut Swig was demanding the players agree to in order to keep the Barons alive. MacAdam was among those who wanted no part of it. "The only paper I'm signing is the one which indicates I want to be a free agent if I'm not paid in two weeks,"[60] he said.

"That's just an incredible cut we were asked to take," added Bob Murdoch, who was almost ready to return following knee surgery. "If the owner were a guy who had almost gone down and out trying to save our team and needed our help to keep the shirt on his back, I'm sure the guys would do almost anything to help. But here's a millionaire asking us to accept that we should play for nothing even though he says he has the money to meet the payroll if he wants to. We didn't ask Mr. Swig to buy the team or move it to Cleveland. It's wrong for him not to live up to his contract with us, as it would be if half a dozen of us were to suddenly walk out on our contracts."[61]

Meloche was among the most vocal of the Barons who would've rejected Swig's proposal. "I've had enough. This is not a snap decision. I've talked to my lawyer, and he advised me not to take a pay cut. I know I can play anywhere in this league. I'm different from maybe half the guys on this team."[62] In urging the players to accept Swig's terms, no matter how unpleasant they were, Eagleson had been blunt. He said that as many as 10 to 12 players weren't good enough to be picked up by other teams if the Barons folded. According to Passan, comments like Meloche's and MacAdam's had driven a wedge between the players who knew they'd hook up with other teams if the Barons collapsed, and those who knew they'd be out of work.

Dissension wasn't a problem, at least not yet, according to Evans. After the team's squeaker over the Blackhawks, the coach praised his squad. "They haven't taken the opportunity to not play hockey, or look for excuses not to play. They are giving it a hell of an effort. They want some fans and some respect from the media. I haven't heard so many compliments about them as I have lately. That's good because they are giving effort under adverse conditions."[63] The job Evans was doing holding the Barons together wasn't going unnoticed. He was reported to be under consideration for head coaching vacancies that were expected in Los Angeles and Chicago.

In his February 7 column, Passan explained some of the details of Swig's alternate plan. Greenberg would put up $500,000 and so would Gund, who was suddenly back in the picture. A third local investor was being sought to contribute another $500,000. How Greenberg could invest in the Barons wasn't clear, since he was a minority owner of the Washington Capitals. That fact apparently wasn't an insurmountable problem. Finding another Clevelander willing to sink half a million dollars into the Barons might be. However, Greenberg was said to be a close friend of Gund's brother, Gordon, who had that kind of money to invest.

Cleveland's players weren't the only club employees struggling without paychecks. The *Press* revealed on February 7 that Swig hadn't paid the Barons' office staff on January 30, either.

Wing Gary Sabourin, who'd been sidelined since mid–December following knee surgery, was cleared to play on February 8. Evans said he'd ease Sabourin back into action. "He hasn't skated with any effort in seven weeks. In want to be sure he has the reflexes and conditioning before I put him in there."[64]

The league's Board of Governors meeting, scheduled for February 11, was postponed until February 14. "This gives us a little more time to work out things," said Swig, who was still piecing together his alternate plan to save the Barons. "I view this is as a positive thing. They— and I'm just guessing—are looking for a little more time to do something constructive. It's the intent of the league to do something that would be helpful. I am not sure what form that might take. It remains to be seen."[65] In spite of Swig's positive tone, it would soon be revealed that the board meeting was delayed by three days to allow Greenberg more time to salvage the alternate plan, which was falling apart. Swig had been fully prepared to liquidate the Barons had the governors met on February 11 as scheduled. He'd planned to fly to Montreal to meet with his fellow owners and auction off his players to the highest bidders, putting an end to the NHL in Cleveland. Swig had to pay the players the money he owed them for the last two weeks of January by February 17, or the Barons would disband. Apparently, as of February 9, when the postponement of the league meeting was announced, he had no intention of meeting that obligation. He planned to recoup as much of his investment as possible by conducting a fire sale.

The Barons bounced the Kings, 6–3, at the Coliseum on February 9. Two players traded for each other were the opposing goaltenders. The Barons built a 5–0 third period lead against their ex-teammate, Gary

Simmons. Gary Edwards appeared to be headed for his third shutout before the Kings woke up and trimmed their deficit to two goals. An empty net goal for the home team concluded the scoring. Only 3,225 bothered to visit the Coliseum on another Wednesday night.

"It's a good thing we had a big lead," said Edwards of the Kings' late flurry.

"I let the team down,"[66] said a disappointed Simmons, who was seeing his first action for his new team.

Two nights later, the Barons topped the Colorado Rockies, 3–0, at the Coliseum before a Friday gathering of 5,322. Meloche stopped 23 shots as the Oakland/Cleveland franchise notched its 200th victory. It had taken the Golden Seals/Barons almost nine full seasons to accomplish the feat, for an average of roughly 23½ wins per year.

Sounding a lot like some of his teammates at various points in the season when the team managed to string together a few victories, Meloche said the Barons seemed to be hitting their stride. "They know what they can do out there now. There are a couple of them who don't know how good they can be. They are playing scared ... scared of making a mistake."[67]

Stewart said the players met before the game and acknowledged it might have been the last time they'd skate on Coliseum ice. "We talked about how this might be our last game as Cleveland Barons. We decided that if it was, we wanted to go out as winners."[68]

In Boston on February 13, the Barons played what might have been their last game as Cleveland Barons anywhere. They lost the Bruins, 4–2. It was the Oakland/Cleveland franchise's 14th straight defeat in the Boston Garden.

The Barons weren't the only major league hockey team with serious financial problems during the 1976–77 season. Chicago *Daily News* reporter George Vass wrote on February 10 that the 29 clubs of the NHL and WHA would lose a combined $30 million. "Twelve of the 18 teams in our league are losing money," said someone Vass identified only as a "prominent" NHL club owner. The Barons, obviously, were one of those 12 teams. "Among them, they will lose $18 million this season. When you consider that the annual combined gross of our 18 teams is about $64 million, that is a tremendous amount."

The moment of truth was supposed to arrive for the Barons on Valentine's Day. Swig and Greenberg would present their plan to save the Barons to a group of owners who were, frankly, fed up to their eyeballs with the troublesome Oakland/Cleveland franchise, which had wandered aimlessly since it was created for the 1967–68 season. The NHL had sunk more than eight million dollars into the team in not quite nine full seasons. It had averaged less than 25 wins per year. It didn't draw many fans to a small building in Oakland, and was, amazingly, drawing even fewer fans to a much larger building in Cleveland. Included in the money spent by the league to support the franchise was a $600,000 loan to Swig to help him buy the Golden Seals from the NHL, which had purchased them from Charlie Finley. Swig hadn't repaid so much as a dollar of that loan.

Said one unidentified NHL owner of the chances of the Barons living to play another game, "if it's Greenberg, or Greenberg and somebody new, involved in a genuine plan to build a solid franchise, then the governors might bend to be helpful. But if it's Mel Swig coming back to ask for a handout, like he did in Vancouver, forget it. Heck, there are owners in this league swallowing about as much red ink as Swig. They don't have as much money as the Swig family, and they aren't asking for charity."[69]

Another owner, also unidentified, said no one was bothered by the thought of the Barons folding with two months of hockey still on the schedule. "We are no longer upset by the possibility of folding a franchise. Actually, a few owners seem in favor of letting a few weak sisters die."[70] At least some owners had accepted the harsh reality that the league had expanded much too quickly. Adding 12 teams in 10 years had been the height of foolishness. Or, possibly, greed. Owners love getting their cut of a new franchise's expansion fee.

All parties expected the worst when the Board of Governors convened at the February 14 league meeting in Montreal. A secret draft had already been conducted to disperse the team's players. A contingency schedule for the league's remaining 17 teams had been drawn up in the event the Barons folded. If they did, they'd be the first NHL team to disband since the New York Americans in 1941. The same New York Americans Al Sutphin's American Hockey League Barons were asked by the NHL to replace. Sutphin said no.

Rather than voting on the Swig/Greenberg plan, the governors appointed a committee of four club owners to study it and make a recommendation. Bill Wirtz of Chicago, Bob Sedgwick of Toronto, Bob Swados of Buffalo, and John Ziegler of Detroit met until 10 p.m., when they broke briefly for dinner. Then the meeting resumed. Wirtz emerged from the meeting long enough to announce that the players would be paid before the February 17 deadline and wouldn't become free agents. Wirtz said the Swig/Greenberg plan held promise. "We would not be working on a negative agreement,"[71] he said.

League president Clarence Campbell said Greenberg's involvement would save the Barons, if they were to be saved. And it appeared they would be. "Mr. Greenberg has been maneuvering for some weeks to try and put together a group to operate in Cleveland. He has a substantial interest in seeing them continue." Campbell added, "the degree of support they have been able to marshal up to this time does not warrant discontinuing the season."[72]

When the special committee adjourned at three o'clock in the morning on February 15, it seemed that the Greenberg plan had saved hockey in Cleveland. By late morning, the plan was dead. "The proposed deal between Mr. Swig and Mr. Greenberg has completely collapsed," Campbell reported. "Mr. Swig is now working on the infusion of capital to keep the team alive. The stumbling block was a fundamental difference in what was expected to be the agreement between Mr. Swig and Mr. Greenberg. The league's part of the deal had been satisfactorily agreed to by everybody."[73]

A stunned Peter Larsen met with Cleveland reporters to declare the Barons all but defunct. Larsen had been appointed president of the Coliseum just eight days earlier. "A firm offer of one million dollars to complete the season, plus another commitment to raise another three million to four million so the franchise could continue beyond this year, was placed before Mr. Swig this morning. The offer was rejected. We believe the whole proposal is out the window now," said Larsen. "There is nothing more that we can do to keep the team in Cleveland. I don't know what else we could do. Mr. Greenberg was flabbergasted by what happened. He was stunned. Mr. Greenberg worked two weeks to arrange the deal. He even went so far as to convince potential investors at his bedside at his home."[74] Greenberg had been suffering from a severe case of the flu and had canceled several trips to Cleveland because of it. He flew back to Washington immediately after negotiations with Swig ended.

"It is our indication that with the rejection of the offer, the team is finished," Larsen reaffirmed. "The only person who could have saved it is Sandy Greenberg. It is finished."[75] If Larsen was right, he'd find himself in charge of a three-year-old facility that would be empty most of the time.

The usual blame game followed the collapse of the Greenberg plan. Greenberg was astounded that Swig rejected his proposal. Swig said he was just as astounded that Greenberg marched into the meeting and announced that he had an idea which Swig could either accept or reject. It was non-negotiable. He could take it or leave it, and he chose to leave it. It hadn't bothered Swig when he gave the players an ultimatum on February 2: accept a 27 percent pay cut or the club folds. But when he was on the receiving end of Greenberg's "non-negotiable" offer, he didn't like it.

Other sources claimed the villain was once again George Gund III, who was still vacationing in South America. Gund was supposed to have contributed $500,000 to the Greenberg plan. For some reason, he backed out, just as he'd done to Swig in December. That left Greenberg in need of a million dollars to save the Barons. It was money the NHL didn't believe he could find.

Swig wasn't ready to pronounce his hockey team dead. "There are solutions, but we haven't finished them, by far,"[76] he said. The league enabled Swig to meet the tardy January 30 payroll by advancing him $175,000. The advance came with a catch: the Barons would be the CLEVELAND Barons in name only. Tired of microscopic crowds at the Coliseum, the Barons, as soon as the logistics could be worked out, would play their home games either on neutral ice, or on the home ice of the opposing team. "Some Barons games will be played on neutral ice, but I don't know how many,"[77] said a league official. Only if no alternate rink was available would the league bite the bullet and allow the game to be played at the Coliseum ... where it could be reasonably expected that no one would show up to watch.

The Barons' February 16 home game against Toronto would be played as scheduled. "At one point, the Maple Leafs game was off," said the official. "Then the league decided it did not want any violations in the free agent agreement with the players."[78] In other words, the NHL didn't want to risk creating a loophole by which the Barons could declare themselves free agents since the game hadn't been played ... in breach of their contracts.

February 16 was a bad day for 19 players under contract to the Barons, or their Salt Lake City affiliate. The parent club informed defenseman Glenn Patrick and right wings Frank Spring and Phil Roberto that they'd been released. Spring had been productive since being recalled from Salt Lake City, scoring 10 goals. Roberto's wife had just given birth, and he'd moved his family to Cleveland just two days before being terminated. He'd played 21 games for the Barons and been paid for only 10 of them.

"When a guy sticks a knife in your back and can't face you.... I've got hard feelings for the man right now,"[79] growled Roberto. "I hear about differences between millionaires like Mr. Swig and Mr. Greenberg and Mr. Gund. But how does it solve a millionaire's problem by not giving me the month's pay that I earned? I just can't understand it."[80] Roberto criticized Swig for letting acting GM Howell deliver the bad news to himself, Spring and Patrick. Howell had tears in his eyes after giving them their releases.

That was a small part of the purge. Thirteen Salt Lake City players were released, as were three players owned by the Barons who'd been farmed out to clubs in the International Hockey League.

February 15 was supposed to have been payday for the Barons, who'd just received their checks from January 30 ... thanks to an infusion of cash from the league. The players didn't get paid for the first two weeks of February on the 15th, and they wasted no time signing a paper to be delivered to Swig announcing their intent to become free agents if he didn't come up with the money he owed them within 15 days. Alan Eagleson assured the players they had that right. The NHL disagreed.

The pressure became too much for defenseman Len Frig. During the 5–3 loss to Toronto at the Coliseum on February 16, Frig flew into a rage after a third period score by the Leafs' Inge Hammarstrom. His tirade drew a 10-minute misconduct penalty from referee John McCauley. On his way to the penalty box, Frig threw his stick against the board, then removed his gloves and heaved them toward the box. He topped off his performance by removing his jersey and tossing it on the ice. The performance was witnessed by 4,308 fans who'd given the players a standing ovation when they took to the ice for their pre-game warm-ups.

After the game, Frig unleashed his frustrations ... which were undoubtedly shared by many, if not all, of his teammates. "I've been with this so-called organization for three years, and it keeps telling us everything is going to get better. For three years, it's been getting worse. It's as if they are going to make us stand up and rebel. Right now, I think a lot of players are playing for themselves and not playing for the betterment of the organization. They are turned off by the organization. It's like waiting for the end of the world."[81]

Spotted at the game was a banner reading simply SELL MEL.

The rebellion Frig mentioned might take the form of a boycott of the Barons' next game, versus the Colorado Rockies at the Coliseum on February 18. "The players have been informed of the legalities involved," said Stewart. "I've asked them to sleep on it, and we will make our decision after our morning skate."[82]

"It doesn't look good right now," admitted one player. "It will not take a unanimous vote. It will take a simple majority. Hopefully, it will be almost unanimous. We don't want it split down the middle."[83]

Said another player, "we can go on playing here and not get paid. Or we can get suspended and still not get paid. But when you're suspended, at least you're not taking the risk of getting hurt. That's the big thing right now."[84] The players were worried about who'd pay their medical bills if they were injured on the job. And a suspension from the league was a distinct possibility if they chose not to take the ice against the Rockies.

Stewart said of his teammates, "some of them are mad. They are all very frustrated and disappointed at the way things have been done. We don't know any more now than we knew two weeks ago. These are not very nice circumstances to be under."[85]

Swig was tired of being portrayed as the villain in the confusing affair and met with Evans and Howell on February 18 to explain the situation. He told his head coach and his general manager that he'd been given no choice by the league but to trim the Barons' roster to the bare minimum. He'd been given enough money to pay just 27 players, necessitating the release of Patrick, Roberto and Spring in addition to 16 minor leaguers. "He wanted to make clear he wasn't the ogre in the thing and that his hands were tied,"[86] said Evans. But Swig's hands weren't tied. He'd admitted in late January that he had the money to meet the Barons' payroll, but had decided not to spend it in order to force the issue. How could the team's employees (office staff included) view him as anything but a Scrooge?

Howell said Swig understood how his employees felt. "Nobody likes to take the criticism he is taking, but he understood."[87] That, too, must've been hard for the employees to swallow ... particularly the office workers who didn't have six-figure contracts as many of the players did and lived from paycheck-to-paycheck. Swig was a multi-millionaire. There was no way he could empathize with his unpaid employees.

Swig also told Evans and Howell that John Ziegler had renewed negotiations with Sandy Greenberg. It seemed unlikely that Greenberg would simply walk away and wash his hands of the whole mess in Cleveland. When he purchased the Coliseum, he said his goal was to have an event in the building 365 days a year. And now he was willing to accept the fact that one of his tenants was in danger of going belly up? Ziegler hoped to revive Greenberg's interest in saving the Barons, and their remaining home games in the Coliseum.

After their morning skate on February 18, the Barons voted overwhelmingly not to report for their game against Colorado that evening. Ziegler was informed and hastily reached an agreement with Eagleson and Stewart that satisfactorily addressed all of the players' immediate concerns. The boycott ended almost before it started. Some of the Barons, assuming there'd be no game, left the Coliseum. When the problem was satisfactorily (but temporarily) fixed, they were hastily summoned back to work. Ninety minutes before the game, however, the boycott was almost restarted. Stewart received a telegram informing him that the National Hockey League and Swig flatly rejected their claim that they'd be free agents if Swig hadn't paid them by March 2. Stewart wasn't able to reach Eagleson, but he contacted Ziegler, who reaffirmed the league's position. If the players weren't paid by March 2, the Barons would fold and the players would be subject to a dispersal draft. They'd go where they were told to go. They would NOT become free agents. The telegram almost led to a strike, but the players chose to proceed with the game, largely because they trusted Eagleson, who'd promised them the NHLPA would support their position. The Barons tied the Rockies, 3–3, as a crowd of 5,191 watched. A few of those fans brought a Mel Swig doll with them. They hung it in effigy from the Coliseum's second level.

After a brief break for an actual hockey game, the vigil for the Barons resumed. Stewart said he'd been told Gund was returning to the United States on February 22, and he was expected to rejoin Greenberg in his effort to save hockey in Cleveland. As far as the players were concerned, they were fed up with the whole thing and had decided to bring the uncertainty to a close within five days. Stewart told Swig that "if by Tuesday noon of next week [February 22nd] the situation is not rectified, or we don't get paid in full, or Mr. Greenberg does not step into the picture, then we will become free agents." Stewart didn't elaborate as to what the players would consider the situation being "rectified." He said Eagleson had assured the players of the full support of their union if they wound up declaring their free agency. They could be certain of a bitter fight with the owners over the issue.

Stewart was asked how Swig responded to the ultimatum. "He said he didn't give a damn,"[88] answered the player representative. At that point, neither did most Clevelanders. They'd been through a similar situation exactly a year earlier, when a missed payroll almost resulted in the Crusaders folding. Major league hockey ... at least in Cleveland ... was a bad joke. Who cared anymore?

The players' goal was to resolve the situation, regardless of what that resolution might have been. They were sick and tired of one reprieve after another, followed by another crisis. Their ultimatum was meant to force Swig's hand once and for all, and it sent shivers through the office of Coliseum president Peter Larsen. "This puts terrible pressure on us to pull the parties together and proceed," he warned. "We want the team. I believe the terms have been revised, based on some new information. The offer to Mel has been revised. We haven't firmed up the revised offer because there is no firm handle. That's what is wrong with this time frame."[89]

Another problem with the time frame was that it wasn't revealed at what time Gund was due back in the country. If it was early in the day, it would have given the parties an extremely limited amount of time to meet Stewart's noon deadline. If it was later in the day, the deadline would have already passed. However, Gund hadn't been personally involved in the negotiations. He was letting his lawyer do his talking for him, so his continued absence shouldn't have posed a problem. Swig's stubbornness and indecision did. He vacillated from one day to the next between seemingly wanting to keep the team going, then wanting to auction off the players and recoup as much of his original investment as possible. One flustered (and, not surprisingly, unidentified) associate of Greenberg's said Swig simply wouldn't tell the Coliseum's owner what he wanted in exchange for selling his hockey club.

According to a league source, "the money differences between the two guys aren't so big that they couldn't be worked out. But it remains to be seen if the personal differences can be settled."[90] Gund was reportedly mad at Swig for making him out to be the villain for pulling out of the December agreement—an agreement that, Bob August had written, Swig's lawyer had booby-trapped. But Gund refused to talk to the media, nor did he appoint a spokesman to speak for him. No one knew what he was thinking. Greenberg wouldn't talk to the media either, but he at least allowed Larsen to speak for him. Swig was happy to talk, but his arguments didn't sway anybody. He spent an hour explaining to Bob Schlesinger how the whole ghastly mess wasn't his fault. Schlesinger's response in the column he wrote based on the interview was "hogwash!"

Schlesinger wrote that Swig was threatening to sue Gund for backing out of the December agreement to take majority control of the team. He was threatening to sue the NHL for anti-trust violations and threatening to drive the Barons into bankruptcy. Schlesinger wrote that the people threatening to sue Swig could form a single-file line stretching from Richfield back to Oakland. Broken down into its simplest form, Schlesinger's analysis called the Barons' debacle a snit between two men whose families were worth hundreds of millions of dollars, but who somehow couldn't, or wouldn't, cobble together $200,000 to meet the team's payroll.

Evans made a startling confession after the loss to Toronto. For the past three weeks, since chaos had broken out in Richfield, he hadn't been trying to win games. With the demise of the Barons a distinct possibility, he was more concerned about giving his players a fair chance to show their abilities to the scouts in the stands. "I'm not coaching by using the best players as much as I could," he said. "I'm playing everybody to showcase them, so they can get jobs in case the club goes under. It's unfair to sit somebody down in a case like this." As for the noise that surrounded him and his players, he said, "I've given up listening to everything. It's come to the point where I've said 'the hell with it.' I'm going to wait and see what happens."[91]

Evans' admission that he was putting his players on display rather than trying to win drew no backlash or criticism, even from Swig. The players undoubtedly appreciated it. So did Swig, since he still hoped to sell those players to the highest bidder if the Barons folded ... despite published reports that a secret dispersal draft had already been conducted. As for Evans, he was held in high regard throughout the NHL. He wouldn't have trouble finding a job for the 1977–78 season, and he knew it.

The Barons took the ice in Pittsburgh's Civic Arena, better known as The Igloo, on Sunday, February 20, knowing they might be performing as a team for the last time. They were deadly serious about their February 22 deadline for a resolution of the team's status, which could've resulted in their free agency.

"I just hope I put [the uniform] on again," said Bob Girard. "I don't know what will happen. I hope we keep playing. I want to play hockey. I love to play hockey."[92]

"Maybe it's a bad thing to say, but I just wanted to get the game over with as soon as possible," said Mike Christie. "I can't get motivated out there. All I'd like to do is get back to playing hockey instead of the way it has been."[93]

"I hope everything is settled," said Stewart. "And I hope that means Mel Swig completely separates himself from the club. The players have no respect for him after he told us he doesn't give a damn what we do."[94]

"I don't play any more until I get paid," said Gary Sabourin. "If I don't get paid, I will demand to be traded or sold. If I'm not good enough to make it with another team, I'll pack it in." Sabourin spoke for all of the Barons when he said, "this has gone far enough."[95]

The Penguins, a team with financial woes of their own, took advantage of Cleveland's understandable lack of motivation for a 4–1 victory.

The National Hockey League team owners met to discuss the Cleveland crisis in the ironically named Baron Suite of New York's Waldorf Astoria Hotel. The meeting lasted six and a half hours and resolved nothing. One frustrated owner was heard muttering "15 guys with 15 different solutions"[96] when the meeting recessed. One of the points of contention was the dispersal of the players if the league let the Barons expire. The wealthier owners wanted them made available to the highest bidders. The owners with less cash insisted on a draft.

The February 22 deadline set by the players to have their demands met passed. Negotiations continued. The players didn't declare their free agency. But Stewart said they wouldn't play the game scheduled against Buffalo on the 23rd.

Stewart had a busy morning on February 23. He took part in the

Barons' morning skate at the Hudson Ice Barn, then drove to Cleveland Hopkins airport to pick up Eagleson. He chauffeured the head of the players' association to the site where the Barons were to meet with Bill Wirtz and Ziegler, representing the league's Board of Governors. Eagleson would reaffirm the union's commitment to support the players if the team and the league failed to meet their demands, and they unilaterally declared their free agency. Ziegler and Wirtz would try to talk them out of their hardline stance. If they failed, they'd make sure the players understood they'd have a fight on their hands if they pursued free agent status. The league wouldn't stand for it.

While the players were busy in Cleveland, Swig and his lawyer were in New York for a second day of meetings with attorneys representing Gund and Greenberg. The news that trickled back to northeastern Ohio wasn't promising. "From what I understand, the new deal with Greenberg and Gund is not coming through," said Stewart. "It looks more doubtful than a few days ago. If they can't come to an agreement, they can't approach Swig." Stewart was asked if the players would back off their threat to strike and agree to play that night's scheduled game against Buffalo if word of progress in the negotiations came from New York.

"As of right now, I don't think we would play in that event," he answered. "I'd still have to ask the players and have them vote on it."[97] For the past three weeks, there'd been one story after another that a deal to save the Barons was close. Then it wasn't. Then another one was close. Then it wasn't. The players were sick of it. They had already ignored their self-imposed deadline of noon on February 22 to declare their free agency. They were in no mood to make any more concessions.

Ziegler wasn't optimistic when he spoke to reporters as the talking continued. "There is the possibility of a sale by Mr. Swig. There is the possibility of the league taking over the franchise and running it until the end of the year. There is the possibility of the franchise winding down and the players being sold. The first two possibilities seem remote, but they are possibilities."[98]

Ziegler's comment was the first hint by a league official that the players might be auctioned off if the Barons folded. Prior to that, the NHL had insisted that a dispersal draft would be (or had already been) held to allow for the orderly distribution of the players, rather than a wild free-for-all with the teams waving checkbooks and competing for the available talent. That was the solution Swig wanted. An auction would enable him to recoup some of his losses, and he needed money to repay a $2.5 million loan he'd been given by the Union Bank of San Francisco when he purchased the team.

Once their deadline had passed, a number of players said that even if a miracle saving the team occurred, they'd refuse to play if Swig continued to own it. As Stewart had said, the players had lost respect for their boss. Many of them said they were still waiting for Swig to reimburse them for their moving expenses to Cleveland, which he was obligated to do under the basic agreement between the NHLPA and the owners. The club was also behind in paying the players' medical expenses.

In response to a question he was undoubtedly tired of hearing, Stewart said on the afternoon of February 23, as negotiations dragged on in New York, "unless we see the money in the bank or a guaranteed salary, we won't play hockey for the Cleveland Barons. We have to stick to our agreement. We won't do any playing unless there is solvency."[99]

Within hours of Stewart's statement, the Barons achieved that solvency, thanks to a sizable contribution from an unexpected and unlikely source. Gund didn't save the Barons. Neither did Greenberg. Alan Eagleson did. It was announced late in the afternoon on February 23 that $1.3 million had been secured to keep the Barons alive for the rest of the season. Swig contributed $350,000. The NHL put up $350,000. And the NHLPA borrowed $600,000, with the stipulation that the money was to be used to pay the players' salaries for the rest of the year. Eagleson believed strongly that it was in the best interests of everyone that the Barons finish the season, and when push came to shove, he put the union's money where his mouth was. The $1.3 million was enough to allow the Barons to pay their operating expenses for the rest of the 1976–77 season. Cleveland's game against the Sabres at the Coliseum that night would be played as scheduled. None of the team's eight remaining home games would be transferred from the Coliseum.

"We thought it was hopeless yesterday," said a weary Stewart, who drew praise from the Cleveland media for the calm and dignified way he handled a very difficult situation. "We want to give our appreciation to Mel Swig and his family for donating $350,000 to this franchise. He's shown he has faith in us by putting up the money. He's said some things he shouldn't have, and we said some things we shouldn't have. I've been annoyed at times with him, and he's been annoyed at times with me. But now it's all over. I hope the pressure we've gone through this last month can be forgotten."[100]

Said Swig, "as of last Monday night, I didn't think there was a chance of this thing going. Now we're going to invest to insure and make sure this franchise is on as solid a footing as we can make it." He didn't sound as if he planned to sell the team, or dissolve it, at season's end.

Swig reiterated his belief that he'd been unjustly cast as the villain in the nerve-wracking series of events. "I was the villain in the eyes of

Alan Eagleson (left), president of the National Hockey League Players Association, addresses the media along with a frustrated group of Cleveland Barons players on February 22, 1977. Eagleson kept the club alive by borrowing $600,000 on behalf of the NHLPA to be used to help beleaguered owner Mel Swig make payroll and keep the Barons from folding midway through the 1976–77 season (Michael Schwartz Library, Cleveland State University).

the press and players when, in fact, I felt I had done everything in my power to continue running the operation. I didn't have to. Then came the time when I said, 'hey, this is it.' It was time to call a halt."[101]

Ziegler admitted that he'd given up all hope of keeping the Cleveland franchise going. "Last night, I would have bet anything I wouldn't be here announcing this."[102]

Swig said he hoped the agreement would give him and his hockey team a clean slate in northeastern Ohio. It amounted to "an invitation to Cleveland to take another look. We bet on the community once before. We're going to take a positive approach."[103] And Cleveland would take another look at the Barons. But not at the Coliseum on February 23 against the Sabres. Amid the confusion, it was surprising anyone showed up for the game. It was surprising anyone knew there was a game to show up for.

Some players were happy to let bygones be bygones. "I'm very happy. I thought there was no chance," said Bob Murdoch. "It was completely out of my mind that we'd be playing tonight. I was set to leave. The threat of a boycott made a difference. We forced their hand. Now there's a whole new feeling on the club."[104]

Not all of Murdoch's teammates shared his "whole new feeling." Al MacAdam didn't. MacAdam was downright angry that the Barons didn't fold and he had to play out the season in Cleveland. "I was really ticked off before the game when I heard the news," he growled. "It takes a lot to get my goat, and my goat was got. I was upset when the decision was made for us to stay here. There is no guarantee the team is going to be sold yet."[105] MacAdam claimed 75 percent of the Barons weren't happy about the rescue and preferred to be somewhere else. He hinted that he might retire rather than put on a Cleveland uniform again.

"Are we supposed to be thrilled?" asked Mike Christie. "I hope it's not like it's been every other year, where we'll wait around all summer to find out where we're going to be playing, or if we're going to be playing at all."[106]

"The only way this will be worth anything for us in the long run is if somebody buys the team and straightens the whole thing out,"[107] said Gilles Meloche, who went public with a request to be traded. Rumor had it that if the Barons had folded, Meloche would've been on his way to the New York Rangers.

"I felt all along something would happen to save us," said Harry Howell. "If it wasn't someone appearing on the scene, then it would have been the NHL itself. I have the utmost respect for the players for the way they have performed under adverse circumstances."[108]

While glad the Barons had been saved, Passan and Schlesinger sided with Meloche. The infusion of money to get the club through the rest of the season was little more than the slapping of a Band-Aid on a sick elephant. The Swig/Gund partnership had been irretrievably broken. Only the sale of the Barons to a stable ownership with lots of money (and a willingness to spend it) was going to save hockey in Cleveland. And there was no guarantee that was going to happen.

The Barons dressed only 12 players in their 5–3 loss to the Sabres on a night none of them had expected to go to work. Somehow 3,185 fans got the word that the game was on, and made their way to the Coliseum to celebrate the fact that hockey would stay in Cleveland, at least through the third of April.

Evans gave his players the day off after the Buffalo game to unwind and gather their thoughts. "He thanked us for performing as well as we did under the circumstances," said Stewart. Evans also served notice that it would be business as usual with the crisis having passed. He was coaching to win, and he expected his players, both the happy and the unhappy, to play to win. "He also said that if we continue to play hockey here, we will play to 100% of our capabilities. And if we didn't [intend to], he wanted us to let him know, because we weren't going to be playing under him,"[109] Stewart said. None of the angry Barons told Evans they planned to give less than their best the remainder of the season.

The Barons gave the New York Islanders their best shot on Friday, February 25, but lost, 2–1. The crowd at the Coliseum was 6,449. It was the sixth largest crowd of the year. Ralph Klassen scored Cleveland's only goal. The Barons got off 37 shots while limiting the Islanders to 24, two of which made it past Meloche. "That's the story of our life," moaned Evans. "Good effort, no win. We just don't have enough goals."[110] Evans was pleased to be complaining about events on the ice rather than off the ice for a change.

With the defeat, the Barons departed Cleveland for an eight-game, 18-day road trip. They'd be in for a pleasant surprise when they returned.

7

Meanwhile,
Back at the Ranch

Their financial problems behind them, at least until the end of the season, the Barons could concentrate on playing hockey. Seventeen games remained on the schedule, including six crucial contests at the Coliseum. Not crucial as far as the standings were concerned. Though not mathematically eliminated from playoff contention, the Barons were going nowhere but to their off-season homes after their April 3 game in Chicago. But the attendance at those half dozen games might decide if the team played in Cleveland in 1977–78, or somewhere else ... or not at all.

The Barons opened their longest road trip of the year, eight games, with a 5–3 loss to the Canadiens on February 26. They followed it with one of their better efforts, a 5–2 victory over the Blues in St. Louis on February 28. The Blues, despite a losing record, were in first place in the Conn Smythe Division, which they'd eventually win. The game was the Monday night NHL "Game of the Week," and the Barons, given up for dead less than a week earlier, gave a good accounting of themselves before a national TV audience.

"We had very good passing," said coach Jack Evans of his team's victory. "We played a solid hockey game and checked well. We had some scoring opportunities in front of their net and we didn't give up too many scoring opportunities ourselves." He admitted that his players had spent most of the month of February distracted by Mel Swig's problems. "That occupied your thoughts 24 hours a day, and you didn't even look at the standings."[1]

The players who looked at the Adams Division standings on March 1, the morning after the victory over St. Louis, saw:

Buffalo	38–19–6	82	228–175
Boston	35–21–7	77	234–197
Toronto	29–26–9	67	250–225
Barons	18–35–10	46	180–222

On the last day of February, the Barons announced that the price of nine-dollar tickets at the Coliseum had been reduced to seven dollars. Having barely dodged a bullet aimed at the club's heart, the front office began to take seriously the need to promote the team and lure fans to its remaining home games.

Technically, the Barons still had a slim chance of catching the Maple Leafs for third place. Realistically, that wasn't going to happen. And that may have worked in the club's favor as it headed for Toronto and the third game of the trip. The Barons had posted victories over their other Adams rivals, but hadn't beaten the Maple Leafs. "In those earlier games, we had our problems because of the added pressure on us to win," said Al MacAdam. "Because we're so far behind, maybe everybody will be more relaxed."[2]

MacAdam said he didn't think the Maple Leafs were 21-points better than the Barons, but he couldn't argue with the standings. "The scores don't show that. They seem to show that they are that much better. I don't know what it is. They seem to be so loose against us. Even in the warm up they talk and joke and are relaxed. We're uptight for some reason."[3]

On March 2, the Barons turned the tables on their tormentors in Toronto with a 4–1 victory. The Leafs put the pressure on their guests throughout, sending 18 shots at goalie Gary Edwards in the first period. He stopped them all. The Leafs out-shot the Barons but came up short. Cleveland's third-place deficit was reduced to 19 points.

Evans credited the nine goals scored in the victories over the Blues and Maple Leafs to unexpected contributions. "We are getting goals from guys we weren't getting them from before. Bob Girard has four goals in the last three games, and Ralph Klassen is starting to score."[4] Before the season began, Evans said he wanted the Barons to score 50 more goals than the 278 the Golden Seals had scored in 1975–76. The Barons wouldn't come close to achieving that.

Bob Stewart credited Evans for the Barons' improved play over the past four games. He said it began after the lackluster loss to Buffalo at the Coliseum on February 23. Evans excused the team's poor performance because they hadn't expected to play that night. Word of the infusion of cash that saved the franchise reached the Coliseum just a few hours before game time, and a game most of the players anticipated would be canceled was played as scheduled. It was hard for them to get fired up for it. But Evans had lectured his charges afterward and told them what he demanded in terms of effort for the rest of the season.

"I hate to say what would have happened had he not said that and brought us back to reality," explained Stewart. "The morale now is even better than when we had that six-game unbeaten streak on the road earlier this season. I can compare it to the way we were entering the season. The guys are together now. It's all built up from what Jack said. Everything is coming to a head."[5]

The hot streak Evans referred to couldn't have come at a better time for Girard. He admitted after the Toronto game that he'd instructed his agent to explore the possibility of jumping to the World Hockey Association. The Quebec Nordiques owned his rights, and he was strongly considering signing with them for the 1977–78 season. "It's not very encouraging not knowing what the future holds and what we all will be doing after June. So we are fending for ourselves as well as the team right now."[6] Quebec was one of the more stable franchises in the increasingly unstable WHA.

Cleveland's modest winning streak reached three with a 2–1 victory over the Flames in Atlanta on March 5. Playing with only four defensemen, the Barons were out-shot 36–19. Gilles Meloche made 35 saves. It was only the Barons' second victory in which they'd scored just two goals.

Like the Barons, the Flames had been plagued by financial problems. Club ownership announced in December that it wouldn't be able to meet its next payroll. Rather than asking for a bailout from the league, the Flames launched an immediate ticket drive. The community responded, and the money raised by the sale of those tickets kept the Flames burning for the rest of the season.

From Atlanta, it was on to New York for the Barons. They lost to the Rangers in Madison Square Garden, 4–3. Still, Evans was pleased with his club's resurgence since the players had been assured they'd be paid for the rest of the year. "They are playing at their potential. The only thing we're doing differently is scoring goals. We were working as hard before and creating the scoring chances, but we weren't scoring. Also, we aren't giving up any more goals than we were before."[7] That statement came back to haunt Evans on March 10 in Philadelphia. The Flyers routed the Barons, 7–2.

Adding insult to injury, Philadelphia head coach Fred Shero wasn't happy with his team's performance, despite the resounding victory. "I didn't think we played that well tonight," Shero complained. "We were

Barons goaltender Gilles Meloche turns aside a shot by Stan Jonathan of the Boston Bruins in a game at the Richfield Coliseum during the 1976–77 season (Michael Schwartz Library, Cleveland State University).

not playing with that much intensity. Maybe the players thought they were. It's tougher to play against a team like this instead of, say, Boston or Montreal."[8] Although a few players, such as Boston's Gerry Cheevers and the Rangers' Phil Esposito, had showered the young Barons with praise earlier in the year, Shero's remark indicated how far they had to go to earn some real respect around the NHL.

Two nights later, back in New York (Uniondale to be exact), the Barons absorbed another beating, this one from the Islanders. The Barons' Len Frig scored the game's first goal. The Islanders scored the next eight. Final score: New York 8, Cleveland 3.

Regardless of the fact that the Barons were playing with just four defensemen, 15 goals in two games was more than Evans could stomach. The team returned to Richfield for a couple of days before flying to Washington to conclude the road trip, and Evans put his players through a grueling practice at the Hudson Ice Barn, after which he held a team meeting. He said he had "plans" to end the Barons' three-game losing streak. "I am certainly going to have to do something to shake things up,"[9] he said.

The final game of the trip, against the Capitals in Washington, was "Guaranteed Win Night" at the Cap Centre. If the home team failed to beat the Barons, every fan would get a free ticket for the Capitals game against the Colorado Rockies. It should be noted the Caps wisely didn't schedule the promotion when the Canadiens or Flyers were in town.

Barons majority owner Mel Swig was back in Cleveland in early March and said he was in almost constant contact with representatives of Coliseum owner Sandy Greenberg. "I haven't talked to any other possible buyers who want to keep the team in Cleveland," Swig said. "If there are any such investors, they'd probably be talking to Sandy."[10] Bob Schlesinger in the *Press* said he believed it to be very important that a sale of the Barons to local investors be completed by the end of the season ... which was rapidly approaching.

There was good news from the team's sales department. Tickets for five of the six remaining home games were selling well. Through 34 home games, the Barons had been averaging an anemic 5,100 fans per date at the Coliseum. The advance sale for the visit by Minnesota was 7,500; games against Atlanta, Buffalo and Vancouver had advance sales of 8,000 tickets, and the game against the Islanders had an advance sale of 8,200 tickets. Only for the season finale against the Flyers were sales lagging. Just 4,000 tickets had been sold for that game. It was anticipated (and hoped) that the crowds at all six games would exceed the 10,000 mark.

The Barons spoiled "Guaranteed Win Night" by trampling the Capitals, 5–1, on March 15. Meloche lost his shutout on a goal by Craig Patrick in the third period. Each fan in the crowd of 7,374 left the Cap Centre with a free ticket to Washington's game against Colorado the following Friday. The victory was historic in that it completed the first season series sweep ever by the Oakland/Cleveland franchise. The Barons beat the Capitals five times in five tries.

The eight-game road trip broke down as it should have. The Barons defeated the teams they should have, or at least could reasonably be expected to. They lost to the teams they should have lost to.

Buffalo was a team the Barons couldn't reasonably have been expected to defeat, and they lived up to that expectation when they returned home on March 16. The Sabres scored five goals over the last two periods and posted an easy 6–2 victory. But the atmosphere in the Coliseum had changed. There were 11,189 fans in attendance. It was the second largest crowd of the year.

Swig didn't enjoy St. Patrick's Day. His former friend and general manager, Bill McCreary, filed a lawsuit against him in Summit County Common Pleas Court on March 17. Summit was the county in which the Coliseum was located. In the suit, McCreary claimed Swig had slandered him by accusing him of stealing money from the team in articles that had been published in newspapers in both Cleveland and San Francisco. In researching this book, I saw no such statement by Swig in either of Cleveland's papers, the *Plain Dealer* or the *Press.* The suit also claimed Swig had reneged on terms of McCreary's contract and failed to reimburse him for expenses (such as moving from Oakland to Cleveland) covered by his contract. McCreary asked for more than three million dollars in damages. Swig had no comment on the suit.

Evans' goal for his team was to win 28 games ... one more than it had won in 1975–76. In order to achieve that objective, the Barons would have to win seven of their 10 remaining games, all of which were against teams either fighting for a playoff spot, or to improve their playoff position. "It doesn't matter who we meet at this time of year, they're going to be tougher to beat,"[11] said the coach.

The Barons started fast against the Minnesota North Stars at the Coliseum on March 18, then stalled. Cleveland scored twice in the game's first five minutes, with the goals by Wayne Merrick and Ralph Klassen. They didn't score again in the remaining 55 minutes. The North Stars scored twice in that time and left town with a 2–2 tie. The Barons' injury list grew longer when Rick Hampton broke a wrist bone. How long he'd be sidelined wasn't immediately known. It was the only one of the Barons' last six home games that didn't draw a five-figure crowd, and it didn't miss by much. The attendance was 9,165.

The NHL's schedule gave the Barons just two matinees, and both were in late March. On Saturday, March 20, Cleveland defeated Atlanta, 5–4. For the second straight game, the Barons skated to a quick start. Goals by Whitey Widing, Bob Murdoch and Girard gave the Barons a 3–0 lead in the game's first six minutes, much to the delight of the crowd of 10,829. The lead grew to 5–1 late in the second period before the Flames fought back.

"We almost blew the game after playing so well," said a relieved Evans. "In the first period, we played perfectly. We were on them on them quickly, and we didn't give them time to do anything. But when we get a lead, we tend to get a little cautious. We didn't skate as well in the second period as the first."[12] Or, Evans might have added, in the third period. Meloche stopped 37 shots as his teammates hung on for the victory.

After losing their first three games to division rival Toronto, the Barons suddenly found the key to beating the Maple Leafs. They visited

Maple Leaf Gardens on March 21 and romped to a 7–2 victory. The "3-M" line of Dennis Maruk, Al MacAdam and Murdoch scored four goals. Edwards made 35 saves. But all hope of catching Toronto for third place in the Adams Division had long since faded.

Two days later in Buffalo, the Barons bowed to the Sabres, 4–2. Acting general manager Harry Howell coached the club in Evans' absence. Evans had been given permission to go home to San Diego due to a serious illness in his family. "I would have liked to face a different team in my first game," Howell admitted. "The Sabres are tough at home. I wasn't nervous, but I was concerned because of our manpower. I have to give the team credit. They played well despite it."[13]

Swig said he'd received a revised offer for the Barons from Greenberg on March 22. "I've received a first draft of an offer and we're moving on it," he said. "Moving slowly."[14]

The Barons were playing short-handed as the season wound down. Due to injuries, and releases during the massive purge of mid–February, only 13 players (not counting goaltenders) dressed for the March 25 home game against Vancouver. Evans addressed his team on the need to keep its cool due to the lack of manpower. He wasn't happy when Frig's volcanic temper got the best of him (as it often did) in the third period. Frig unloaded (verbally) on referee Gregg Madill, earning a 10-minute misconduct penalty. When Frig continued to argue with Madill, he was assessed a game misconduct. When that didn't stop the verbal barrage, Madill slapped Frig with a gross misconduct penalty. In all, Frig racked up 32 penalty minutes in the third period. That was added to the nine minutes he'd accumulated earlier in the contest, giving him a dubious franchise record of 41 minutes for the game. The game misconduct penalty Madill assessed Frig was his fifth of the season, resulting in an automatic two-game suspension.

"We were supposed to avoid all this,"[15] grumbled Evans. He wasn't quite as upset with the result of the game, which ended in a 4–4 deadlock witnessed by another robust crowd of 11,816.

In spite of Frig's absence for the next game, a matinee against the powerhouse Islanders, Cleveland's defense held the visitors to just 19 shots on goal. Unfortunately, Meloche stopped only 13 of them in a 6–3 defeat. "I looked like a fool out there," said a perplexed Meloche of his performance. "Every good chance they got, it went right in. They just waited and made the perfect play. There were times when play was at the other end of the ice for five minutes, then they came back and bang, it was in."[16] The Islanders had played at home the night before and arrived in Cleveland at three o'clock in the morning. If they were fatigued, they didn't show it.

A crowd approaching 14,000 had been anticipated for the game. That figure was overly optimistic. The attendance was 10,794.

The Barons visited Minneapolis on March 29 and lost to the North Stars, 4–2. "We knew when we came here it would be a tough game because of the North Stars playoff situation," said Evans. "This was a must victory for them, and we were in a hornet's nest."[17]

Wednesday, March 30, was the Barons' last scheduled game at the Coliseum for 1976–77. Off-season developments would determine if it would be their last ever. "We are working to make it not the last game," vowed Swig. "And I think we are making progress. We've got until June 1st. Right now, we are proceeding as though this thing is going to be in Cleveland."[18]

"We are all waiting for some confirmation there will be a team here next year," said Evans. "We're optimistic there will be. What could have been more difficult than what we've been through? We've all accepted the fact we'll play out the remaining games and see what happens. The players, naturally, are concerned. They have homes here and want to know whether to sell or keep them. They have all these problems."[19]

The Barons' problem that Wednesday was dealing with the Philadelphia Flyers. They battled the Flyers to a 2–2 tie. As 10,216 fans departed the Coliseum, the public address announcer told them, "We hope to see you all back here next fall."

"I'm very optimistic," said MacAdam, who'd resisted the urge to retire rather than play the final weeks of the season in Cleveland. "I wasn't in February. Greenberg cannot afford to lose 40 nights here. With the right promotions, the team will do well here. With a few changes in personnel, our team can be more consistently productive."[20]

"This is not a playoff team, but it is progressing," said Mike Christie. "If we can just keep up our progress, this won't be a bad place to live and play."[21]

Maruk didn't want to be put through an ordeal similar to that of the previous summer. "They had better make up their minds soon. I don't want to be waiting all summer. It'll be too hard on everybody that way."[22]

"I think the team will be here next year," said Murdoch. "I was surprised at the number of people who showed up. I didn't think it would jump like that and stay steady."[23] The Barons had drawn 63,004 fans to their final six home games, an average of 10,668 per game. But there was more to those numbers than met the eye.

Meloche, who had demanded a trade and who'd hoped to go to the Rangers when it appeared the Barons were about to be liquidated back in February, said he wouldn't have a problem with returning to Cleveland ... under the right conditions. "If they settle this thing [ownership] once and for all, it's okay with me. But if they're going to go through the same thing again, no."[24]

Swig met with the players the morning of the last home game and told them to expect a restructuring of the team's finances within a month, if not sooner. "We've been making slow progress and right now I'm feeling very positive about the whole thing. I'd say we'll have a deal set by May 1st, if there's going to be a deal." The players had heard promises from Swig before. The promise they wanted to hear (and him to keep) was that he'd sell the team to an individual or a group with lots of money and be out of their lives forever.

As to the surge in attendance in the final month, Swig said "obviously, what we did at the end of the season was what we should have done right from the start. If we had the right information, then we would have done it."[25] What Swig meant by "the right information" isn't clear, but the comment shows again how the necessary preparation for transferring a sports franchise wasn't done. Swig moved his team to Cleveland blindly and hoped everything would work out.

Among the incentives the Barons offered was a free soft drink and hot dog for each ticket purchased. It helped, but that alone didn't explain attendance more than doubling for the last six home games.

In downtown Cleveland, demolition had begun on the Cleveland Arena, the home of the original Barons of the AHL from 1937 until early in 1973, and the home of the Crusaders from 1972 until 1974. The building sat empty after the Crusaders and Cavaliers moved to Richfield in the autumn of 1974. The site where so many memories had been created would, within days, become a vacant lot at the corner of East 36th Street and Euclid Avenue.

The Barons concluded the 1976–77 season with a pair of road games. They were bombed by the Blues in St. Louis on April 2, 9–2. The next day they defeated the Blackhawks in Chicago, 4–2. Greg Smith scored the tie-breaking goal in the third period. Dave Gardner scored twice, the second an empty-net tally with 13 seconds remaining. Meloche made 34 saves. The Blackhawks, members of the weak Smythe Division, were headed to the playoffs despite a losing record. They'd accumulated 63 points for the season. The Barons had accumulated 63 points as well. In the much stronger Adams Division, all they earned was a last-place finish. Twelve of the NHL's 18 teams made the post-season. The Barons weren't one of them.

"It was good to win the last one, particularly against those guys,"[26] said Meloche. His career started with the Blackhawks. He played two games for Chicago before being traded to the Golden Seals. The final Adams Division standings:

Boston	49–23–8	106	312–240
Buffalo	48–24–8	104	301–220
Toronto	33–32–15	81	302–285
Barons	25–42–13	63	240–292

The Barons were the only Adams Division team not to score 300 goals. Not only had they failed to meet Evans' goal of scoring 50 more than the 278 they'd accumulated in their final season in Oakland, they'd scored 38 fewer. They'd averaged exactly three goals per game. To compete with the Bruins, Sabres and Maple Leafs, the Barons needed more firepower. Whether or not that was a moot point would be determined over the next month.

8

Who Wants to Buy a Slightly Used Hockey Team?

Another one bit the dust.

On the day the Barons played their second last game of the season, and possibly the second last game of their existence, another major league hockey team went out of business. The Phoenix Roadrunners of the World Hockey Association announced on April 2 that they'd "suspend operations" after finishing their schedule the following week. In their three years in the WHA, the Roadrunners had lost five million dollars. "I probably should have closed a year ago," admitted owner Karl Eller. "It must have been misguided optimism and sheer stupidity that made me continue.[1]

"It simply comes down to the fact that it isn't fair to our families to continue pouring a tremendous amount of money into a losing cause," said Eller, sounding much like Mel Swig when he'd talked about "pouring money down a rat hole." Eller said, "we can simply no longer put forth the tremendous cash drain to keep the Roadrunners in business." Then he added an ominous note for major league hockey. "There's going to be a great falling out in the hockey business in the next three to six months."[2] The NHL was in financial trouble, and the WHA was staggering. How might that "falling out" affect the Barons?

As far as NHL President Clarence Campbell was concerned, the league's Cleveland franchise was kaput. "I haven't heard of anybody who would want to resuscitate it," he told Rich Passan in the *Plain Dealer* on April 4. "I wouldn't say it is in a moribund state, but it's close to it. There is no indication of any move to take it over by any one."

Passan reminded Campbell about Sandy Greenberg. Campbell dismissed the owner of the Coliseum as a potential owner of the hockey team that played in it. "I know Mr. Greenberg is a very nice fellow. But I don't think he is in a position where he can underwrite that kind of shift. I think it would be wonderful to have the club remain there, but he has got to have help. I haven't any reason to believe he can do it. He hasn't said he can or made any overtures to do it."

Campbell said Swig was no longer responsible for the Barons. "Swig's liability ended as of yesterday. He has no further financial responsibility. The league and all its supporters contributed what it agreed to. There is no question about Cleveland being an appropriate place for hockey, but we're not talking about potential. It's there, but it may have to be screened out. Cleveland has a beautiful building. If it isn't the best building, it's one of the three best in America, and the area has sufficient enough background for us to know the people are knowledgeable. But that isn't what is required. What is needed is working capital to sustain the operation and gain the necessary support. Local ownership is also important."

Campbell disregarded the spurt in the Barons' attendance during their six March home games. "I am assured there was a fair amount of paper," he said, dismissively. As far back as mid–March, Bob Schlesinger had reported in the *Press* that the Barons were distributing free tickets in an effort to get Clevelanders interested in hockey. He gave no indication of how heavily the Barons had papered the house, but the impressive attendance numbers at the Coliseum for the club's last six home games apparently had to be taken with a grain of salt the size of the Rock of Gibraltar. Such a surge in ticket sales for a team that had been largely ignored for five and a half months, and had no chance of making the playoffs, defied a logical explanation.

Greenberg didn't have the cash needed to buy the Barons and run the team by himself. He needed deep-pocketed investors. Two such investors existed, but whether or not they could be enticed to rescue their hometown's hockey team remained to be seen. When the question was who might buy the Barons and keep them in Cleveland, the answer was invariably George Gund III, and possibly his brother Gordon. That the brothers had the fortune to operate the Barons (most likely at a substantial loss for a few years at least) was a given. But did they want to? Families like the Gunds didn't acquire their huge fortunes by squandering their money on bad investments.

According to Schlesinger, Gund had backed out of the plan Greenberg presented to the NHL in Chicago in February because Swig insisted that the Barons' massive debt, believed to be in the neighborhood of five million dollars, be paid off before he'd sell the team to anyone. Swig was demanding a "pay now, buy later" plan, as in he wanted the debt he'd accumulated paid in full before the new owner took over the team. Schlesinger estimated that, paid incrementally, it would take from five to 10 years to eliminate the debt, and Gund had no intention of waiting up to a decade before taking control of the Barons. Swig was adamant that the new owner assume the team's debt and allow him to recoup at least some of the money he'd "poured down a rat hole" during his ill-fated foray into professional hockey.

If Gund, or Greenberg, or someone else, did buy the Barons, they'd be faced with a myriad of immediate problems, not the least of which was the fact that head coach Jack Evans' contract was about to expire. He was asked after the season-ending victory in Chicago about rumors that he'd be coaching the Blackhawks in 1977–78. "Right now, I'm still employed by the Barons, so it's premature to speculate on anything," Evans responded. "But first, there is the matter of getting assurances that we'll be back in Cleveland, that we'll have a team at all, and then negotiating a contract with me."[3] Like his players, Evans had gone without paychecks during the season that had just ended, and he was no more willing to endure that hardship again than they were.

One of Cleveland's best players was also a free agent. Wing Bob Murdoch scored 23 goals while missing a large chunk of the season after knee surgery. On a team desperate for offense, Murdoch's scoring ability would be missed. He wanted to sign an extension in the summer of 1976, but the Barons weren't interested. In the interim, the price had risen substantially. "I hope I'm back in Cleveland next season. But you can bet it's going to cost them a whole lot more than when the season began,"[4] he said. Murdoch's bargaining position was enviable. He was just 23, and his peak years figured to be ahead of him. If he hit the open market, he was likely to have plenty of suitors.

Passan sat down with Evans for a lengthy end-of-season interview that filled a full page of the *Plain Dealer* on April 10. Evans admitted that he'd almost left town for San Diego on February 23, the day after the deadline established by the players to have the Barons' future resolved, one way or another. The situation hadn't been resolved, although the players had backed off on their promise to declare themselves free agents ... a declaration the NHL vowed to fight vigorously. Still, all signs pointed to the franchise folding. Evans' brother, Glen, had come to town for a visit, and the two were on their way to Hopkins airport for Glen's flight. As they passed the Coliseum, Evans suggested they stop and check on the situation ... just in case a near-miracle was about to be achieved. The *Plain Dealer*'s headline that morning indicated the end had come for Cleveland's NHL team.

"Some of the players were in the dressing room," Evans said. "The phone rang, and it was Eagleson. He advised the guys to stick around because it looked like something was going to break, and there might be a game. So, we waited until noon, and a call came again and said we were going to play. If I had not stopped [at the Coliseum], I'd have purchased a ticket and probably gone. It's a good thing I stopped here out of habit to check things out."

Passan asked Evans to list the season's best moments. "As far as a single game was concerned, the 1–0 loss to Montreal was very satisfying. It was our best game of the season. There were other satisfying moments. It was very satisfying to see the players play as well as they did when they were not getting paid and having all the problems. It was a real satisfaction to work with a group of kids like them."

The season's worst moment may have been the loss to Buffalo on February 23 ... the game few, if any, of the players expected to play. Evans said the atmosphere on the bench and in the dressing room that night was almost toxic. "They played that game in bitterness, you might say, because a great majority of them were hoping the team would go under. They were anticipating going to other clubs and getting with a financially sound organization and possibly a chance for a playoff berth. It took a while to get over that, the fact we were playing again." It was after that game Evans held a meeting and informed his charges that, like it or not, they were stuck in Cleveland for the rest of the season, so they'd better stop whining about the late paychecks and tiny crowds in the Coliseum and play the best hockey they were capable of playing. Bob Stewart credited that meeting with improving the Barons' attitude for the six weeks that remained in the season.

Evans told Passan that the lack of support in the team's new home had a negative impact on the players, whether they cared to admit it or not. Some didn't, but many did. "The players felt like they had no fans," he confessed. He said that during the team's years in Oakland, there had been interaction between the players and the fans within the community. That hadn't been the case in Cleveland. "The fans would come to the games, then go their way while the players went another. There was no feeling of togetherness. That crisis did one thing. It brought the fans and players closer together." It also brought a lot more fans to the Coliseum ... even if many, or most, of them hadn't paid for their tickets.

Evans discussed what he wanted to do with the Barons in 1977–78, with the caveat that he was well aware of the chance there'd be no Barons in 1977–78. He again steered clear of the rumor that he'd be the new head coach of the Chicago Blackhawks in the coming season. "I'm still an employee of the Cleveland Barons," he said.

Swig had intimated that he expected a deal, or at least the framework for a deal, to divest himself of his hockey team would be in place by May 1. On April 26, he announced that he'd reached the final stage of negotiations to give Greenberg the option to purchase the Barons.

"The contract is drawn up and subject to final word review by the attorneys," he explained. "It's now been reduced to the legal stuff, but it's very important."[5] Swig said he and Greenberg had agreed on a price for the team. He had dropped his earlier insistence that the new owner cover all the team's debts before he'd relinquish the club. Swig said he would sell the Barons at a sizable financial loss, and that he'd watched three million dollars go down the drain while operating the team during the 1976–77 season.

The reclusive Greenberg, who rarely had anything to say, followed his usual pattern after Swig broke the news of the negotiations. He couldn't be reached for comment. Richard Paisner, a man identified as an associate of Greenberg's, said, "my basic feeling is we are still in negotiations. Not much can be said when we are in negotiations. It's best not to say anything until there is something firm to report."[6]

Greenberg had competition in his quest to own the Barons. A syndicate headed by businessman Emil Bernard was said to be confident that it could top Greenberg's offer. "It's a long way between getting the money and closing the deal," said Bernard. "I think I'm close to a deal. A piece of paper is nothing. When the money is up and he is officially named by the NHL, then I'll know it's a deal. I have as good a chance as anyone of buying the club."[7] Bernard was reported to be studying the Barons' lease with the Coliseum, their broadcasting contracts, and their parking and concessions deals before making a formal offer to Swig. His syndicate wasn't considered a serious contender to buy the team ... at least not by the Cleveland media.

On April 30, Greenberg and Swig signed a "conditional agreement" for Greenberg to buy the Barons. It didn't have much meaning since Greenberg still owned stock in the Washington Capitals and had to acquire financing to pay Swig for the Barons and then operate the team. He'd have to convince the NHL's finance committee, and then the Board of Governors, that there'd be no more desperate middle of the season requests for cash to meet payrolls, or any other reason, once he took over. That financing, if Greenberg was able to acquire it, was expected to come from George Gund III. Gund's younger brother Gordon might also be involved.

"I'm relieved that the franchise has a reasonably good chance of staying in Cleveland," Swig said before returning to San Francisco. "It's good to see the fruits of my labor come to fruition. The league already knows Sandy is of good moral character and all that. It's just a matter of demonstrating that he has sufficient financial support to operate the team in an acceptable manner. I'm sure it will sit well with the NHL owners having the building ownership involved with the team."[8]

Again, Greenberg was unavailable for comment. In his stead, Coliseum president Peter Larsen said, "with a commitment to winning and sound business principles, both of which we plan to bring to the Barons, we believe we can achieve the kind of success the Cavaliers have enjoyed."[9] The Cavaliers set a franchise attendance record during the 1976–77 season and drew 19,545 to their only playoff game at the Coliseum.

The league had set a June 1 deadline for a resolution to the Barons' future. The next league meeting was scheduled for May 11. Greenberg wasn't able to secure the financing necessary to consummate his purchase by that date, but he explained how he planned to do it to an "ad hoc" committee of NHL owners charged with the responsibility of putting an end to the league's Cleveland problem once and for all during the first week of May.

Greenberg told the "Cleveland Committee" that he planned to offer 45 limited partnerships in his ownership syndicate to selected wealthy Clevelanders, at a price of $150,000 each. The payments could be spread over a four-year period. If all 45 were sold, it would raise $6.75 million, with which he'd operate the Barons. As an added inducement to invest, anyone purchasing a partnership would receive a tax shelter. The prospectus, technically titled a "confidential preliminary placement memorandum," given to each potential investor was 100 pages in length.

Bob Swados, owner of the Buffalo Sabres, was a member of the "Cleveland Committee" and shared his opinion of Greenberg's complicated plan on the night before the Board of Governors meeting. "The special committee was generally of the view that the plan presented could be presented to the Board of Governors if Greenberg can come up with the conditions contained in the plan. All we've done so far is reach an understanding of what the league would require. We will be making good progress if the Greenberg group can deliver on the things we indicated would be required to make a sensible deal."[10] It sounded like a lot of gobbledygook masking the fact that Greenberg didn't have the cash to buy the Barons from Swig and then operate them to the satisfaction of the NHL.

Swados later got to the point. He said he expected the finance committee to accept Greenberg's proposal if it included "sufficient cash on the table ... sufficient working capital, that is."

The Board of Governors met for three hours on May 11. Greenberg's proposition wasn't discussed. He was scheduled to talk to the governors the next day. Before that meeting, Swados said the "odds are he will get a favorable, conditional recommendation from the finance committee."[11] Swados wouldn't spell out the conditions Greenberg would have to meet (although proving he had the money to run the team was obviously among them), and he said some of the conditions had already been met.

Greenberg explained his plan to the governors on May 12 and was given conditional approval to proceed. He had until the league's next meeting, scheduled for June 6 through the 8th, to meet the league's conditions.

Greenberg had decided his original plan to recruit 45 investors was too ambitious. The amended plan he presented to the governors called for 25 investors paying $150,000 over a period of four years. The first payment of $30,000 would be due immediately. That would raise $750,000. The limited partners would pay interest at prime rate on the balance of $120,000. Each partner would sign a note and a letter of credit on the balance. Greenberg would use those notes to secure a $3.5 million bank loan. The total package was worth $5.3 million ... most of it borrowed.

Some of that money would go to Swig, who agreed to accept a three-million-dollar, non-interest note payable over seven and a half years. One-point-eight million of that was payable in annual installments of $450,000 with 7.93 percent interest.

The Board of Governors demanded Greenberg have three million dollars in a bank account or in escrow, with the money guaranteeing the Barons could navigate through the 1977–78 season without asking for yet another hand-out from the league. Greenberg would also be responsible for bringing the team's league dues up to date, and for making the remaining payments to Charlie Finley for the league's purchase of the Golden Seals way back in 1972.

Greenberg told the governors that with an average player salary of $65,000 in 1977–78, the Barons, charging an average of seven dollars per ticket, would have to average 11,900 fans per game to break even. That figure would almost double the club's 1976–77 per game average, which had swelled to 6,100 following the papering of the house for the Barons' last six home games.

The folly of trying to recruit 25 "limited investors" had already been proven by the Cleveland Indians, who had more than 50 part-owners during the 1977 baseball season. The team tanked, attendance plummeted, and the club was teetering on the verge of bankruptcy by season's end. A lot of people investing a relatively small amount of money in a major league sports franchise was a prescription for disaster. Nonetheless, the Board of Governors gave Greenberg a chance to prove he could find 25 people willing to invest in Cleveland's staggering hockey team. He had roughly one month to pull it off.

"Plans are now being mapped out to strengthen the team and bring costs and revenue more closely into line," said Larsen, speaking for Greenberg. "I am confident the Barons can be turned into a financially successful team by increasing attendance and placing the franchise on a businesslike basis."[12]

Due to the continuing uncertainly in Cleveland, the league postponed its draft of amateur players from May 26 until June 14, since it couldn't be certain whether there would be 17 teams or 18 divvying up the talent.

Bob August, the witty sports editor of the *Press*, expressed his frustration with the lack of accessibility of the two men who seemed to hold the future of the Barons in the palms of their hands. In a column on May 6, he referred to Greenberg as "the phantom of the Coliseum" and noted that he hadn't been seen ... or heard from ... since the press conference in the summer of 1976 at which he was introduced as the majority owner of the building. "Since then," wrote August, "he has been merely a rumor." August said a reporter (presumably Schlesinger, although the scribe wasn't identified) seeking a comment from Greenberg had recently planted himself outside the door of a room in which Greenberg was supposedly meeting with an attorney. Hours passed, but no one ever emerged. Greenberg spoke only through his employees, usually Larsen.

August also wrote that "George Gund III ... has shared with Greenberg the quality of carrying inconspicuousness to the point of invisibility. Gund-sightings are reported, but from exotic places." Schlesinger had written a few days earlier that Gund was in Europe. August was more specific, writing that Gund, or someone bearing a striking resemblance to him, had been spotted attending the world hockey championship in Vienna, Austria.

If hockey was to be saved in Cleveland, it would be up to Greenberg and/or Gund to save it. The few people in Cleveland who cared about the sport had grown weary of being constantly told that both men were "unavailable for comment."

For a change, Gund was reached by Passan for a comment about a story regarding his investment in Greenberg's plan on May 25. Typically, he had none. Passan's sources said Gund had purchased 13½ units, or slightly more than half of the 25 units Greenberg was trying to sell. The price was $2,025,000. Of that, Gund would pay half a million dollars immediately. The same day in the *Press*, Schlesinger reported that Gund's investment was actually $2,250,000. He had purchased 15 of the 25 available units. The remaining 10 units had also been sold.

According to Lawrence C. Schmelzer, a local financial consultant who was described as Greenberg's "offeree representative" in the deal, "about seven to 10 other local businesses and professional people are buying the remaining 10 units. A lot of them are new names, not involved in sports before." Schmelzer said he and his brothers Jerome, the owner of a public relations and advertising company, and Richard, an attorney, would "probably" buy one of the units. The Schmelzer brothers had previously owned the Columbus Checkers of the International Hockey League. He said they were likely to sink money into Greenberg's plan because it was "a good real estate deal."[13] Schmelzer said the names of the other investors would be made public when the deal was finalized, which he expected to happen in two days. But nothing ever came easy for the Barons. The deal wasn't finalized on May 27 as Schmelzer anticipated, and the investors weren't identified.

"We hope to have the deal completed by the end of the week, but as of now, there's just nothing definite,"[14] said Larsen on June 2.

Evans spent the month of May in limbo. There was a difference of interpretation among Cleveland's hockey writers as to his contract status. Schlesinger claimed the coach's contract had expired. According to Passan, he was under contract until August. He met with Gund personally and was advised to "sit tight" until Greenberg's deal was completed. Coliseum officials assured Evans that once Greenberg assumed control of the Barons, Evans would be given a new contract. But there existed the possibility that Greenberg's deal would fall through, and that weighed on Evans' mind as the days passed and summer approached. "It would be quite a problem for me if I were asked to give a yes or no answer by some other owner before I knew for sure what the Cleveland situation was," he admitted. He'd spent two seasons coaching a group of youngsters he believed were capable of big things, and he wanted to stay to finish the job. But what if there was no job to finish?

"Once those jobs are filled, they're filled, and suddenly there aren't any openings,"[15] he mused. Evans didn't say whether he'd been approached by any other NHL teams.

Evans visited Cleveland early in June to meet with Howell and Larsen and lay the groundwork for a new deal. He wanted a multi-year contract and a raise. Howell and Larsen felt he deserved both. Evans said the two sides were close but reiterated that nothing could be signed until the Barons officially had new ownership. "The changeover has to be made. I don't know if I can actually sign until the deal is affected. I don't anticipate signing until everything is sewn up."[16] The fact that Evans was supposedly coveted by Los Angeles and Chicago, but neither had approached him as of the first week of June, would seem to indicate that Passan was correct regarding the expiration of his contract. Had he been a free agent, the Kings and Blackhawks undoubtedly would have made overtures toward him, and he most likely would've accepted one.

The NHL's owners met at the Queen Elizabeth Hotel in Montreal starting on June 6. Interestingly, neither the *Plain Dealer* nor the *Press* found it necessary to send their hockey correspondents to Montreal to cover it. The long-distance telephone bills Passan and Schlesinger accumulated from their desks at their newspapers may have exceeded the price of a plane ticket and hotel room.

Sandy Greenberg didn't attend the meeting, either. He was represented by Larsen. The Barons' problems weren't the only ones the Board of Governors would have to deal with during their scheduled three-day stay in Montreal. The Colorado, Atlanta and St. Louis franchises were also in trouble financially. Just as the move to Cleveland hadn't solved the Golden Seals problems, the move from Kansas City to Denver hadn't saved the Scouts/Rockies. The Rockies had reportedly lost more than twice as much money as their ownership had budgeted for. The Flames had been forced to conduct an emergency sale of season tickets two months into the season to keep the club from folding, or at least asking to be propped up by the league. And the Blues had a unique problem. They were drawing plenty of fans, but their rent was so expensive they couldn't break even despite selling out most of their games. But the Barons were still the league's biggest headache. And they quickly became an even larger one.

Swig hadn't planned on attending the meeting. He thought his involvement with hockey ended when he signed the letter of intent to sell to Greenberg. But it wasn't working out that way. "I hadn't expected to be coming to Montreal, but since it appears I still own the team, I guess I have to show,"[17] he groaned. Swig hoped to leave Montreal as the former owner of the Barons. Some of the NHL's owners hoped they'd leave Montreal with the Barons as a former hockey team.

Larsen presented Greenberg's plan to the finance committee on June 6. He hadn't been able to come up with the cash the owners felt he needed to run the team properly. George Gund III was his only backer. The seven to 10 other Clevelanders who, according to Lawrence Schmelzer, had agreed to purchase one of Greenberg's "units" for $150,000 had all changed their minds.

"I heard this morning that Greenberg was out and Swig was back and the franchise may fold,"[18] players' union president Alan Eagleson said bluntly. If ownership reverted back to Swig, disbanding the franchise would've been the only option. Swig was through with hockey, and the players had made it clear they wouldn't play for him again.

Bob Swados wasn't as pessimistic as Eagleson. He had a

long-winded and complicated assessment of the latest crisis. "My understanding is that Mr. Eagleson's remarks are premature," he said. "There are apparently some problems in that they are not able to come up with the total dollars contemplated. Apparently, they ran into some problems and were not able to raise the money [the owners] felt was prudently proper to run the club. I wouldn't go so far as to say the deal is off. It's just that the provisions of the original deal couldn't be worked out at this time."[19] Put more succinctly, Greenberg had been given until June 8 to raise a minimum of three million dollars with which to operate the Barons in 1977–78. Gund had pledged $2,250,000. The other potential investors had declined. Gund was only obligated to pay half a million dollars up front. That left Greenberg $2.5 million short of the amount of operating capital the finance committee demanded. Swados said the committee could extend Greenberg's deadline to give him time to recruit more investors. But from where? It was obvious that no one in Cleveland was interested in sinking a penny into the city's NHL team. Except for Gund.

The reclusive minority owner flew to Montreal and met with the finance committee on June 7. On his shoulders rested the fate of hockey in Cleveland. To assume ownership of the Barons, Gund would have to pay Swig $500,000 immediately. He'd be responsible for the $1.8 million note still owed by the league to Finley for its purchase of the Golden Seals from him five years earlier. He'd also be responsible for the franchise's $3.4 million in debts and $300,000 to cover "incidentals" which weren't defined. The finance committee demanded Gund post $1.95 million in "earnest money" and $2.45 million in cash. The total package amounted to $6.95 million. Gund had the money to meet the finance committee's demands. But would he?

"Somebody has his hand on the rope," said an unidentified league executive. "It's now a matter of pulling it."[20] A number of owners would've gladly pulled on that rope. Several made no secret of hoping the Barons would fold, allowing their teams to acquire some talented players through a dispersal draft. The players, much to their dismay, would not become free agents.

While Gund considered his options, rumors swirled around Montreal. One suggested that the owners of the WHA's Cincinnati Stingers would buy the Barons, merge the two teams, and then apply for membership in the NHL. The membership fee was $2.5 million, and some owners hoped a few of the WHA's more stable franchises, such as the Stingers, would seek membership. That could've raised as much as $7.5 million for a league looking for ways to enhance revenue.

Gund met with the "Cleveland committee" on June 9. He offered

$2.5 million in operating capital to run the Barons for the 1977–78 season. The committee preferred at least three million, and $3.5 million would've been better. "The deal is still alive," Swados said. "There is a strong possibility things can be worked out. What I'm not so certain about is whether the league will go along with a deal that does not have a strong base."[21] Gund's offer couldn't have had a shakier base than Greenberg's, which the committee had signed off on. And Gund's offer was good enough for at least one team owner.

"I don't see how we can kick a team out of the league with a guy like Gund ready to back it with two million dollars out front," said the unidentified executive. "People here know the assets and the reputation of the Gund family. Assuming the deal the Barons are bringing in makes any sense at all, I think it will go through."[22]

Meanwhile, Howell tried to conduct business as usual in the front office while waiting to learn whether he had a job or not. "I've tried to maintain the idea that we will be in business and am proceeding along those lines,"[23] he said.

And the Barons were still in business. The owners approved the transfer of ownership from Swig to Gund and his brother on June 9. Gordon put up $300,000 to join George as owners of an NHL team. The league decided that $2.4 million was sufficient operating capital. Under the agreement, the Coliseum would manage the Barons' business affairs. George Gund was asked if he believed the time, effort and money he'd put forth to gain control of the Barons had been worth it.

"Yes, I think so," he answered. "I'll know in a couple of years. On the surface, though, I can say it was."[24] The Gunds wouldn't need a couple of years to evaluate their decision to buy the Barons. It would only take 12 months for them to realize they'd made a bad investment, and to cut their losses.

Gund shot down a rumor that he'd change the team's name to the Ohio Barons. "I haven't heard anything about that," he said. "I don't think that would be agreeable."[25] Howell liked the idea but didn't think it would happen. "I don't think the name will be changed now. You have to give the league a year's notice to change the logo. It's not a bad idea, though. The Ohio Barons takes in a whole area. We are as close to Akron as we are to Cleveland,"[26] said the man who was expected to have the word "acting" removed from his title now that the team had new ownership. There was speculation, however, that the Gunds might rehire former general manager Bill McCreary. The speculation was unfounded.

Barons player representative Bob Stewart was asked for his reaction to the Gunds' purchase of the team. "It's about time everything was settled, one way or the other. This has been nerve-wracking for everybody, including the players and the office staff. This sure will take a lot of the pressure off Jack and Harry. But I won't stop worrying until the money crosses hands."[27] Stewart's caution was justified. This was the Oakland/ Cleveland franchise, and anything that could go wrong usually did go wrong.

With 18 teams apparently in the fold for 1977–78, the NHL held its delayed draft on June 14. By virtue of their 25–42–13 record, the Barons had the fifth selection of the first round and used it on 20-year-old right wing Mike Crombeen, who had played three seasons with Kingston of the Ontario Hockey League. During that time, Crombeen scored 141 goals and assisted on 133 others. The Barons needed offense, and they were counting on Crombeen to provide it.

"Crombeen reminds me physically of Bobby Hull," said Howell. "He's strong, has a good, hard shot and fills our needs on the right side."[28] Crombeen had undergone surgery to repair torn knee ligaments in April, but Howell wasn't worried. "We have been assured his knee is sound, and barring something unforeseen, he will step right in."[29]

Crombeen said all the right things to the Cleveland media. "I'm very happy to be chosen by Cleveland. I've heard a lot of good things about the Barons. I consider myself a Bobby Hull–style winger and skating is one of my assets."[30] Crombeen had been drafted by the Edmonton Oilers of the WHA, and the Barons would have to compete with them to get his name on a contract. First, ownership of the team had to be officially transferred from Swig to Gund. The process seemed to be proceeding without a hitch, until the NHL's owners met on June 23 in Chicago.

In its edition of the 23rd, the *Plain Dealer* reported that the Cleveland franchise was once again on the verge of extinction. Retiring league president Campbell, whose successor would be chosen by the owners at the meeting, was quoted as saying a deadline of 1:00 that afternoon had been established for finalization of the transfer of ownership. If it wasn't met, the franchise would fold. Campbell said the deal should've been completed two weeks earlier, but problems had arisen.

In a rambling statement, the 72-year-old Campbell said, "I think there will be a National Hockey League team in Cleveland next season. Nothing more remains to be done but to exercise the agreement of the sale of the club. It can be ironed out in 10 minutes. I don't think there is anything wrong. Recent thoughts have made them fumble around. They have had deadlines of June 1st, June 9th, and June 21st to complete this agreement and this meeting can't be adjourned forever. The problem was that they failed to execute the agreements to execute the closing the first time."[31]

If there was a problem, Swig, who didn't make the trip to Chicago, wasn't aware of it. "As far as I'm concerned, I don't know of any problems. To the best of my knowledge, the deal is complete,"[32] he said.

Campbell quickly recanted his original statement and claimed his comments had been misconstrued. "All the Board of Governors really wanted was a progress report at the time of the deadline, and the report has been made to the satisfaction of the NHL. They have completed the closing of the transaction as far as we are concerned with all of the requirements necessary."[33]

George Gund said there was never any danger that the deal would fall apart, as so many other deals to save the franchise had. "There has never been any snag in the deal. All that has been involved in completing the deal in the past few days have been some minor technical matters. The problem of logistics in getting a very complicated deal through had to be reworked in Montreal two weeks ago and are completed." Gund admitted that he'd hoped the league would give him more time to finish the deal. He wasn't pleased to hear Campbell's erroneous comments.

"I am really sorry to hear this," he said of Campbell's statement about the league's deadline and the possibility the Barons would fold. "It is really too bad this came out. An extraordinary amount of paperwork, including sending couriers to San Francisco, is holding up the deal. But I can assure it will be resolved ... and there will be a Cleveland Barons team in the National Hockey League next season." Gund reiterated that the deal he reached with Swig was "kind of complex" and joked that "I hate to see what the lawyers' fees will be."

Gund said he thought Campbell's misstatement could be attributed to a decade-long accumulation of frustration with the Oakland/Cleveland franchise. "This goes back to 1967 and the team has been a drag to the league, and they didn't want to see it happen anymore."[34] But it would happen again, and quickly, in spite of Gund's best efforts and intentions.

The deal closed on June 23. Gund paid $5.2 million to take control of the Barons, or $1.75 million less than the original estimate of June 7. Swig received $1.5 million. One-point-eight million went to Finley, to complete the league's purchase of the Golden Seals from him five years before. It also relieved Swig from that obligation, and the savings meant he was essentially paid $3.3 million for his hockey club. The NHL got $600,000 to repay a loan it had given Swig to assist his purchase of the Golden Seals. Three hundred thousand was set aside for unspecified "incidentals." Two million was earmarked for covering the Barons' operating expenses for the 1977–78 season. It wouldn't be enough.

Swig was no longer burdened by the ownership of the Cleveland

Barons. He said he felt "very, very relieved. This has been like a noose hanging around my neck, having to continue to worry about it." He told Cleveland's hockey fans he was leaving behind a team that was ready for a breakthrough season. "I'll tell you this. This isn't self-serving because I won't be part of it. But every hockey expert here at these meetings tells me that this is one of the best young clubs in the league. If they add two players from the junior draft who can help right away, Cleveland will have a very, very competitive hockey team." The Barons thought they'd done that with the drafting of Crombeen and second-round pick Danny Chicoine. Both were expected to be impact players immediately.

Taking advantage of the benefit of 20/20 hindsight, Swig admitted that not nearly enough preparation had gone into the transfer of the Golden Seals to Cleveland. "We got started too late, and we didn't know the market. To put it bluntly, we screwed up. I really think you'll have people running the thing now who know what they're doing, and the program will be a great success. I think they'll put 19,000 fans into the building a couple of times and the thing will take off. I've always felt that Cleveland was a good hockey town."[35]

No sooner did George and Gordon Gund assume ownership of the Barons than a rumor arose that they'd merge the team with the Indianapolis Racers of the WHA. "That's absolutely false," said an angry Howell. "That's ridiculous."[36] And it was.

Gund left Chicago and headed for Cleveland. He took part in a news conference at the Coliseum on June 25 to introduce the Barons' new ownership. "I would say this is a partnership with the Coliseum. Sandy Greenberg spent a lot of time on this transaction. I would consider it a financial transaction for the money and time Sandy has put in on this."[37] Although Gund may have considered Greenberg a partner in his hockey team, the ever-reclusive owner of the Coliseum was not present at the press conference. He was represented by Larsen. In the team's new power structure, George Gund was chairman of the board. Larsen, president of the Coliseum, added the responsibility of president of the Barons. As such, he reported to Gund. But it would be revealed during the upcoming season, Greenberg held the power of the purse strings. Not the Gund brothers.

Gund said Evans had signed a new contract to coach the Barons. The length and financial terms weren't announced. Howell was reported to have signed a new deal as the team's general manager. But the report was in error, a fact that wouldn't be revealed until late in the 1977–78 season. Howell spent the season working under a handshake agreement with the Barons. Ticket prices for the 1977–78 season were set at $8.50, $7.00 and $4.50. The most expensive ticket in 1976–77 had been $10.

"We are confident that the hockey franchise can be turned into a success here," Gund said.[38]

The Barons had new, and essentially local, ownership. However, their long-term future in Cleveland was hardly assured. The Gund brothers had put up enough money to satisfy the National Hockey League that they could operate the team for the 1977–78 season. Beyond that, there were no guarantees.

9

A Second Chance

The National Hockey League had been given a reprieve in Cleveland. Or maybe it was the other way around. Cleveland had been given a reprieve in the National Hockey League. Deposed owner Mel Swig admitted that he'd made a lot of mistakes when he'd transferred the California Golden Seals to northeastern Ohio. George Gund III had a ringside seat from which to witness those mistakes and learn from them. Gund knew that the NHL's brand alone wasn't enough to entice Clevelanders to venture to the Coliseum in large numbers to watch his hockey team. Promotion and community involvement were needed, as was a vastly improved product on the ice, if the Barons were to succeed.

The summer of 1977 passed quietly. Gund and his brother, Gordon, got to work repairing the Barons' tattered image. Newly appointed general manager Harry Howell made no trades, so improvement on Cleveland's 25-win season would have to come from within. The team, according to people who should've known, possessed a wealth of young talent. Whether that talent was ready to blossom remained to be seen. It was up to head coach Jack Evans, freshly signed to a new multi-year contract as a reward for his commendable work in two years at the helm, to oversee that blossoming.

Thirty-nine players reported to training camp at Kent State University on September 21. That was 15 fewer than had reported to Kent the previous September, and Evans was grateful. He'd felt that the cattle call of 1976 hadn't given him sufficient time to work with the players who had a legitimate chance of earning a place on the Barons' 20-man roster. "We are bringing in people who have indicated they have the potential of making the big team, now or in the future,"[1] he said of the players on hand. Several of the club's draft picks fit that category.

The Barons' main need was for offense. First round pick Mike Crombeen and second round choice Danny (Chico) Chicoine were expected to provide it. Crombeen scored 56 goals for Kingston in 1976–77, and Chicoine scored 54 for Sherbrooke of the Ontario junior league.

In the team's first light scrimmage (meaning no hitting was permitted), Crombeen scored twice and Chicoine once.

"It might be different when they start hitting,"[2] Crombeen admitted sheepishly. It would be different for Crombeen when they started hitting. Much different.

"All I can do is my best and hope I make it," said the 19-year-old Chicoine. "If I have a good camp, you never know. I think I should learn to skate a little faster. Jack Evans told me to shoot more."[3]

Evans had praise for goaltender Gilles Meloche and veteran defensemen Bob Stewart and Jim Neilson after the first scrimmage. He was pleased with everyone in camp, at least in the very early stages. "The enthusiasm of the veterans was very pleasing. They're working hard. Overall, the skating was very good. From the oldest veterans to the newest rookies, everyone has been really gung-ho."[4]

Two rookies and two veterans were missing. Whitey Widing and Brent Meeke defected to the World Hockey Association over the summer. Widing would play in 71 games for the Edmonton Oilers. Meeke was cut in training camp, and his career was over. Rookie forward Mike Boychuck and rookie defenseman Jeff Allan, the Barons' sixth round draft choice, were no-shows when camp began. Boychuck never played in the NHL. Allan proved to be a wasted draft pick. He'd play four games for the Barons in 1977–78, and two games for Cincinnati of the WHA. That was the extent of his career.

Reg Kerr, a 19-year-old left wing who was one of Cleveland's two third-round draft picks, showed up even though he didn't have a contract. Kerr had been drafted by the WHA's Houston Aeros but rejected their offer. "It was not a bad contract," Kerr said of his decision to spurn the Aeros. "But the way things are going in the WHA, I was not sure. I didn't want to play half a year there and then not get paid. I wanted my contract guaranteed. They would not do it."

Kerr had also rejected a contract from the Barons, reportedly because he wanted more money than Howell offered. He reported to training camp unsigned. "I wanted them to see me more," he explained. "And the way things have gone, I feel good."[5] Kerr scored 101 points playing for Kamloops, British Columbia, in 1976–77.

The Barons began their exhibition season after just five days of two-a-day practices. That was fine with Evans. "My theory is that a game is really the best practice. We'll get a look at a lot of players in a hurry."[6] He got his first look under game conditions in a 5–2 victory over Detroit in Windsor, Ontario, on September 27. Meloche and Gary Edwards split time in goal for the Barons. Goals were scored by Al MacAdam, Dennis Maruk, Ralph Stewart, and rookies Kris Manery and John (Butch) Baby.

The next night in Port Huron, Michigan, the Barons lost to St. Louis, 7–6. Kerr, who didn't get off the bench in the game against the Red Wings, took three shots against the Blues and scored with each one. Wayne Merrick, Mike Fidler, and Dave Gardner scored the other goals. Like Kerr, Gardner was in camp without a contract. He was a free agent who hadn't drawn any interest from the rest of the NHL over the summer.

Kerr's perfect night (three shots, three goals) got his coach's attention. "You have to be impressed," said Evans. "Since he came to camp, it seems whenever we send him out there, he scores a goal."[7] And goals were what Evans was looking for from Cleveland's draft picks, such as Kerr.

The stretch of three exhibitions in three days ended with a 5–4 victory over Pittsburgh at Kent State's ice arena on September 29. The Barons scored three first period goals and coasted from there. The Penguins scored a pair of goals in the closing seconds to make the result more respectable. Evans came away impressed with the performance of rookie defenseman Owen Lloyd, who spent his time on the ice throwing his weight around. "He looks for people to hit," said Evans, who wanted to improve the Barons' physicality. "He also hits cleanly. He doesn't cross-check or use the elbow [either of which would earn a penalty]. They are good, stiff checks. He hits people and hurts them."[8] Evans had watched his club get pushed around often during the 1976–77 season, and he was looking for players who could put a stop to it. Lloyd appeared to be the type of player Evans was seeking.

The game on the Kent State campus drew a capacity crowd of 1,200. Tickets cost $3.75.

Since taking ownership of the Barons in late June, the top priority of the Gund brothers had been selling season tickets. Their efforts weren't paying off. Coliseum president Peter Larsen announced on September 27 that the team had sold just 2,000 season tickets in three months. It proved to be an omen.

Gardner agreed to a one-year contract during training camp. He felt he was worth a longer deal, but Howell didn't. He had no bargaining leverage since no NHL team made him an offer over the summer, when he was a free agent. Gardner's 16 goals and 22 assists in 1976–77 were far less production than the Barons had expected. "I have to show them what I can do," said the 25-year-old center. "I did it in junior hockey, and I did it in spurts during the years here. But I wish they had more confidence in me with more than a one-year contract. I'm a little upset. I figure I did more for them than they thought."

Jumping to the WHA hadn't been an option. "If I can't play in the NHL, I don't want to play hockey,"[9] Gardner said.

The Penguins routed the Barons in Pittsburgh, 9–4, on October 1. Cleveland's goals were scored by rookies Jim McCabe and Manery and veterans Maruk and Bob Murdoch. The Barons had 29 shots on goal. The Penguins had 33, and the Barons stopped just 24 of them.

The first roster trimming was made after the loss to Pittsburgh. Cleveland's new farm team was Phoenix of the Central Hockey League, and nine players were demoted there. Goalie Jim Warden; defensemen Darcy Reiger, Owen Lloyd and Dave Syvret; centers Vern Stenlund, Rick Shinske and Angie Moretto; and right wings Ken Kuczyk and Guy Lash were sent out west. Lash was the first of the Barons' draft picks to be found not ready for the big time. The roster was reduced by one additional player when Gary Sabourin's balky knee, which had caused him to miss more than two months in 1976–77, sidelined him again. He'd be out of action a minimum of six weeks.

With 1,200 fans watching, the Barons lost their second and final home game of the exhibition season, 5–2, to the Red Wings at Kent State's ice arena on October 8. It was Detroit's first win in eight pre-season games, and Evans didn't like anything he witnessed from the Barons' bench that evening. The Red Wings, dubbed "mayhem makers" by Bob Schlesinger in the Cleveland *Press*, spent 60 minutes pushing the Barons around. Detroit had been a terrible team in 1976–77 but figured if it couldn't beat its opponent on the scoreboard, it would beat them up physically. That mentality carried over into the 1977–78 season.

"We need to work on everything," Evans complained after the loss. "The power play didn't work, we gave up a goal while short-handed, we were overpowered in the corners, and we were overpowered in front of the net." The Barons weren't making the progress their coach wanted to see as the regular season approached. "We seem to be going backwards since the opening game in Windsor. We are becoming less physical. We should be getting sharper. I can't put my finger on it. If we hope to make the playoffs, we can't lose games to Detroit through intimidation."[10] One reason the Barons were less physical than in their first encounter with the Red Wings was because defenseman Owen Lloyd, who drew praise from Evans for his willingness to mix it up with the opposition, had been sent to Phoenix.

Howell agreed with his coach that his team had to be more aggressive. "They just have to become a little more muscular. I don't want them to be goons. I just want them to dish it out a little instead of taking it all the time." Howell was critical of the Barons' veteran players. "The draft choices aren't being pushed around. The rookies handled themselves well."[11]

The Barons broke camp on October 7 and sent eight more players to the minor leagues. Forwards Paul Tantardini, DeWayne Endicott, Greg Agar and Jim McCabe and defensemen Gary Soetart, Tom Anderson and Mark Toffolo were demoted to Toledo of the International Hockey League. Left wing Grant Eakin was sent to Phoenix. The Barons' roster was sliced to 23 players. They wouldn't have to get down to the limit of 20 until after the regular season started.

The Barons were northeastern Ohio's new kids on the block. Under Swig, the team had made no effort to connect with the fans and ingratiate itself with its new community. The Gund brothers knew that needed to change, and on October 10, they gave the fans a chance to voice their opinions to the people in charge. Those who called the club's office on that day could speak to George Gund III, Coliseum president Larsen, general manager Howell or community relations director (and former Cleveland Crusader goalie) Bob Whidden. The office was open from 9:30 a.m. to 6:30 p.m., and fans were encouraged to call with questions or comments on anything pertaining to the Barons or the NHL. About 200 calls were received. Some Clevelanders cared about the Barons, but not nearly enough.

Although season ticket sales had been slow, Larsen was optimistic about the Barons' home opener versus the Washington Capitals on October 15. Advance sales indicated a crowd of between 12,000 and 15,000.

The Barons finished the exhibition season with victories over their former Salt Lake City farm team in Utah, and over the WHA's Edmonton Oilers in Edmonton. In June, it had appeared that a merger between the NHL and WHA was imminent. The plan fell through, but the fact that the two leagues had scheduled exhibitions against each other was an indication that an amalgamation was inevitable, with both organizations losing money. A merger would come at the end of the 1977–78 season.

Cleveland completed the preliminaries with a record of 4–3. It was time for the Barons' second ... and last ... season to begin.

10

New Faces, New Season, Same Script

For the second straight season, the Barons opened against the Los Angeles Kings. The 1977–78 season began in Los Angeles, and Jack Evans was nervous. Not about his team's prospects for the upcoming season, but about opening night. He said he always had butterflies on opening night. "I don't think there will ever be an end to them," he said of the first-game jitters. "I experienced them in my first pro game, and they are still there. I don't ever remember them disappearing."[1]

Cleveland's star center, 21-year-old Dennis Maruk, said he hoped the Barons could put the trouble and turmoil of the previous season behind them. "We'll have to win a couple of big games like we did against Philadelphia last year," he said. "If we can play .500 on the road, beat some big clubs on the road, and then come home, we'd probably bring more fans out."[2] The lack of fan support in their new home had affected the players the year before, and the situation wouldn't improve in 1977–78.

The Barons didn't open the season with a win on the road. The Kings had given them problems in 1976–77, and those problems continued in 1977–78. Los Angeles won the season opener, 2–0. Cleveland's defense allowed just 28 shots against goalie Gilles Meloche, who stopped 26 of them. But Cleveland's offense managed just 24 shots, none of which made it past Kings netminder Rogatien Vachon.

Cleveland's newspapers weren't giving the Barons any assistance in their effort to increase their visibility in northeastern Ohio. Neither paper saw fit to send their hockey writer with the team to Los Angeles to cover the first game of the season. Readers of the *Plain Dealer* saw only a wire service preview with a note in bold print that the Barons trailed after two periods. The game began at 11:00 Cleveland time and was still in progress when the morning paper went to press. Readers of the afternoon newspaper had to settle for a brief wire service summary of the action.

Rookie right wing Danny Chicoine didn't return to Cleveland with the Barons. He was demoted to Phoenix following the loss to the Kings. After scoring 54 goals in the Ontario junior league and being drafted in the second round, Chicoine would play in only six games for the Barons. He wouldn't score.

Cleveland's media had hammered at Mel Swig's ownership of the Barons for its lack of promotion throughout its first year in northeastern Ohio. The ownership of George and Gordon Gund wasn't going to make the same blunder, and the promotions started with the team's home opener. First of all, ticket prices had been slashed across the board. The schedule-maker had cooperated by giving the Barons an opponent they figured to beat. Cleveland had swept its five-game season series from the Washington Capitals in 1976–77. The best promotion was sending the paying customers home happy by winning the game. And a lucky few of those customers would go home with a bonus: a free copy of the multi-million selling album *Hotel California*, personally autographed by rock star Glenn Frey of the Eagles. Frey would also drop the ceremonial first puck to start what everyone hoped would be a new era in Cleveland hockey. But he wouldn't sing.

In addition to Frey's appearance, all the ladies in attendance would receive a carnation, and fans were invited to bring skates for a free whirl around the Coliseum ice after the game. The post-game skates had proven popular in the late stages of the previous season and were expected to become a regular attraction at Barons games.

There was one ominous note: Coliseum president Peter Larsen's estimate of a crowd ranging from 12,000 to 15,000 had been scaled back substantially. In the *Press,* Bob Schlesinger speculated that opening night would draw "well over 10,000" fans. It didn't, but Schlesinger came much closer than Larsen to accurately predicting the attendance.

The Barons drew the kind of crowd to their second home opener that they'd anticipated drawing to their first. There were 10,253 fans in the Coliseum to watch what Rich Passan described as a "very dull game." But at least the home team won, 4–2. Evans was pleased with his team's performance in the first and third periods. Of the middle period, he said, "we became disorganized in that period. Nobody passed the puck for a while."[3] Cleveland's goals were scored by Dave Gardner, Ralph Klassen, Fred Ahern, and rookie Kris Manery. Meloche turned away 30 of Washington's 32 shots on goal.

The game was played on a Saturday night, meaning no coverage in the *Press*, which didn't publish a Sunday edition. In the *Plain Dealer,* the simple headline on the first page of the sports section read BARONS WIN. Underneath were a few paragraphs of Passan's game story.

The bulk of the story was buried on page 14. Such treatment of the home opener for any of Cleveland's other teams would have been unthinkable.

On Tuesday, October 18, the Cavaliers opened the 1977–78 NBA season at the Coliseum. A crowd of 15,192 watched them squeeze past the Chicago Bulls, 91–88. The next night, the Barons beat the Kings, 3–1. Attendance was a meager 3,252.

Meloche had allowed five goals in the Barons' first three games. He knew he'd have to be stingy throughout the upcoming season. "This is a team that is not going to score many goals,"[4] he said. In the victory over Los Angeles, the goals had been scored by Ahern, Maruk, and Bob Murdoch.

Following the successful (at least on the ice) opening of the home season, the Barons made a quick two-game trip to the middle west. They out-scored the North Stars, 7–4, in Minneapolis on October 20. Gardner scored twice, and Mike Crombeen tallied his first NHL goal. Klassen, Maruk, Al MacAdam and Wayne Merrick provided the rest of the offense. Meloche stopped 31 shots.

Before the next game in St. Louis, Bob Stewart reflected on the Barons' 3–1–2 start. "It's nice to start off this way. The idea is to keep going," he said, conceding that it was far too early to draw any reasonable conclusions. "After 10 games, we'll take a closer look. The next six games are very important. In the first 10 games of a season, the young players are getting the butterflies out of their system. After the first 10 games, you can sit down and look at the way the lines are performing. You can see what has to be worked on."

Four games had been enough, however, to convince Stewart the Barons were a playoff-caliber team. "This team is capable," he said. "The more I see other teams, the more I think we've got a playoff team."[5]

Evans attributed the quick getaway to his club's improved mental state. "The team and myself feel more secure and relaxed, knowing that the franchise is stable. We hear no rumors of folding, or not receiving paychecks."[6]

The Barons extended their winning streak to four with a 3–2 victory over the Blues on October 22. Murdoch scored a pair of goals, and defenseman Greg Smith lit the lamp for the first time in his NHL career. It almost wasn't enough, as Garry Unger of the Blues appeared to have tied the game by slipping the puck past Meloche with a fraction of a second remaining in the game. The sharp-eyed judge behind Cleveland's goal ruled, however, that the puck hadn't entered the net until a split second after the buzzer ending the game had sounded. Meloche faced 53 shots. The Barons managed just 17. The loss was the Blues' fifth without a victory. The Barons improved to 4–1–2.

As hard as it may be to believe, the four-game winning streak was the longest in the 10-year history of the Oakland/Cleveland franchise. Which provides proof of just what a miserable excuse for a major league hockey team had been foisted on Cleveland when the Golden Seals relocated in the summer of 1976.

The next day in Cleveland, the winning streak ended. As a crowd of just 5,910 watched, the Barons lost to Pittsburgh, 3–2. Maruk scored both goals. Meloche recorded 23 saves for the weary Barons, who finished a grueling stretch of four games in five days in three different cities.

"It's really a bitter defeat," said a dispirited Evans. "The guys were expecting to win this one."[7] Adding to the bitterness was the loss of defenseman Mike Christie, who aggravated an injury sustained in the season opener in Los Angeles. Somehow, Christie had managed to play on a left foot with a cracked bone (or on a broken ankle, depending on the source of the information) for almost two weeks before the pain became unbearable. Projections were that he'd miss at least three weeks. The loss of Christie sent Harry Howell shopping for reinforcements.

"I'll have to look around and see what's available," said the general manager. "All the teams I talked to before said they wanted to wait two weeks to see how they did. Those two weeks are up now. We'll see if anybody is willing to trade."[8]

After a day off, the Barons returned to the ice at the Coliseum on October 25 ... their fifth game in a week. They looked tired and lost to the Rangers, 5–0. "They overpowered us skating and physically," lamented Evans, who found no lack of effort among his players. "But there were tired people out there tonight. Sure, it was a bad loss, but I'm not going to start blaming people. They played well in six of the first seven games. It's just unfortunate they got beat this badly at home."[9] It was fortunate not many fans witnessed the blowout. The attendance was just 4,556. And that got the attention of Rangers star Phil Esposito.

"I think they have a heck of a hockey club," Esposito said. "I can understand their predicament here. It must be difficult to play in front of an empty house." Having started his career with Boston and then joining the Rangers, Esposito wasn't accustomed to playing in front of empty houses in his home arena. "This rink is gorgeous. Somebody told me they play better on the road. It would be such a boon to hockey if more people came. Maybe they would respond to larger crowds."[10]

Meloche turned away 24 shots in the loss to the Rangers. He'd played every minute of the Barons' seven games. Meloche's back-up, Gary Edwards, was asked if he was upset with Evans for leaving him on the bench. "Whatever my feelings are will be my own," he told Passan, who was probably looking for a headline-grabbing quote from a disgruntled player after a depressing defeat. Edwards provided no satisfaction. "I've been through this sort of thing before. All I can do is practice and play as well as I can. But it's not good to not play for a long time."

Edwards said he wouldn't force his way out of Cleveland by asking to be traded, as he'd forced his way out of Los Angeles the season before. If it was any consolation, the man the Barons had traded to the Kings to get Edwards, Gary Simmons, wasn't playing either. Simmons was growing cobwebs on the Kings' bench watching future Hall of Famer Rogatien Vachon stymie enemy attackers.

Edwards did say that his teammates were in a much better mood than they'd been when he was sent to Cleveland in February. "They seem much happier. I have no idea why. Perhaps it's because they are winning. Maybe it's because the financial situation is better."[11]

Through seven games, Cleveland's first round draft pick, Crombeen, had scored only one goal. Evans was certain that would change. "It's just a matter of time before he breaks out scoring goals," the coach assured. "Mike has speed, a good shot, good hockey sense, and is very strong."[12] The Barons weren't going to be as patient with their third-round selection, Reg Kerr, who was sent to Phoenix after contributing nothing in the loss to the Rangers. On the young season, Kerr had no goals and two assists.

"He needed seasoning," said Howell of the decision to demote Kerr. "He was losing his confidence a little bit. He wasn't doing the things he was doing in training camp. He wasn't driving for the net and taking a lot of shots."[13]

Rumors floated throughout the closing months of the 1976–77 season that Evans was high on the Chicago Blackhawks' list of potential coaches. So was Bob Pulford, who'd stepped aside in Los Angeles during the 1976–77 campaign. The Blackhawks signed Pulford as their head coach and general manager, and he set about toughening up the squad. That toughness was on display at the Coliseum on October 28. "They gooned it up,"[14] was the way Mike Fidler described the first period, during which the visitors were whistled for seven penalties. The Barons scored on only one of those seven power play opportunities. The Blackhawks won, 4–2.

"After tonight, everybody knows we can be intimidated," griped team captain MacAdam. Asked what he thought management should do about that, MacAdam answered, "make some trades and hire somebody to mash some heads in. Then get the team together and have each of them stick up for everybody."[15]

Evans was seething after watching his team get pushed around for

60 minutes on its home ice. "If you're not going to be aggressive, you're in the wrong kind of game. You have to have an eye for an eye and a tooth for a tooth. We are capable of retaliating. We did on several occasions last year. If we don't this year, we are going to be in a lot of trouble. You have to play this game belligerently and claim your share of the ice."[16]

Evans wasn't alone in bemoaning his team's willingness to be intimidated. Schlesinger called the Barons "polite." Passan said they were "timid." Passan noted in his column that he'd gotten a letter from a frustrated fan who was tired of hearing about how well the Barons could skate. The fan said if he wanted to watch skating, he'd visit the Coliseum when the Ice Capades came to town. This was hockey, and the fan wanted to see HITTING!!!

The man whose job it would be to toughen up the Barons, if they were to be toughened up, didn't think they had been passive against the thuggish Blackhawks. "I don't think we were intimidated," said Howell. "That didn't enter it at all. Sure, I'd like to have a mean, aggressive, high-scoring team. But you can't make people what they aren't. Yes, I'd like to see them a little tougher. Okay, a lot tougher."

Passan and Schlesinger were pressuring Howell to trade for an enforcer. Howell hadn't yet made a trade as Barons general manager. And he didn't think he needed to make one to add muscle to his team's roster. "I think we have individuals on this club who, if they pull together, will make an enforcer unnecessary. I've seen it happen with this club before. It's a question of all of them sticking together. I don't know why it's not happening now, though."[17] It was easy for the writers to criticize Howell for not making any deals in his brief time in charge of the Barons, but he wasn't in a position of strength. The Barons didn't have many players other teams wanted, and parting with one (or more) of them in exchange for someone whose sole purpose was to throw his weight around wasn't wise.

Cleveland's goals against Chicago were scored by Fidler and Manery. Meloche recorded 25 saves. The Friday night crowd was 6,273 ... the second largest of the young season.

The Blackhawks prevailed in the second game of the weekend home-and-home series, winning in Chicago Stadium, 6–1, on October 30. Gardner's fourth goal was all the offense the Barons could muster. Cleveland whiffed on all five power play chances. But the Barons did show some feistiness. Rookie defenseman Darcy Reiger, recalled from Phoenix to replace Christie, piled up six minutes in penalties in the first period.

The Barons had followed their club-record four-game winning streak with a four-game losing streak.

October closed with the NHL's Adams Division standings looking like this:

Buffalo	5–2–2	11	27–18
Toronto	4–1–2	10	31–22
Boston	3–3–2	9	26–26
Barons	4–5–2	8	22–29

In spite of their problems, the Barons were just three points behind the division-leading Sabres. In the off-season, the league had added a "wild card" playoff spot, enhancing Cleveland's chances to qualify for the post-season.

In practice on November 1, the Barons lost center Ralph Klassen for six to eight weeks. A hard hip-check by teammate Bjorn Johannson tore ligaments in Klassen's left knee. Fortunately, he wouldn't need surgery.

"The frightening part is they are getting injured by their own people," sighed Evans. "Christie had his foot broken by Gilles Meloche's stick. Then Klassen is hip-checked by Johansson."[18]

Howell was mystified by the wave of injuries that decimated the Barons in 1976–77 and continued in 1977–78. "It's hard to explain. In my first 16 seasons, I missed 17 games. There were never injuries 20 years ago like there are now. Then, all kinds of guys played 65 to 70 games out of a 70-game schedule."[19] Howell's playing days weren't that far behind him. He retired after the 1975–76 season, at the age of 43, after playing 31 games for the Calgary Cowboys of the WHA.

Thanks to a hat trick plus one by Maruk, the Barons tied St. Louis, 4–4, at the Coliseum on November 2. Maruk said he was inspired playing against the Blues' center Garry Unger. "I like to play against the best in the league, and he's one of the best. He's one of the superstars in hockey. I hope I can become one."[20] Gary Edwards made his first start in goal for the Barons and stopped 22 shots. The attendance was a meager 4,461.

Cleveland's injured list grew during the game against the Blues. Defenseman Butch Baby was hit in the face by a puck and rushed to a hospital for emergency surgery. Doctors were able to fix Baby's nose, but he'd be lost to the team indefinitely. With a roster spot open, the Barons recalled Danny Chicoine from Phoenix.

Cleveland split a home-and-home series with the Red Wings on November 6 and 7, winning at Detroit, 4–3, and losing at the Coliseum, 4–1. Just two games after scoring four goals against St. Louis, Maruk was benched by Evans for ineffective play in the second period of the loss. So was his line mate, Bob Murdoch. "They weren't doing anything. They were on the ice for two [Detroit] goals. They were in trouble with every line I put them in against. I had to do something,"[21] said the coach.

Maruk wasn't pleased to spend half of the game on the bench. "I'm not going to talk about tonight," he said. "I'm not going to say anything. He's the coach. We got no warning. He just said we weren't skating and put us on the bench."[22]

Detroit head coach Bobby Kromm explained how his team won. "We took away their speed,"[23] he said simply. The Barons were a finesse team. A few well-placed bumps and checks could take them out of their rhythm, and other NHL teams knew it. They'd employ that strategy until the Barons found a way to counter it.

A crowd of 6,687 watched the loss to the Red Wings. It dropped the Barons' record at the Coliseum to 2–4–2.

"The team seems to click on the road," said Howell. "They have to get this out of their heads. They have to think they can win at home. This is where they have to make it."[24] Through seven home games, the Barons were averaging just 5,800 fans at the Coliseum. Though it was early, the marketing effort being made by the Gund brothers, which started with a trimming of ticket prices, wasn't having any effect.

Gary Sabourin hadn't played a game for the Barons in 1977–78, and he wouldn't. His injured knee didn't respond to treatment and would need surgery. He'd miss the entire season.

With a record of 3–2 away from the Coliseum, the best thing for the Barons was a road trip, and they opened a five-game journey against the Penguins on November 9. Pittsburgh had lost five games in a row. The Barons put a stop to that, losing, 5–3. The Penguins spurted to a 4–0 lead and held off a mild Cleveland rally. Maruk scored twice and Fidler added the other goal.

Through 13 games, the Barons had scored only 34 goals. Seven of them came in a victory at Minnesota in the season's first week. Mac-Adam, who seemed to have lost his scoring touch like all of his teammates except Maruk, said concern was setting in. "At first, when certain guys weren't scoring, they said 'wait, we'll break out any minute.' Now after 13 games, those people are starting to worry,"[25] he said.

Said Evans, "we are averaging 2½ goals a game, but that is not enough to win in this league."[26]

After the loss to Pittsburgh, the Barons sent Baby and Johansson to Phoenix. Injuries and lack of offense had the club shuffling its personnel on a regular basis.

In mid–November, the Barons found themselves once again worried about the future of the franchise. Alan Eagleson, the executive

director of the NHLPA who'd borrowed the cash on behalf of the players' association that kept the Barons alive in February, was once again
predicting their demise. He told newspapers in Boston and Toronto that
Gund would fold the team before the end of the season.

"Yes, I said the franchise was in a shambles, but that was from a
fan's point of view. [The fans] have not shown any interest in the club,"
said the attorney who served as agent for five of Cleveland's players. "I
am not going to say Cleveland is in great shape. Ticket sales and interest do not reflect well on the future of that organization. I made no time
reference. But how long can a man like George Gund go on losing two
million dollars a year? You can't back away from the facts. Pride is one
thing, but unfortunately, it does not pay the bills."[27] Eagleson acknowledged that the Gund brothers had the personal fortunes to absorb huge
losses running the Barons but posed the totally reasonable question of
how long they'd be willing to do so.

Gund was contacted at his home in San Francisco and quickly
answered Eagleson's comments. "That's just more bull, and you can
quote me on that!" he seethed. "This is more of his maneuvering. Of
course I'm worried about the attendance. But we haven't done as much
yet as we hope to do. This franchise is on a solid financial foundation."[28]
Gund accused Eagleson of urging his clients on the Barons to play out
their options and get out of Cleveland, a charge Eagleson dismissed as
"garbage."

Added Larsen, "I am aggravated beyond words. His comments are
detrimental to hockey and our efforts in Cleveland and also the players he represents. I wish he would keep his remarks to himself. We don't
want the fans threatened with a 'show up or else' approach. If we did,
they would say 'go take a jump!' We are trying to build something here."[29]

The Barons were in no danger of folding during the 1977–78 season. But there could be no denying, or ignoring, the fact that hockey fans
were avoiding the Coliseum just as they had the season before. Eagleson
knew whereof he spoke when he questioned how long George and Gordon Gund would be willing to lose boatloads of money on a team northeastern Ohio didn't seem to care about.

One day after Eagleson's comments were printed in the *Plain
Dealer* (curiously, nothing was written about the incident in the *Press*),
the Barons lost to the Bruins in Boston, 3–1. Crombeen scored Cleveland's only goal. "I can see why they never get blown out of any building,"
said Bruins head coach Don Cherry of the vanquished visitors. "They
make you earn every goal. They're a tough team to play."[30]

"Actually, we played well," said Evans. "We had a lot of chances to
win the game, but we didn't. I thought my team played well for the first

half of the game, but then...,"[31] his voice trailed off. There was no need to finish the thought. But then the Barons had found a way to lose, to an admittedly superior opponent, as they almost always did. Once again Cleveland found itself short-handed as Gardner didn't dress for the contest. He was battling a blood infection in his left ankle. His return was uncertain.

From Boston, the Barons flew cross-continent for a pair of games on the west coast. The first was against the Canucks in Vancouver, and they jumped to a quick 2–0 lead on goals by Maruk and Fidler less than six minutes into the contest. Merrick and Crombeen scored later in the game, but the Canucks fought back. Mike Walton's goal with less than two minutes remaining gave Vancouver a 5–4 victory.

"Collectively, this was the worst game we've played all season," moaned Evans. "Four goals should win most any game, especially when you get a fast start on the road. But there were a lot of errors at both ends of the ice."[32] The Barons couldn't afford to lose games in which they scored four goals, since four goals was an offensive explosion for them.

In Los Angeles, Cleveland tied the Kings, 1–1. Former King Gary Edwards stopped 47 shots. His cocky teammates shouted, "Who's Vachon?" in the dressing room afterward. Edwards had matched the Kings' ace goalie save-for-save and then some, as Los Angeles managed more than twice as many shots on goal as the Barons. Kings coach Ron Stewart wasn't as impressed with Edwards as his teammates were.

"What can you do when you have 48 shots?" Stewart groaned. "I don't know if we're not bearing down. We had enough chances to win five games."[33]

Evans continued to bemoan his team's lack of scoring punch. "We are working hard. I can't ask for any more effort. We are creating scoring chances. We've got to break out sooner or later."[34] It would have helped if top draft pick Crombeen had been contributing. Evans said he'd spoken with the youngster following a brief benching.

"We had a talk several games ago. I hadn't played him for a couple of games, and he wanted to know what was the matter. I told him he was hesitating and not doing the things he did as a junior. I suggested he play to his strengths and see what happens. He seems to have agreed and that's what he is doing now."[35] Evans rejected the thought that the Barons simply lacked talent. He insisted he was coaching a club with playoff potential.

The Barons wrapped up their trip with an embarrassing 7–2 loss to the Rockies in Denver. The ledger showed no wins, four defeats and one tie.

"All I can say is I'm disappointed with what we've accomplished so far," said Evans when the club returned to Cleveland. "We need more goals, and we're giving up too many goals. I don't know what it is. Some of these people were able to score before. I thought we'd have a better team than this. I still hope we can come back. I can't believe we can't score more goals."

The coach admitted he was beginning to get discouraged. "It certainly is depressing. Who can live with losing? It's starting to affect the players and myself. We're getting edgy. Nothing is working for us. It certainly is getting to us."[36]

In their constant search for more offense, the Barons recalled right wing Ken Kuczyk from Phoenix and sent Chicoine to replace him on November 22. It was Chicoine's second demotion of the season. The Barons' second round draft pick was contributing even less than Crombeen.

Howell had taken a lot of grief from Passan and Schlesinger for failing to swing a trade ... any kind of trade ... to at least create the illusion that the Barons were trying to improve themselves. On November 22, he sent wing Reg Kerr to the Blackhawks for defenseman Randy Holt. The 24-year-old Holt had the distinction of holding the Central Hockey League record for penalty minutes (411) in a season. With Chicago in 1977–78, he'd accumulated 20 minutes in the penalty box. The front office touted the trade as proof of its commitment to "toughen up" the Barons. Holt was expected to be the enforcer the writers had been begging Howell to obtain.

If the Barons could defeat the Montreal Canadiens at the Coliseum on the night before Thanksgiving, each fan would be able to exchange their ticket stub for a ticket of equal value to the December 7 game against Washington, or the February 1 contest against Detroit. The catch was that the ticket stubs had to be exchanged at a Coliseum box office immediately after the game. Since the two-time defending Stanley Cup champions from Quebec were bringing a 12– 3–2 record into the game and hadn't lost on the road all season, it appeared highly unlikely the box offices would be stampeded after the contest.

11

One Shining Moment

Watching the Barons play hockey night after night was enough to make a grown man cry. Coliseum president Peter Larsen admitted as much after the game against Montreal on November 23.

"When Maruk got that breakaway and scored, I went crazy," he said. "I even had tears in my eyes."[1] Larsen was in good company. The largest Coliseum crowd to witness a Barons game, 12,859 fans, went crazy with him … except the scattered few who'd made the trek to Richfield to root for the mighty visitors. Some may even have shed a tear or two of their own.

For one magical evening, hockey in Cleveland was just as Mel Swig and George Gund III had envisioned when they'd transferred the Golden Seals. The Coliseum wasn't even close to being sold out, but crowds of almost 13,000 would have been highly acceptable. And those in attendance made enough noise for 20,000 people. The short-handed Barons took a 2–0 lead on goals by Bob Murdoch and Dennis Maruk, and then held on desperately. By the time the visitors awoke and realized they had a chance to lose to their lowly hosts, it was too late to get the mighty Montreal machine in gear. The Barons spent the game's final frenzied minutes fighting off charge after charge by the Canadiens, buoyed by the support of their biggest crowd ever, many of whom clapped their hands, stomped their feet, and screamed "defense, defense!" at the top of their lungs.

Barons 2, Canadiens 1. This was what Swig and Gund had in mind. Unfortunately, it turned out to be just a mirage. But it was fun while it lasted. Some of the patrons didn't want the evening to end. They hung around the Coliseum tooting bullhorns for an hour and more afterward. No one asked them to leave.

"Jack wanted us to concentrate on defense," said Dave Gardner. "We knew the offense would come." Gardner credited the work of future Hall of Fame goaltender Ken Dryden for keeping the Canadiens from being trounced by the inspired Barons. "If it hadn't been for Dryden, we could

have been ahead 5–1."[2] Gardner said the unexpected victory couldn't
help but boost the team's sagging morale. "This is going to bring everyone closer together. We just beat the best hockey team in the world. And
if we can beat them, we can beat anybody."[3]

Gardner's coach agreed. "It could do wonders," said Jack Evans.
"Why shouldn't it? It will give our guys considerable confidence. A performance like that will be very beneficial to them."[4]

Said Maruk, one of the evening's heroes, "no doubt about it, you
beat the Canadiens and it's a big thrill. Never mind those eight-goal
games, I'll take this anytime."[5]

Said another of the evening's heroes, goalie Gary Edwards, who
stopped 27 shots and steadfastly refused to allow the puck to elude him
in the closing minutes as the Canadiens tried feverishly to at least tie the
score and avoid embarrassment, "if we play like we did [tonight] you'll
see a big improvement. If we play within our abilities ... we will score
our goals. We will beat the teams we're supposed to beat. And we will
also take our share of points from teams like Boston, the Islanders, Philadelphia and Toronto. The reason the game is so important is that we
know, in our minds, we are capable of doing it."[6]

The epic win was the first for the Oakland/Cleveland franchise at
home against the Canadiens since 1970. Overall, it was the franchise's
first victory versus the Canadiens in the past 16 meetings between the
clubs. But in spite of the optimism it generated, the game was nothing
more than the type of Herculean effort every doormat can muster a few
times each season against a powerhouse such as Montreal. Edwards
was mistaken about the Barons being ready to win their share of games
against the NHL's strong teams, and they'd prove it quickly.

There was one downside to the victory. Defenseman Bob Stewart's left knee stiffened, and he wasn't able to make the trip to Philadelphia for the game against the Flyers the night after Thanksgiving.
The knee had been surgically repaired 16 months before. The already
short-handed Barons would meet one of the NHL's best teams even
more short-handed.

The Flyers wasted no time bursting Cleveland's bubble with a 7–2
victory on November 25. Gardner and Rick Hampton scored the Barons' customary complement of goals. Edwards, who'd been an impene-
trable fortress in the upset of the Canadiens, was more like a swinging
door against the Flyers. The game was low-lighted by a 10-minute brawl
that forced the officials to end the first period 42 seconds early. The time
was tacked on to the second period.

If the Barons had been able to score two goals against the Blues the
following night at the Coliseum, they would've salvaged a tie. But they

only scored once, and St. Louis skated off with a 2–1 victory ... its first on the road against the Oakland/Cleveland franchise since late November of 1972. After almost 13,000 fans were lured to Richfield to watch the Canadiens, the Blues drew a paltry "announced" crowd of 4,497. That represented the number of tickets sold. There were about 3,200 spectators in the seats. A typical blustery late November night in northeastern Ohio made travel hazardous and discouraged all but the hardiest fans from risking the trip to the Coliseum on the slick and slippery roadways leading to the building.

After the close defeat, Evans repeated a familiar refrain. "We've got to score goals. All we can do is keep working at it and hope they go in."[7] He said he was out of ideas for jump-starting the Barons' offense. "When you are averaging two goals a game, all you can do is hope to give up one. I have tried every line change I can make." For the first time, he let slip the possibility that the Barons just couldn't compete. "Maybe we just don't have the people. You can show them to the net, but the final move is up to them."[8]

At the very least, the Barons were consistent. They scored two goals in the first game of a home-and-home series with Adams Division rival Toronto on November 29. It was the fourth time in five games Cleveland had scored twice. The Maple Leafs scored three times before more than 16,000 delighted fans in Maple Leaf Gardens. The Barons returned the favor, 5–3, the next night in front of a much smaller crowd at the Coliseum: 3,930. A fluke goal off the stick of Mike Fidler in the third period proved to be the game winner.

"We out-skated Toronto [last] night, only to lose by a goal," said Fidler. "These four-point games are absolute must-win situations. We couldn't let two in a row get away from us."[9]

On the morning of December 1, these were the Adams Division standings:

Boston	13–5–2	30	71–52
Buffalo	14–6–2	30	77–59
Toronto	12–5–2	27	71–54
Barons	7–13–2	16	54–77

As December opened, Howell was reported to be in serious trade negotiations with the Red Wings and Blackhawks. The *Plain Dealer*'s headline asked: WHO'S COMING? A number of names were mentioned, but none wound up in Cleveland. Nobody left, either.

The Barons would get a chance to pick on someone their own

size in their next game. The Washington Capitals were at the tail end of a horrendous stretch which had begun on October 26. The Capitals hadn't won a game during the entire month of November. They entered their home match with Cleveland winless in their last 17 games (0–12–5). They'd scored just 30 goals in those games.

"I didn't think all the words you can write will be able to tell you what myself and the players are going through," said Caps coach Tommy McVie. "I've never been through anything like this in my life."[10] The Barons extended McVie's misery with a 3–2 victory at the Cap Centre on December 2. Maruk scored the winning goal with a minute-and-a-half to play.

"When they made it 2–2 I was concerned," said Evans. "They had played well the whole game. But Denny came up with the big play when we needed it."[11]

The Bruins, who visited the Coliseum the next night, were headed in the opposite direction. Boston was undefeated in its past 12 games (7–0–5) and continued the streak with a come-from-behind, 4–4 tie. Cleveland skated to an early 3–0 lead, but Gilles Meloche withered under a Bruin attack that produced 52 shots on goal. It was a promotional night at the Coliseum, and the first 10,000 fans to enter the building were to receive a Barons pennant. Since the crowd was just 6,636, management had 3,364 pennants left over. They presumably wound up at the souvenir stands. It isn't unreasonable to assume some of them were still on sale when the season ended. Barons souvenirs weren't a hot item in northeastern Ohio.

Howell, the Barons' rookie general manager, had fanned in his effort to trade with the Red Wings or Blackhawks (or both), but he wasn't giving up. "I am going to pursue trades because I know there are some severe deficiencies on our club," he understated. "Frankly, I believe we need more scoring, which is obvious. That is the primary concern."[12]

The early returns on Howell's first trade were promising. Randy Holt gladly accepted his role as Cleveland's enforcer. "When I see some of our little guys getting pushed around," said Holt, explaining his job, "I make sure that I warn whoever is shoving or elbowing our guy that I am ready to protect him. And if he continues to harass our guy, he has to answer to me."[13] It was particularly important that Holt watch out for Maruk, Cleveland's smallest but most productive player.

While his general manager searched for fresh talent, Larsen expressed the opinion that the Barons had turned the corner. "Our effort in beating Montreal and Toronto and tying Boston demonstrates that, when we play our game, we're there. We're capable of winning most games."[14]

But the Barons weren't capable of winning their game against

Washington at the Coliseum on December 7. It was one of the games to which the attendees of the November 23 contest versus the Canadiens could've obtained a free ticket, but few had taken advantage of the offer. There were only 3,842 fans in the seats, and they watched the Capitals end six weeks of frustration with a 5–3 victory.

"What are you going to say? We played bleep-bleep hockey," said an agitated Evans afterward. "Our worst game of the year. We played worse periods, but not a worse game. There was no rhyme or reason to give up five goals."[15] The only positive for the Barons were the season's first goals by Ken Kuczyk and Rick Shinske.

Cleveland lost a game to Washington but gained a player. Howell traded unproductive (no goals, four assists) right wing Bob Girard and a second-round draft pick to the Capitals for 30-year-old center Walt McKechnie. McKechnie was familiar with his new home, having played for the American Hockey League Barons in 1970–71. He'd seen action with five NHL clubs, including the Golden Seals from 1971 to 1974. His career totals were 123 goals and 205 assists. But McVie decided McKechnie was a rotten egg and benched him. The Capitals viewed the trade as a case of addition by subtraction.

"I tried to get him to tell me what was bothering him," said McVie of his effort to get through to McKechnie. "So we could work it out. I had him in to talk four or five times. But it didn't work out."[16]

Howell wasn't worried about McVie's low opinion of the newest Baron. "I've talked with a lot of people who know Walter, and I feel he will perform for us with no trouble. Maybe we need a trouble-maker. Actually, I like to let a guy get a fresh start."[17]

McKechnie said he had no idea why McVie soured on him. "They really cut me up badly. They think I quit on the team and said so publicly. I did everything they asked me to. They used me as a scapegoat." A club that hadn't won in its past 20 games needed someone to blame for its problems, and McKechnie was that guy. "I'm just glad Harry Howell and Jack Evans want me. I have a lot of hockey left in me. I'm not anywhere near through playing."[18] What McKechnie didn't say was that being traded from Washington to Cleveland was like being transferred from Alcatraz to Devil's Island.

McKechnie joined his new team in Buffalo on December 8. The Barons lost to the Sabres, 5–2. They managed only 23 shots on goal while allowing 41. The trip back to Cleveland was canceled by an early December snowstorm. The Barons couldn't leave their hotel. They were snowbound for two days and wound up going directly to Philadelphia for their next game. They played like a team that had been confined to a hotel for 48 hours.

The Flyers mangled the Barons, 11–1. Maruk's goal with 66 seconds left on the clock avoided the additional embarrassment of a shutout. Unfortunately, the Barons were able to leave Philadelphia, and arrived in Cleveland to find the Canadiens waiting for them.

Any resemblance between the almost surreal night of November 23, and the night of December 9, was purely non-existent. The Canadiens wanted revenge for the humiliation they'd suffered during their first visit to the Coliseum, and they got it, 5–1. Despite allowing five goals, Rich Passan praised Meloche's goaltending as "superb." There were almost 8,000 more empty seats in the Coliseum than there had been on the night before Thanksgiving. The attendance was 5,026.

Evans sounded like a coach whose team had been out-scored 16–2 in its last two games. "I thought our players tried very hard," he said. "It's

Barons goaltender Gilles Meloche is congratulated by teammates Al Mac-Adam (25) and Walt McKechnie after a rare victory at the Richfield Coliseum during the 1977–78 season (Michael Schwartz Library, Cleveland State University).

not easy for them. They're giving their best effort night after night after night, and they lose. It's a credit to the team that they keep on coming back."[19]

As if the Barons didn't have enough problems, they appeared to be in danger of losing their top farm team. It was reported by the *Plain Dealer* on December 15 that Mike Leonard had "withdrawn" as owner of the Phoenix Roadrunners of the Central Hockey League, although he said he'd be willing to join a new ownership group, if one could be put together. The Arizona desert wasn't proving to be fertile ground for the winter sport. The Roadrunners of the WHA had failed in Phoenix, losing five million dollars in the process, and now the CHL was going down the drain. CHL president Bud Poile, whose office, ironically, was in Phoenix, said the league would assume control of the Roadrunners if necessary.

Larsen announced in mid–December that the Coliseum had scheduled an exhibition game between the Barons and the touring Kladno team of Czechoslovakia on January 4. That was quite a surprise to the Buffalo Sabres, who were scheduled by the NHL to visit the Coliseum that night. With the Sabres' permission, their visit was rescheduled for January 12.

Evans held a team meeting before the Barons clashed with the Flames in Atlanta on December 15. He told his players he was confident they were playoff contenders. Bob Stewart appreciated the pep talk and said he agreed with his coach. "The guys have to realize how important it is to win and how close we are. It should not be Jack's job. We don't have a Stanley Cup championship team, but we do have a playoff team."[20] The Barons performed like a playoff team that night, doubling up the Flames, 6–3.

Two nights later, Cleveland turned in a sparkling effort in a 4–2 victory over the New York Rangers at the Coliseum. It didn't hurt that Rangers star Phil Esposito was injured less than five minutes into the contest and didn't return. Meloche stopped 32 shots. The Barons' goals were scored by Kuczyk, Shinske, Rick Hampton and Kris Manery, an unheralded rookie who was playing much better than the club's two top draft picks. Evans expressed the opinion that it was his team's best game of the season. It was too bad only 4,929 fans saw it.

The following night in Boston, the Barons led the Bruins, 1–0, going into the third period. The Bruins scored twice in the final 20 minutes to pull out a tight victory.

Northeastern Ohio's hockey fans would be able to watch the NHL's Monday night "Game of the Week" again in the winter months of 1978 ... provided they were night owls. The games telecast in January, February and March of 1977 had drawn a sufficient audience to convince the management of channel 43 to carry the contests again, but not live. Only the NHL All-Star game could be viewed as it happened. The rest of the games would be shown via tape delay, starting at 11:00 p.m., meaning a typical game would end about two o'clock in the morning. The first delayed broadcast would be on January 9.

Passan called the Barons' December 21 match-up with the Flyers at the Coliseum a typical "non-display" of hockey by the home team. It wasn't as bad as the 11–1 humiliation the Barons had suffered in Philadelphia 10 days earlier, but it was bad enough. Cleveland lost, 5–0. The Barons managed just 25 shots on goalie Bernie Parent. The Flyers took 44 shots on Cleveland's goal. As was the case with many Philadelphia games, a bench-clearing brawl was included, although the players waited until just 34 seconds remained in the third period before dropping their sticks and gloves and punching each other, which gave those in the crowd of 5,112 who hadn't headed for the Coliseum's parking lot something to scream about.

Evans, who was getting tired of facing reporters game after game to explain another defeat, took the lacing philosophically. "Philadelphia is the best team in the league right now," he said. "Even better than Montreal. I thought we played a good game considering the team we were up against."[21] The comment illustrated just how far the Barons were from becoming one of the NHL's elite clubs.

Two nights later in Madison Square Garden, the Barons made a better showing against the Rangers but still fell, 5–4. The goals were scored by Maruk, Manery, Murdoch, and Kuczyk. Edwards made 18 saves. "We made four mistakes, and every one cost us a goal,"[22] said a discouraged Evans.

In the *Plain Dealer* on Christmas Day, columnist Dan Coughlin looked back on the year 1977 in Cleveland sports and suggested that George Gund III and his brother Gordon had done the city no favors by coming to the rescue of the Barons. Coughlin said that while the jury was still out, there was plenty of evidence that the Barons should've been allowed to expire quietly at the NHL meeting in June. Doubtless there were many NHL owners who agreed and were tired of watching their teams play in front of 12,000–15,000 empty seats in the Coliseum. So were George and Gordon. The Gund brothers had cut ticket prices and were vigorously promoting their sad-sack team. One promotion began the day after Christmas. The Barons started taking their practices on the road, occasionally conducting them at local ice rinks and opening them to the fans, free of charge. After practice, the players would be available to pose for pictures and sign autographs. The first open practice was held in Lakewood on December 26.

After a three-day Christmas break, the Barons opened a four-games-in-five-days stretch with a visit to Montreal on December 27. Evans wasn't thrilled by the scheduling. He called it "a character builder, but I've had enough of that. I'd like to get spoiled by some victories."[23] The Barons couldn't have been reasonably expected to spoil their coach versus the Canadiens, and they didn't. The game was tied at 1–1 after the first 20 minutes. The Canadiens scored four goals in the second 20 minutes and won, 5–3.

Bruins coach Don Cherry wasn't happy after his club's 5–5 tie with the Barons at the Coliseum the next night. Neither was Evans. For some reason, Cherry was agitated by the small crowd of 5,617. Maybe he was insulted that so few Clevelanders turned out to watch a team as good as his, particularly during the days between Christmas and New Year's, when people were off of work and kids were home from school. According to both newspapers, Cherry ranted that "the franchise has to be helped! You may as well know that!"[24] Cherry's evaluation of the state of hockey in northeastern Ohio was hardly a news bulletin.

Evans was unhappy about his team's inability to hold a 3–1 lead after the first period. The Bruins, like the Canadiens the game before, exploded for four goals in the second period. The Barons rallied from a goal down twice to earn the tie, but that didn't satisfy Evans. "Coming back from a goal behind twice to tie a team as good as Boston isn't bad. But when you're ahead of any team 3–1 on your home ice and don't win the game, you can't be that pleased."[25]

The Barons didn't rally against the Maple Leafs on December 30, falling behind quickly and succumbing meekly, 5–0, amid a shower of boos and jeers from the crowd of 6,520 at the Coliseum. Evans said the fact it was Cleveland's third game in four days was no excuse for the lethargic effort. "They shouldn't be tired," he moaned. "We just never got going. We weren't skating the way we were against Boston the other night."[26]

Toronto goalie Mike Palmateer said it was one of the easiest shutouts he'd ever earned. "Yeah, it was a pretty easy game. I had a heck of a lot of protection. They played so well it wasn't funny."[27] Evans and the fans agreed. It wasn't funny. The frustrated coach ordered his players to report to the team's practice facility at 10:00 the next morning. They wouldn't skate, however, since they'd have to catch a bus for Pittsburgh and a New Year's Eve game with the Penguins after the session. But they would watch a tape of the loss to the Maple Leafs, and Evans would have lots of criticism for his team.

As 1977 ended, the Barons weren't Cleveland's only team wondering what had happened to the fans. The city's red-hot love affair with the Cavaliers had peaked, and even though the team was winning and headed for the playoffs, attendance was down 30 percent from the previous season. Cleveland State University's basketball team, which had never been able to excite the populace, drew an "announced" crowd of 651 to its game against Eastern Kentucky on December 30. The game was played in Cleveland's Public Auditorium, which seated approximately 10,000. Attendance at Indians games had declined for the third straight season.

Thanks to the "wild-cards" introduced by the NHL for the 1977–78 season, the Barons entered their last game of 1977 just four points out of a playoff spot, even though they'd won just two of their last 13 games. Directly ahead of them was Pittsburgh. With a chance to pick up two points on the team in front of them, the Barons instead lost to the Penguins in the Civic Arena, 6–3, on December 31. Cleveland's goals came off the sticks of Hampton, Fred Ahern and McKechnie. For the third game in a row, the Barons were torched for four goals in the third period. The loss dropped their record against the Penguins since moving to Cleveland to a laughable 0–7–2. These weren't the Canadiens, the Bruins, the Flyers, or the Islanders. They were the Penguins, and they were just four points ahead of the Barons in the race for the conference's "wild card" playoff spot. But the Oakland/Cleveland franchise hadn't beaten Pittsburgh since 1975.

When the clock struck midnight on December 31, ushering in 1978, the Adams Division standings showed:

Boston	23–7–2	52	139–90
Buffalo	21–7–2	49	128–92
Toronto	21–10–4	46	127–93
Barons	10–23–4	24	94–146

Two and a half months of hockey was in the books, and the Barons had won just 10 games. Technically, they were in the thick of the chase for the wild card. But few, if any, fans in Cleveland were buying management's insistence that the club was a genuine playoff contender.

Although he couldn't say so, Howell knew the Barons were pretenders. But he was almost powerless to do anything about it. That would change quickly in the new year.

12

Just Teasing

When a sports team isn't playing well, as the Barons weren't as the 1978 portion of the 1977–78 season began, rumors spread that the head coach or manager's job is in jeopardy. Those rumors hadn't started in Cleveland about Jack Evans … yet … and Evans' boss, general manager Harry Howell, wanted to make sure they didn't. The Barons had enough problems without the players wondering about the status of their coach.

"I'm satisfied with the job Jack Evans is doing," Howell said emphatically. "Changes have to be made. We have to improve the team. But I want to make it understood Jack Evans' position with the team is solid."

Howell said he'd meet with some of the players … without specifying which ones … and ask them, point blank, why the Barons weren't producing the way he and Evans thought they should be. He said there'd be no threats. "What can I threaten them with?" he asked. "Demotion? Trade? It might affect some players, and others it won't. I don't believe in threatening players. All you can do is get them upset." In the Barons case, telling a player he was on the trading block was hardly a threat. Many of them would have welcomed the chance to leave Cleveland for a team with a shot at the playoffs, and that played in a building in which there were fans in the seats.

Demotion was a threat, and Howell thought he may have to use it. "Maybe I should bring up a couple of kids from the minors and send a couple of veterans down. That's something Jack and I will have to talk over." But any NHL-worthy players in Phoenix had already been summoned to the parent team.

Howell was frustrated by the Barons' inconsistency. They occasionally looked like contenders, but more often like doormats. "This club has a lot of talent, but it is not getting used every night. Maybe it's the individual. I don't think it's that hard to 'get up' for two hours work for 80 games." Howell absolved Evans of any blame for the players' failure to be properly motivated. He'd played the game for two decades and never needed anyone to motivate him. "I don't buy not being able to 'get up' for

80 games. A coach can get a team up, but it's up to the individual to get himself up for the game."[1]

Bob Schlesinger revealed in the *Press* that Howell's hands had been essentially tied as far as making personnel changes by the agreement that transferred the Barons from Mel Swig to the Gund brothers. As announced at the time, the agreement put the Coliseum in charge of the team. What wasn't explained was that all personnel moves had to be approved by Coliseum president Stu Giller, who had taken over for Peter Larsen in September. According to Schlesinger, the Gunds couldn't spend their own money on their own hockey team without Giller's okay. Negotiations were underway to amend that agreement, and Schlesinger expected them to be concluded within days. The shackles would then be removed from Howell, and he could start remaking the Barons the way he wanted.

Evans blamed the New Year's Eve loss to Pittsburgh on a harsh December schedule. "I think it's a little bit of fatigue," said the coach. "We had 15 games in December. That's a lot of hockey."[2] It was a game every other day, on average.

The Barons lost their first game of 1978, 5–4, to the Flyers in Philadelphia on January 3. Dave Gardner, Bob Murdoch and Kris Manery scored, with Manery finding the range twice. The Barons managed just 18 shots on goal.

International competition came to the Coliseum the next night as the Barons hosted Kladno of Czechoslovakia. Kladno played a typical European-style game, relying on speed and finesse and very little checking. The Barons took advantage of the lack of physicality on the part of their opponent for a 4–3 victory. The crowd was 7,117.

"Any team that lets us skate, we'll give them a good game,"[3] said Evans.

"It was nice for a change to be in a game without all that goon stuff,"[4] said Greg Smith, who tallied one of the Barons' goals. The others were scored by Wayne Merrick, Ralph Klassen and Manery. Gilles Meloche and Gary Edwards split the goaltending duties in the exhibition.

Kladno's coach was surprised by the loss, his team's only defeat in its four-game tour of the United States. "We had the attitude it would be an easy game," said Bohuslav Prosek. "We had never seen Cleveland play before. We had a message they were not very good."[5]

It was back to NHL competition for the Barons on January 6, and they made quick work of the visiting Vancouver Canucks, 6–1, before 5,037 fans on "puck night." The first four thousand kids were to be given free pucks. Unless 80 percent of those in attendance were children, the promotions department had plenty of pucks left over. The Barons fired

44 shots at Canucks goalie Cesare Maniago, who'd frustrated them in the past. Meloche faced only 26 shots and turned back all but one. Evans thoroughly enjoyed the rare laugher. His enjoyment didn't last long.

The next evening in Uniondale, New York, the Barons dropped a 5–3 decision to the Islanders. They managed just 16 shots on goal and allowed the Islanders 36. Dennis Maruk scored twice, and Bob Stewart added the other Cleveland goal. "We made mistakes in the second period that shouldn't have happened," lamented Evans. "I don't know what I can do to eliminate those mistakes. It's inexperience, and it always happens under pressure."[6] If a game was close, the Barons seemingly always found a way to lose. Little did Evans know that two of the players who'd helped the Islanders beat his club would find themselves in Barons uniforms just days later.

Negotiations to eliminate Giller from the personnel decision-making process were completed during the first week of January. The Gunds could spend money, and Howell could make deals, without asking permission from the president of the Coliseum. He wasted no time getting to work.

On January 9, the Barons traded left wing Klassen and right wing Fred Ahern to Colorado for right wing Chuck Arnason and left wing Rick Jodzio. On the surface, it appeared to be nothing more than cosmetic, a trade made to get rid of two unproductive players while adding two new players who'd been unproductive for their old team. Howell, of course, didn't agree. He said Arnason could help the Barons offense.

"When he plays regularly, Arnason can be a 20-goal scorer in the National Hockey League. He is an excellent passer, shooter and skater. He is an excellent offensive player."[7] Arnason had played in 29 games for the Rockies and scored 12 points (four goals, eight assists). The 26-year-old had amassed 88 goals in 347 career games. He said his problems in Colorado stemmed from the team's emphasis on defense. Arnason wanted to be free to concentrate on scoring, and that was what Howell wanted him to do. The general manager said he wasn't concerned about Arnason's defense.

Howell was concerned about Jodzio's defense. "He was obtained for two reasons. He is a good defensive hockey player, as well as a fighter." In other words, Jodzio would join Randy Holt as the Barons' second enforcer. Howell denied that the 23-year-old Jodzio's hockey skills were minimal and that he earned his living by fighting. "I know Rick very well and he wants to play hockey. Rick will do exactly what we ask of him. He will not like what he sees in some of our games. I don't think we'll see any of our players pushed around."[8]

As for the departing players, Ahern had seven points on three goals and four assists. Klassen had just one goal.

Having added some scoring punch and some muscle with the acquisition of Arnason and Jodzio, Howell set out to give his young club some sorely-needed veteran leadership. He swapped Merrick and a Player To Be Named Later to the Islanders for left wing J.P. Parise and defenseman Jean Potvin.

"I'm looking forward to Potvin helping us more on the power play," said Howell. "And he is not that bad defensively. He can get the puck out of our end." Of the 36-year-old Parise, Howell said, "I've always been an admirer of his. He gives 100% at all times. He's a real digger and not a bad scorer."[9] Parise's numbers for the Islanders were 12 goals and 16 assists for 28 points. Potvin had scored only one goal, but he was a defenseman. Scoring wasn't his job.

Parise wasn't anxious to leave a Stanley Cup contender for one of the NHL's bottom feeders, but he accepted his fate. "My goals were set on winning a Stanley Cup with the Islanders. This is a helluva hockey club. Not being able to participate in the Stanley Cup is a downer for me. But it's something I have to accept. I'm leaving a club with 63 points and coming to a club with 26. You don't need a computer to figure that one out."

Parise tried to find the silver lining to the situation. "I need to be positive. We're only nine points behind a playoff spot. When I came to New York, it was the same way. We never made the playoffs. When I got here, things changed around. A lot can happen in 40 games. I'll do the best I can to see the Barons participate in the playoffs."[10]

In two days, Howell had addressed what he saw as his team's major weaknesses. Not enough scoring, not tough enough, and too young. "It is very evident we are short on experience, especially in close games. It has cost us many games over the season. The added experience definitely will help us,"[11] he analyzed. With Cleveland in the throes of a second consecutive brutal January weather-wise, there was some question as to whether the new players could make it in time for the Barons next game, at the Coliseum against the Islanders. They did, and paid immediate dividends.

On January 7, Potvin and Parise helped the Islanders beat the Barons. On January 11, they helped the Barons defeat the Islanders, 5–3, in a nearly empty Richfield Coliseum. Rather than being critical, the newspapers praised the 2,074 fans who defied abominable conditions to attend the contest. None of the new Barons scored, but their presence was felt in the dressing room. Rich Passan told his readers in the *Plain Dealer* "a new feeling pervades the club now. The losing syndrome is a thing of the past." It was a hasty and ultimately inaccurate conclusion to reach after just one game had been played.

Evans liked the way Parise, Potvin, Arnason and Jodzio made themselves at home. "They were talkative and showed some leadership, reminding everybody what they had to do."[12] The newcomers must've reminded Maruk, McKechnie, Manery, Al MacAdam and Rick Shinske that they needed to score, so they did. Meloche rejected 27 shots, and the Barons had a victory over a quality opponent.

Jean Potvin confided after the game that he'd never played against his brother, Islanders center iceman Denis Potvin, before. He wasn't sure how he'd react if he found himself fighting his brother for a loose puck. That situation didn't come up.

Howell wasn't finished dealing, although the trade announced on January 12 was actually the completion of the earlier deal with Colorado. The Barons sent defenseman Mike Christie to the Rockies for defenseman Dennis O'Brien. Cleveland would be O'Brien's third team in a month. After seven years with the Minnesota North Stars, he started the 1977–78 season with Toronto. He was released by the Maple Leafs in December and signed by Colorado.

Christie, who'd been outspoken about his unhappiness with the Barons the year before, during the payroll crisis, was reluctant to depart. "I hate to leave," he admitted. "It would be nice if we had won the last 10 games. Parise and Potvin have brought a winning attitude to this team and are leaders. I hope this isn't a spur of the moment thing for these guys. I hope their winning attitude is an inspiration for the rest of the team. I think that has been the major problem. There were too many guys losing for too many years."[13]

Evans was sorry to lose Christie. He "disliked giving Mike up. It's unfortunate these things have to happen. He performed well for me, and I'm thankful for that."[14]

The victory over the Islanders started a four-games-in-four-nights stretch for which the Barons had only themselves to blame. More specifically, for which the players had management to blame. The schedule called for three games in four nights before management scheduled the exhibition against Kladno for January 4 and rescheduled that night's game with Buffalo for January 12. The Sabres may have been flat for the trip to Cleveland they weren't supposed to have to make and lost to the Barons, 6–3. Hampton scored twice. MacAdam and Maruk also lit the lamp, and Potvin and Parise notched their first goals in Cleveland uniforms. Another miserable night weather-wise led to another paltry crowd of 2,110. It must be understood that "miserable" meant treacherous. Getting to the Coliseum was downright dangerous on many nights that the Barons played, and the show they usually put on didn't justify people taking the chance of winding up in an accident (or worse) on a snow or ice-covered Interstate 271 or state route 303.

Parise seemed to have shaken off the disappointment of losing his chance to play on a Stanley Cup champion. He had praise for his new teammates after they took care of the Sabres. "Coming from the Islanders, we always said this was a helluva hockey club. They never got the points they should have. Maybe they should be told they are good. We have to have 20 leaders on this club. The Islanders are not as talented a club as the record shows. They have patience and discipline. I'm sure we can do the same thing with this club. Why not?"[15] Parise seemed to be suggesting the Islanders were a team that was better than the sum of its parts, and the Barons could be the same, with coaching and some veteran leadership, which he had been acquired to provide.

There were asterisks next to one of Hampton's goals, and also Mac-Adam's. The Sabres accidentally kicked two pucks into their own net. Hampton and MacAdam were the Barons nearest to the puck and were credited with goals they didn't actually score. That was the kind of thing that generally happened TO the Barons, not FOR them. The loss to Cleveland snapped Buffalo's 11-game unbeaten streak.

The inspired play by the suddenly vibrant Barons continued the next night, as they took down the Maple Leafs, 5–2. The weather had improved somewhat, but the crowd was only 4,527 at the Coliseum. Cleveland put the game away with third period goals by Parise, Jodzio and MacAdam. Edwards had a relatively easy game in goal, facing just 20 Toronto shots.

"I haven't seen spirit like this in the 6½ years I've been with this club," said Stewart, who'd seen just about everything during his career with the Oakland/Cleveland franchise. "Cripes, are we ever looking good!"[16]

Potvin was excited, too. "I definitely see something happening here," he said. "This is a gutsy hockey team. We've beaten three great hockey teams in three straight nights in the third period. The guys could have said they were tired and used it as an excuse, but they didn't. They worked hard and got what they deserved."[17] What they deserved was their third win in three nights, which Schlesinger told his readers had never been achieved by an NHL team before. That seemed unlikely, and Schlesinger didn't cite the source of his information. But it sounded impressive.

Parise said the Barons would be psyched up for their visit to Pittsburgh the next night. They were chasing the Penguins in the race for a wild card playoff spot, and even though it was just the middle of January, the game was crucial. The Barons needed to prove they could beat the Penguins. They failed.

Four games in four nights, possibly coupled with the emotion of the three victories at home and the addition of four new players, caught up to the Barons, and they fell at the Civic Auditorium, 4–2. Maruk and Mike Fidler scored, but two goals weren't enough. "We couldn't get any offense going," said Evans. "I wanted to believe we had enough left."

Evans said he wasn't disappointed by the defeat in Pittsburgh, which dropped the Barons' record against their turnpike rivals to 0– 8–2 over the past two years. "How could I be disappointed? Six out of eight points is a good track record. The luster is still there. The loss is disappointing, of course, because it would have put us two points behind Pittsburgh. Sure, it hurt. But I have to be realistic, too."

Evans said the attitude of the players had taken a 180-degree turn since the previous January, when they had reason to wonder if the team was about to collapse and if they'd ever get paid again. The trades had improved morale dramatically. "It helps for the players to know management is doing what it can to improve this club,"[18] he said.

The NHL announced its All-Star rosters on January 16. Dennis Maruk was on the roster of the Prince of Wales Conference. "This is great news. I love it," said the Barons' star. "I didn't think I'd get there. I never thought of being in the All-Star game in the first three years."[19] Maruk was tied for 13th in the league in scoring with 43 points.

After watching the new-look Barons in action for four games, Evans said "it's a much better team. We are capable of giving any other club in the league a run for its money. There has to be a renewed respect for this team. The other teams can't look at us as passive anymore."[20]

Even with four new players and a new, positive attitude, the Barons were no match for the Canadiens at the Coliseum on January 18. The defending Stanley Cup champs roared to a 7–0 lead after two periods as 7,110 fans groaned … those that hadn't come to enjoy the wizardry of the visitors, that is. And many of those in attendance had. Those rooting for the Barons must've wondered how their team could possibly have beaten the same Canadiens back in November, holding them to one goal. Cleveland made the loss semi-respectable when Arnason, Parise, MacAdam and McKechnie scored in the third period, long after the issue had been decided.

"It was embarrassing to have that many goals scored against you in your own building," said Evans. "But it was nice to see they didn't quit. I was disappointed in the first two periods. We did not play well. Certainly not the way we played the previous four games."[21]

Parise said his new teammates seemed to be in awe of the mighty Canadiens. He said his former teammates in New York had that problem for a long time before reaching the point that they knew they were worthy of sharing the same ice with Montreal. The young Barons weren't there yet. And they never would be.

Two defeats had chipped away at the confidence the Barons seemed to be developing after Howell's trades. A walloping in Buffalo eroded that confidence further. The day after being routed by the Canadiens at home, the Barons journeyed northeast on Interstate 90 and were smoked by the Sabres, 9–2. Cleveland's defense allowed the Sabres 48 shots at Meloche, and he stopped only 39. Evans wasn't pleased by the results of the last two games, but he felt there were extenuating circumstances that explained his club's poor performances.

"Those are two of the top teams in the league, and they wiped us out," he said. "But we are being worked to death."[22] Evans pointed out that the Barons had played 31 games in the past 61 days. An average of a game every other day. That was a staggering workload. And there were two more games to play before the All-Star break.

After surrendering nine goals to the Sabres, the Barons struck for nine goals against the Rockies at the Coliseum on January 23. Only 5,226 fans were on hand to enjoy the 9–4 romp. Immediately afterward, the players boarded a bus for Hopkins airport and then boarded a plane for Boston, where they'd take on the Bruins the next day. That summed up the schedule for the past two months, and it was little wonder the players were dragging.

Weary or not, the Barons stunned the Bruins in Boston Garden, 3–2, in the final game before the All-Star break. They fired just 15 shots at Bruins goalie Gerry Cheevers. Arnason, Murdoch and Fidler put the puck past him. Edwards faced 29 Boston shots and turned away 27. The victory ended a 24-game winless streak in New England for Cleveland's hockey teams. The Barons were 0–5 against the Bruins, and the Crusaders never beat the New England Whalers on their home ice in 19 attempts.

After the rare victory in one of hockey's hallowed buildings, Evans talked about his team's playoff chances. "I still think we have a good chance of making the playoffs," he said. "We have to concede a few of the spots, but I think it's very possible for us to beat out either Pittsburgh or Detroit for a spot. We don't think it's out of sight at all."[23] Sparked by Howell's trades, the Barons ended the first half of the season by winning five of eight games and earning 10 points.

A year earlier, the All-Star break had been a traumatic time for the Barons. It was when Swig told his fellow owners he needed financial help to keep the club alive for the rest of the 1976–77 season, and a month of turmoil followed. The Gund brothers didn't attend the mid-season NHL meeting pleading poverty as Swig had. But they were losing money

Barons goaltender Gilles Meloche, with help from defenseman Jim Neilson (15), turns back a scoring attempt by Larry Wright (25) of the Detroit Red Wings in a game at the Richfield Coliseum (Michael Schwartz Library, Cleveland State University).

operating the Barons, and the NHL's new president, John Ziegler, was watching the situation in northeastern Ohio closely.

"Cleveland is soft," he said. "The attendance has been inconsistent. But the ownership there has made a commitment to Cleveland that Cleveland should be proud of. The response to a team playing pretty good hockey has to be discouraging to the owners." Ziegler was charitable to call the Barons' attendance "inconsistent." With the exception of a handful of games, attendance had been consistently poor. But he was also charitable when he said the Barons had been playing "pretty good hockey." With the exception of the spurt after Howell's trades, the Barons had spent the 1977–78 season playing pretty bad, dull hockey.

Ziegler said with the Gunds in control, the franchise was meeting all of its obligations. "From the standpoint of meeting the schedule and payrolls, paying the bills and meeting their commitments to the league,

Cleveland is not a problem. Hopefully, something can be done in Cleveland that will produce the kind of attendance we like to see." Then he sounded a note of warning for Cleveland's hockey fans. "The response has not been encouraging so far."

Ziegler said the Barons were one of several NHL clubs that would lose at least one million dollars during the season. He acknowledged that, when they purchased the Barons, the Gunds made a three-year commitment to the city. But he added that they were under no obligation to continue losing money. "When you lose millions, even when you're dedicated to the game, you have to permit them to re-examine the situation."[24] And the Gunds would re-examine the situation at the end of the season.

On behalf of the Barons, Howell gave the league's scheduling committee a list of 50 potential playing dates at the Coliseum for the 1978–79 season. Sixteen of them were Saturdays. Even though the Barons weren't drawing any better on Saturdays than any other day, Howell felt the club needed to play at home on Saturday nights as often as possible. He told the scheduling committee that the league's established franchises would pack their arenas whenever they played. But the struggling Barons needed to play at home on Saturdays. They needed to make Saturday night "hockey night" in Cleveland, as it had been in the 1940s and 1950s.

The Wales Conference All-Stars beat the Campbell Conference All-Stars, 3–2. Maruk played nine shifts but didn't score and didn't take a single shot on goal.

The Barons entered the second half of the season trailing the Rangers by five points for the Wales Conference's wild card playoff spot. The Rangers had compiled 41 points. Detroit and Pittsburgh were right behind with 40 points. The Barons had 36.

"This is the first time in the six years I've been with the club that we're close to the playoffs at this point," enthused Stewart. "This team is on the way up. The team knows it can win after beating Boston. And I'm being quite honest."[25]

A Thursday game against the Blackhawks in Chicago started the season's second half. The Barons barely made it. Their flight out of Cleveland Wednesday evening was delayed by an hour, and they flew through a snowstorm that struck Cleveland shortly after they left. Chicago was on the periphery of what northeastern Ohioans called "the white hurricane." Nearly a half century later, the blizzard of January 26, 1978, remains the worst winter storm in Ohio's history. The Blackhawks considered postponing the game but decided to play after learning that the Barons had arrived from Cleveland. The wire service writer who covered the game noted that the tiny gathering of 527 in Chicago Stadium should have made the Barons feel right at home. Chicago won, 5–0.

The Barons trip from Chicago to Minneapolis was only slightly less harrowing than the trip from Cleveland to Chicago had been. They arrived at 1:00 in the morning on the day of the game. They scored twice in the second period and managed to beat the North Stars, 2–1. Then they got on a bus to the airport and got on a flight to Cleveland for a matinee game against the Atlanta Flames about 12 hours later.

The well-rested visitors took advantage of the Barons' weariness and skated to an easy 6–2 victory. Northeastern Ohio was still digging out from the massive blizzard of three days earlier, and only 3,221 made the trek on icy roads and through sub-zero wind chills to the Coliseum for "Jim Neilson Appreciation Day." The Barons honored their 37-year-old veteran defenseman, who was playing in his 1,000th NHL game.

The loss to Atlanta was the Barons' final game in January. As February began, the Adams Division standings looked like this:

Boston	31–11–6	68	189–117
Buffalo	26–10–12	64	173–131
Toronto	26–15–7	59	169–134
Barons	17–30–4	38	147–204

Cleveland had no hope of catching the Maple Leafs, but the Wales Conference's wild card playoff spot was within its grasp. The Rangers, Red Wings and Penguins were in the hunt as well, and the Barons next game was at the Coliseum against Detroit.

"There are no more excuses," said Evans bluntly. "We've used the scheduling, the number of games we've played, the clubs we've played and everything else. We have to run at this thing and see what we can do. Everything is in our favor ... the way we want it. We have to be able to take advantage of it."[26]

The Barons beat the Red Wings, 2–0, on February 1 to move within one point of the visitors in the standings. Arnason and Nielson provided all the offense Meloche needed. The crowd of 7,841 was better than average, but still disappointing. A gathering of better than 10,000 had been projected.

Meloche made 26 saves in registering his 11th career shutout. "This is the closest I've come to the playoffs at this time of year. Usually, we've been hopelessly out of it by now. It's no problem getting up for the

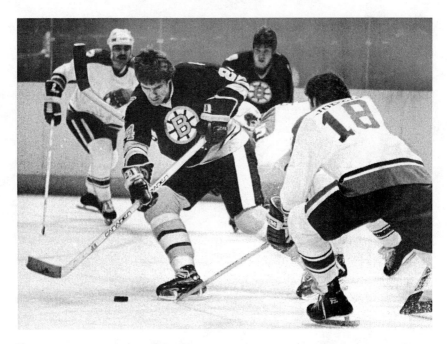

Barons defensemen Greg Smith (5) and Rick Jodzio (18) put the squeeze on Terry O'Reilly of the Boston Bruins (24) while an unidentified teammate closes in from behind in a game at the Richfield Coliseum during the 1977–78 season (Michael Schwartz Library, Cleveland State University).

games now."[27] Meloche echoed the sentiments of his teammates who'd been with the Oakland/Cleveland organization for most, or all, of their careers.

Arnason's goal versus the Red Wings was his sixth in the 12 games he'd played since being acquired from Colorado. In those 12 games, the Barons were 7–5.

The Gund brothers got the second, and final, glimpse at what the NHL was supposed to have been in Cleveland when the Barons tied the Islanders, 2–2, at the Coliseum on Saturday night, February 4. The largest crowd in the team's brief history ventured to Richfield: 13,110. They watched McKechnie score twice and Meloche follow up his blanking of Detroit with a 29-save performance against a much better team.

In his Sunday column the next day, Passan noted the crowd and pleaded with the front office to be prepared for more ... as long as the Barons kept winning. And he expressed the opinion that there was no reason to believe they wouldn't. But they didn't on that Sunday, losing in Detroit, 4–3, and blowing a two-goal lead in the process.

"The only thing we can try to do about a game like this is forget it," said Potvin. "We dropped a big game in Pittsburgh and came back fighting. There's no reason we can't do it again. Sure, this would have been a big victory, but we've come a hell of a long way in the last several weeks. No one expected us to win every game."[28]

Evans didn't expect his team to win every game it played in February, but he expected it to come close. His goal was for the Barons to post a .750 winning percentage for the month. "The way we're playing, it's a realistic goal," he insisted. "This month, our games are spaced out, so there should be no excuses." If the Barons met Evans' high expectation, they'd add 19 points to their total, and probably assume command of the race for the wild card.

The Sabres came to the Coliseum on February 8 and squashed the Barons, 5–2. Cleveland's goals were scored by MacAdam and Fidler. After the brief offensive spurt in late January, the Barons were again having trouble scoring. And drawing fans. Attendance was just 4,094.

On February 9, George Gund III announced the resignation of team president Peter Larsen. Larsen had stepped down as president of the Coliseum in mid–September to concentrate on running the Barons. He was replaced by John Karr, Vice President of Finance and Administration for Cleveland's Cole International Corporation. Karr's area of expertise was reportedly administration and marketing. His appointment, according to Gund, who made a rare public appearance to introduce the new team president, was temporary.

"We left the door open as to longer employment with the Cleveland Barons," said Gund. "We are hoping to persuade him to stay. His background fits in with what we are trying to do."[29] What the Barons were trying to do was dramatically improve their attendance, which was the lowest in the National Hockey League.

Karr was given $100,000 to spend on advertising for the rest of the season. "The Barons will be leaning in the direction of bigger, more viable promotions," he explained. "We feel the opportunities this year should be taken care of. We want to develop more interest in watching the Barons play."[30]

Larsen had no comment to make about his departure. Passan and Schlesinger didn't accept Gund's claim that he'd resigned for personal reasons. Schlesinger, in a column the day after Karr's appointment was announced, told his readers in no uncertain terms that Larsen did not resign. But neither writer offered any proof that Larsen had been fired.

Passan described the Barons' 4–1 loss to Washington on February 10 as the worst hockey game played in Cleveland in several years, dating back to the days of the Crusaders and the WHA. The Capitals came to town having no victories in their previous eight games, and just one win in their last 16 contests. But the Barons couldn't handle them. Passan said the meager crowd of 4,193 would have been justified in demanding its money back.

Evans was at a loss to explain his team's sluggish performance and went so far as to question their desire. "They all say they want to win," he moaned in the dressing room. "Then they go out on the ice and play the way they did tonight. You have to wonder."[31] He was singing the same melancholy tune the next day. "For years, they were complaining they weren't going to the playoffs. Now they have their chance. Judging from the talk in the room before the game Friday night, I'd have bet 100 bucks they were going out and blow Washington off the ice. This has really thrown me. Jeez, it's depressing.

"We're wasting this home stand," the coach continued. "If they want to make the playoffs, they'll have to bust their butts and give everything they've got every game. We don't have the kind of club that can float through games. They've got to go out and make things happen if they are really sincere about going to the playoffs, they have to bear down and play up to their capabilities and beyond that."[32]

Evans was right about wasting the home stand, but the truth was, throughout their brief existence, the Barons enjoyed no home ice advantage at the Coliseum. Home ice advantage is largely the result of being comfortable in one's building, and feeding off the energy of sizable crowds. The Richfield Coliseum never felt like home to most of the Barons, and their play reflected that fact.

A pair of Sunday matinees at the Coliseum had drawn well at the tail end of the 1976–77 season (when many of the tickets were given away), so the Barons tried another one in mid–February. Before a poor crowd of 6,440, they tied the Islanders, 2–2. Parise scored against his old teammates, and McKechnie's third period goal achieved the deadlock. McKechnie admitted the Barons stunk out the Coliseum against Washington, and hoped the team redeemed itself with a stronger showing against a much better team.

To the doubters, McKechnie said "it seems everybody is writing us off for the playoffs. We know we've got a big battle. We still have a chance."[33]

When Karr was hired as the Barons' new team president, Gund emphasized Howell's position within the organization wasn't affected. Karr was to take care of the business and promotional end. Howell was still running the hockey team. At the midway point of February, Howell speculated that a team would have to earn at least 72 points to grab the wild card. The Barons had a mere 42. They increased that total slightly to 43 by tying Atlanta, 5–5, at the Coliseum on February 15. The Flames led by three goals after two periods. Parise spoke to his teammates at the second intermission.

"J.P. told us if we were going to play that way, we were going to be losers the rest of our lives,"[34] said Holt of the pep talk given by the veteran. Parise said he deserved no credit for the fact the Barons scored three unanswered goals in the third period to pull out the tie. He said he told the players to start communicating on the ice. "If you don't do that, you're forced to play as individuals. And if you do that, you don't win. That's no big philosophy."[35]

Holt took Parise's words to heart and contributed his first goal of the season. Fidler scored twice, and McKechnie and Manery also found the back of the Atlanta net. The Flames managed only 19 shots on Meloche, but five eluded him. A pitiful crowd of 2,696 watched. The day's promotion was a promise that every fan would get a free ticket to a future game if the Barons won. Even though they didn't, management decided to reward the fans anyway. With fewer than 3,000 people in the Coliseum, it didn't amount to much of a financial sacrifice.

Dave Gardner was the hero as Cleveland concluded its home stand with a 3–2 squeaker over Vancouver on February 17. Gardner scored the game-winner with less than a minute to play, saving the Barons from a third straight tie. Parise and Fidler scored the other goals, and Meloche had 17 saves. Attendance at the Coliseum was just 4,589. The Barons wrapped up a stretch of eight out of nine games at home with a record of 2–4–2. They picked up only seven points in the race for the wild card. Their 45 points left them seven behind the Penguins and Red Wings.

It would be a long time before the Barons won another game.

13

Look Out Below!

Their unsuccessful home stand behind them, the Barons hit the road for eight of their next nine games. From coach Jack Evans on down, they were still talking about the playoffs. "We have to get as many points as we can," he said. "We have to look at these games and get as much as we can. We have to play tight checking hockey."[1]

Before leaving, the Barons held a practice at the North Olmsted ice rink and attracted 800 onlookers. Taking practices to the suburbs was proving popular, but the Barons needed some of those people to drive to the Coliseum (which was a significant distance from Cleveland's west side) and buy tickets.

The trip started with a two-game swing through southern Canada. The Barons lost to the Maple Leafs, 5–3, on February 22. Cleveland's goals were scored by Chuck Arnason, Dave Gardner and Bob Stewart. Gary Edwards stopped 31 of Toronto's 36 shots. The Barons could manage only 17 shots against the Maple Leafs' defense.

Next was a visit to the Forum to take on the Canadiens, who hadn't lost a game in 1978. Montreal hadn't been defeated since losing to Pittsburgh on December 17. The Canadiens were unbeaten in their last 27 contests (27–0–5). Evans said of their coach, Scotty Bowman, "I wonder how Scotty can sleep at night, wondering when his team is going to lose. I'd like to be in that position. The law of averages is in our favor. They can't win forever."[2] Evans would soon be unable to sleep at night wondering when (if ever) his team was going to win.

Mathematically, the Canadiens may have been long overdue for a defeat. But it wasn't going to come on their home ice at the hands of the Barons. The visitors succumbed meekly, 5–1. Montreal's Steve Shutt slammed home four goals. Mike Fidler accounted for the Barons' only score. Gilles Meloche was pelted by 45 shots off the sticks of the Canadiens and turned back 40 of them. The Barons were permitted only 23.

Evans admitted after the loss that he was glad the Barons were finished for the season with the defending Stanley Cup champions ... unless they met in the playoffs, which became less likely with every passing day. The coach was asked if his team, which talked bravely about remaining in the hunt for the wild card spot, was hungry enough to compete for it. "I don't know how anybody can't be hungry on this team," he responded. "Most of these guys have never been in the playoffs." He then made a strange statement about a team which had lost 16 more games than it had won. He spoke of overconfidence.

"I don't know if they go into some games overconfident. Maybe they feel they don't have to play as hard to beat certain teams."[3] With a record of 19–35–7, the Barons had no right to feel overconfident against any team. Evans sounded like a coach who didn't have a handle on his players' mental state.

Evans' mental state was one of extreme agitation after his club was overwhelmed by Buffalo, 13–3, at the Coliseum on Saturday, February 25. Making matters worse, the season's third largest crowd was on hand. Most of the 10,324 paying customers had departed long before the claxon sounded ending the game. Those who stuck around were probably from Buffalo. More than 1,000 tickets had been sold to Sabres fans who made the trip to Cleveland, and they thoroughly enjoyed the evening's activities. They screamed for more all night, and their team was happy to accommodate them.

"I'm [bleeping] humiliated," Evans said in his office. He told the reporters to find quotes elsewhere. "I think you should go out and talk to them. I'm not going to say anything." He then admitted that he was in "a state of shock when you get beat like that. This is the worst defeat I've ever experienced as a player or a coach."[4] Buffalo's 13 goals were the most ever allowed in one game by the Oakland/Cleveland franchise. The previous record had been a dozen, scored by the New York Rangers in March of 1976.

Defenseman Jean Potvin said he and his teammates "played like a bunch of midgets. We forgot everything we were taught. If this does not serve as a lesson..." he said, without finishing the thought. He said it might be good that the team was heading for a six-game road trip. "We have a chance to redeem ourselves on the road. We don't want people to think we're that bad. The playoffs are still in view."[5]

The Barons trailed the Penguins by 11 points. Pittsburgh continued to hold the wild card spot.

Evans was still fuming about the spanking two days afterward. "I'm very disappointed and annoyed. There are guys on this club not playing anywhere near what they are capable of. I'll sit down with them individually and find out what's wrong."[6] Those sentiments had been heard before. General manager Harry Howell said almost the same thing in January. He said he'd meet with the players and try to ascertain what the problem was. Right or wrong, when a team doesn't play up to its ability (or its perceived ability), the head coach is held responsible. No one was suggesting (yet) that Evans' job was in jeopardy.

Evans was furious with what he considered poor sportsmanship by the Sabres. He said he wasn't accusing them of running up the score on his beleaguered icers, however, "there is some sort of unwritten code that says you don't do that kind of thing. Most teams won't do it."[7] Evans saw no need for the Sabres to keep firing away at Cleveland's goal long after the issue had been decided. Al MacAdam did.

MacAdam agreed with Evans that the Sabres had poured it on, but he understood why. He said that had the skate been on the other foot, he and his teammates would've done the same thing. Goals and assists look good at contract negotiation time, and MacAdam confessed that he wouldn't have passed up the chance to add to his stat sheet. And he didn't think the Sabres should've been criticized for taking advantage of the opportunity.

Cleveland's six-game trip opened in British Columbia on February 27. With the host Canucks six seconds away from a victory, Kris Manery squeezed the puck past goaltender Cesare Maniago to gain a 3–3 tie. Evans was understandably pleased.

"It was encouraging to see them come back the way they did,"[8] he said.

Vancouver coach Orland Kurtenbach wasn't pleased. "You shouldn't get that kind of result after leading 2–0 in your own building,"[9] he growled. The tie extended the Barons' winless streak to four in a row, but it was better than a defeat, which they appeared to be headed for until Manery's last-second heroics.

The Barons' final game in February was played in Los Angeles. They fell to the Kings, 4–2, on February 28. Both goals were scored by Arnason, who was proving to be a good acquisition. Former King Edwards stopped 23 of the 27 shots he faced. Evans wasn't happy with the result, but he was satisfied with the effort. "I think our team played very well," he said. "We're averaging two goals a game and we can't seem to get that go-ahead goal."[10] To be precise, the Barons were averaging 2.79 goals per game. But that wasn't going to win many games in the NHL.

The Adams Division standings on the morning of March 1:

Boston	38–13–8	84	234–148
Buffalo	35–12–14	84	229–156
Toronto	33–17–10	76	212–167
Barons	19–37–8	46	179–257

With six weeks left in the season, nothing had been clinched yet, but the Bruins, Sabres and Maple Leafs were headed for the playoffs. The Barons trailed Pittsburgh by 10 points for the wild card, but Howell insisted his team was still a contender.

"We're hanging in there," said the GM. "Our next three games are against Colorado, Atlanta and the Rangers. If we win those three games and the other clubs stumble, it will put us right back in there. We could win all three if we play up to our capabilities. We're making mistakes, but at least we're trying out there. I can't demand talent, but I can demand effort."[11]

Cleveland's few hockey fans, by March of 1978, had gotten weary of hearing about their team's "capabilities." Ever since the team arrived in July of 1976, they'd been told they'd gotten an exciting young club loaded with talent that was on the verge of exploding into playoff contention. They had seen no evidence of that claim. And they'd see no evidence in three upcoming games that Howell said the Barons were capable of winning. It wouldn't be long before the effort Howell alluded to was being questioned.

The Rockies were one of the few teams struggling even more than the Barons, on and off the ice. But the best Cleveland could do was a 2–2 tie when it visited Denver on March 3. Arnason picked up a goal against his former teammates, and Rick Hampton added the other. The Barons managed just 18 shots on goal in 60 minutes of hockey. The Rockies fired 35 shots at Meloche, who turned away 33 of them. So much for the first of the games the Barons were "capable" of winning.

The following night in Atlanta, the Flames waltzed to a 9–3 victory. Arnason scored his third goal in as many games. Gardner and J.P. Parise also scored, but it wasn't anywhere near enough. Not with the Barons' defense collapsing in front of Edwards, who was peppered with 42 shots. The Barons got off just 17. So much for the second game Cleveland was "capable" of winning.

After the debacle in Atlanta, a discouraged Evans admitted that it appeared some of his players had quit on him, themselves, and the team. It was a dangerous admission for a coach to make. He wouldn't identify the players he believed had "packed it in" for the season. "I get encouraged some games, then I get depressed," he said. Evans said the Barons' attitude was still positive, yet "the talk and the bounce is still there, but nothing happens. They get out on the ice and then nothing. I thought it was better than it is. But I can't think that way forever. When you win just two games in February and you're fighting for a playoff spot, you have to look at it realistically. I can't make excuses for that."[12]

Howell said he'd been trying to make more trades to rebuild the team but found no takers for the players he was offering ... and that was just about everyone in a Barons uniform, with the likely exceptions of Meloche and Dennis Maruk. "You'd be surprised how many guys have over-rated their abilities," he said. "A good number of them are not wanted by anybody in the league."[13] What Howell didn't say ... but should have ... was that he and Evans were just as guilty as the players of over-rating their talent.

George Gund III still believed in that talent. Gund was in Cleveland to preside over the opening of the Barons' team souvenir shop on Euclid Avenue in the city's downtown shopping district (what was left of it). He said the Barons lacked motivation. "They have the ability," the team's majority owner claimed. "The question is motivating it. There certainly is a lot of room for improvement."[14] He said nothing about Evans, but his comment couldn't have made his coach feel more secure about his job.

The opening of a souvenir shop downtown was interpreted (incorrectly) as a sign that, in spite of the meager attendance at the team's games, the Gunds were committed to their three-year plan to establish the Barons in Cleveland. The end of the first year was approaching.

Rich Passan told his readers in his March 5 column that the Gunds had met with the team earlier in the year and assured them the club was financially stable and would stay in Cleveland. He didn't explain why the owners felt such a meeting was necessary. Passan didn't say when the meeting took place, but it is logical to guess it was in November, shortly after the president of the NHL Players Association, Alan Eagleson, expressed his belief that hockey just wasn't working in Cleveland, and the Barons would fold before the end of the season. The Gunds may have felt it was important to assure their employees that Eagleson didn't know what he was talking about ... at least as far as the team folding. The Gunds had the money to meet every payroll, even if it was coming out of their own pockets and not out of the club's profits, of which there were none. Mel Swig admitted in January of 1977 that he had the money to meet the payroll but didn't think he should continue paying his players out of his personal bank account. Businesses aren't supposed to work that way, and when they do, they don't remain in business for long. And the Barons wouldn't.

Passan said the players promptly thanked the Gunds for meeting their financial obligations on time by kicking them in the teeth with their uninspired performance on the ice, which continued when they were blown out of Madison Square Garden by the Rangers, 6–1, on March 8. The Rangers were one of the three teams the Barons would have to pass in the standings if they were going to grab the wild card. The game's only bright spot was defenseman Butch Baby's first NHL goal. Baby had

been summoned from the minor leagues days before the game, as Howell shuffled personnel in an effort to break his club's slump which, with
every passing game, appeared to be not a slump, but a true indication of
its ability. Veteran defenseman Jim Neilson admitted as much after the
loss to the Rangers.

"Maybe we just don't have the horses," he sighed. Neilson said the
kind of sniping and finger-pointing that often accompanies losing had
broken out in the Barons' dressing room. He said the defensemen were
criticizing the centers and wings for failing to score, and thus putting
more pressure on them ... and on goalies Meloche and Edwards, who
knew they'd lose if they gave up more than two goals. Neilson said the
centers and wings were responding that the defensemen weren't clear-
ing the puck out of the Barons' zone and giving it back to them with a
chance to set something up. "We have to start kicking ourselves in the
rear,"[15] he concluded.

"We've got to get the spark back," said Stewart, who wasn't buying
the claim made by his coach that some of the players had given up on the
season. "It isn't as though we aren't working hard. We are, but nothing is
happening. It is certainly not from a lack of effort or wanting to do well.
What we need is to beat somebody 8–1."[16] There were no such blowout
victories in the Barons' future.

Before finishing the road trip in Toronto, the Barons waived defenseman Dennis O'Brien, who was claimed by division rival Boston. The
Bruins were O'Brien's fourth employer of the 1977–78 season. Cleveland also sent center Rick Shinske to Salt Lake City of the Central
Hockey League. Mike Crombeen, the Barons' first round draft pick, was
recalled. None of that maneuvering helped against the Maple Leafs, who
defeated Cleveland 5–2 on March 11. That ended the six-game trip with
a record of 0–4–2. The Barons were fortunate to have escaped with two
ties considering they scored just 13 goals on the trip ... or as many as the
Sabres had scored against them in a single game.

Evans had a simple message for his players when they returned to
Cleveland. "They have been putting pressure on themselves and beating
themselves. It is getting ridiculous. I told them to relax. They are doing
things they were not doing before."[17]

The Barons had three Wednesday night home games left on their
schedule. Management announced that $4.50 tickets for those games
would be sold for one dollar. The first of those games was against the
Rockies on March 15, and the cut-rate ticket promotion didn't have
much impact. Only 5,266 fans watched the offensively impaired Barons score two goals again. They battled to a 2–2 draw against a Colorado
club that was winless in its last 32 road games. But the Barons couldn't

beat them. Arnason scored another goal against his former team, and Baby added his second NHL goal.

On St. Patrick's Day, all ladies attending the game against Minnesota would receive shamrocks. All adults would get a pair of coupons entitling them to purchase a cup of beer for 25 cents. The promotions were needed since the game pitted two clubs riding 10-game winless streaks. Regardless of the holiday enticements, most Clevelanders, with St. Patrick's Day falling on a Friday, decided they had better ways to spend the evening than watching two also-rans skate at the Coliseum. The North Stars came within two seconds of ending their winless streak, only to watch Gardner score at 19:58 of the third period to give the Barons another tie, 4–4. Al MacAdam scored a pair, and Arnason added the other goal. Meloche made 23 saves. The attendance was 4,089.

The next night in Washington, the Barons played like a team that had partied way too hard in celebration of their tie with the North Stars. The Capitals roared to an 8–0 lead after two periods. Evans mercifully pulled his starting goalie, Edwards, at that point to save him from further embarrassment. According to game accounts, however, Edwards had been a sitting duck as his defensemen took the night off, allowing the Capitals to do as they pleased when they had the puck, which was most of the time. Goals by Mike Fidler, Gardner and Maruk in the final 20 minutes made the score more respectable, although Evans didn't see it that way.

"We were embarrassed," said the coach, who was getting accustomed to post-game post-mortems. "You can't get worse than when the worst team in the league thrashes you soundly."[18]

Maruk's goal gave him 30 for the season but was his first in 14 games. He'd been battling a shoulder injury that hampered his ability to put any muscle behind his shots.

Despite the Barons' plunge, Evans managed to escape the usual scrutiny that follows a coach whose team has nose-dived in the standings. Neither Passan nor Bob Schlesinger held him accountable for the club's dismal performance over the past two months. Schlesinger wrote that he'd gotten correspondence from fans who wondered what Evans was doing to reverse the slide. He said Evans had tried long, grueling practices, instituting a curfew, and tongue-lashings. Nothing worked. But both writers insisted the Barons' ineffective play wasn't Evans' fault. Howell was blameless as well, in their opinion.

Boston visited the Coliseum on March 21 and handed the Barons a 5–3 defeat. That extended the winless streak to 13 straight games, one shy of the Oakland/Cleveland franchise record, set in 1967–68 and equaled in 1972–73. Evans praised his players' effort against one of the NHL's elite teams. "The difference in this game was the Bruins scored on their chances and we did not," said the coach. "But this was one of the best games we've played in a long time."[19] A crowd of 6,117 watched MacAdam, Manery and Arnason tally the Barons' goals. Meloche registered 20 saves.

Management wanted to give the fans something to remember the 1977–78 Barons by. Those attending the game against the Kings at the Coliseum on March 24 received a color team photograph. The players were available to add their signatures to the picture between 6:15 and 6:45 p.m. Once the game began, the visitors had the better of it, skating off with a 4–3 victory. It was Cleveland's 14th straight game without a win, tying the franchise mark for futility ... or for ineptitude. Greg Smith, Parise and Gardner beat Kings goalie Rogatien Vachon, but it wasn't enough. Meloche wasn't quite as good, stopping 32 of the Kings' 36 shots. Autographed pictures of one of the league's worst teams wasn't much of a lure, and only 4,774 ventured to Richfield.

The next night at the Nassau County Coliseum, the Barons rallied for three goals in the final 20 minutes to salvage a 4–4 tie with the Islanders. Arnason's hat trick enabled the Barons to avoid another loss, but the tie set a new franchise record for consecutive games without a victory. It also officially eliminated the Barons from contention for the wild card playoff spot.

Evans didn't think the drought would last much longer. "If we continue to play with the same enthusiasm we showed against Boston, Los Angeles and the Islanders, it shouldn't be long," he said of his team's next victory. With the playoffs no longer a possibility, the coach was asked what he hoped to accomplish in the remaining two weeks of the campaign.

"I'd like to see us win every game," he said. "I think we deserve it. We've suffered enough. If we apply ourselves, there's no reason why we can't do it, or at least come close. It's very depressing the way things have been going. When you're not rewarded with an occasional victory, it's difficult."[20]

Howell was making plans for the 1978–79 season. Understandably, he had no intention of starting the next season with the same cast of characters. "The way we're finishing, we'll make every effort to improve the team. There could be a big turnover."[21]

One of the players expected to remain was Meloche, who had four years left on the six-year contract he'd signed a few months before the Golden Seals moved to Cleveland. "I really believed we would be in [the playoffs] as recently as a month ago," he said of the season that was approaching its conclusion ... at least for the Barons. "We were winning our share of games. It felt good, especially after waiting almost seven years for it." Meloche's mood had soured as a result of the Barons' fall off a cliff. "Right now, though, it's a long season. I just want to get the season over with."[22] He said he'd play as hard and as well as he could in as many of the Barons' six remaining games as Evans chose to use him.

One day less than six weeks had passed since the Barons last won a game. As their coach had predicted, the accursed streak finally ended on March 29 at the Coliseum. With Meloche stopping 32 shots and Arnason scoring twice, the Barons blasted the North Stars, 7–3. Potvin, MacAdam, Maruk, Murdoch and McKechnie added the other goals. The attendance was 5,345.

"I think I forgot how to smile," grinned Meloche. "It sure is nice to win."[23]

"I'm going to savor this one right up until the first puck is dropped in Buffalo,"[24] said Evans. That puck was dropped less than 24 hours later, and the Barons shockingly stretched their winning streak to two in a row with a 5–3 victory. Although their season had long since been shot to hell, there was still the small matter of gaining some measure of vengeance for the humiliation the Sabres had dealt them in front of more than 10,000 fans at the Coliseum the month before.

"A little different than 13–3, eh?"[25] asked Potvin.

"You don't forget something like that,"[26] said Meloche. And he and his teammates didn't. Maruk set the tone by scoring on the game's first shot, blazing the puck past Sabres goalie Bob Sauve just 1:33 into the evening's festivities. It was one of only five shots Cleveland managed in the opening 20 minutes. The Sabres fired 16 shots at Meloche. Had he not been on top of his game, and determined to avenge the earlier defeat, it might've been another long night for the visitors. Arnason, Murdoch and MacAdam also beat Sauve, with MacAdam scoring twice. Meloche pushed 34 Buffalo shots aside.

Stewart played a strong game defensively for the Barons in his last appearance of the season. He was scheduled to undergo surgery to correct ankle and knee injuries two days later.

Reflecting on the brief winning streak, McKechnie had a message for those who questioned the effort some of his teammates had put forth during the 15-game winless skein. "We had a bad stretch and it took a lot out of us. All I know is we did not quit like everybody said."[27]

Evans agreed, at least partially. "We were getting good effort up to a point," he said of the team's inability to win a game in six weeks. "That point was when the other team scored the first goal. It seemed to be the end of the game. That is not the case anymore."[28] Maybe not, but the

Barons allowed their opponents to strike first in their next game, and the winning streak ended at two.

Cleveland lost to a St. Louis club that, despite having won just 18 games, was still in the hunt for the Campbell Conference's wild card playoff berth. The Blues took a 2–0 lead and held on for a 3–1 victory. Fidler scored the Barons' only goal. The Blues final tally was registered into an open net with 13 seconds to play, after Evans had pulled his goalie in favor of a sixth attacker hoping to achieve a tie. The loss was the Barons' final road game of the season. Their record away from the Coliseum was a dismal 8–28–4.

The last three games of the year would be played in Richfield. The first was a 4–2 victory over the Blackhawks, preserved when Hall of Famer Stan Mikita somehow lifted the puck over an unguarded net with Cleveland clinging to a 3–2 edge and less than 20 seconds to play. The net was unguarded because Meloche was sprawled on the ice after making a save, and the rebound wound up on Mikita's stick. Chicago coach Bob Pulford ordered his goaltender, Tony Esposito, to the bench in the final minute, and with one second showing on the clock, Parise took a pass from Maruk and shoved it into the empty net. Smith, Potvin, and Gardner scored the other goals. Meloche, who always enjoyed defeating the team that had traded him away years earlier, blocked 34 Blackhawk shots. It was T-Shirt Day at the Coliseum, but only 5,435 showed up to watch the game and add to their summer wardrobe.

The second-to-last game was a shoot-out between the Barons and Red Wings which ended in a 5–5 tie. As if to confirm McKechnie's insistence that his teammates hadn't quit, the Barons overcame deficits of 4–1 and 5–3 to gain the tie. Cleveland's goals belonged to Arnason, Maruk, Hampton and MacAdam, who tallied a pair. The crowd was 5,410.

Howell wasn't impressed with the Barons' respectable finish. When a playoff spot was within its grasp, the team played its worst hockey of the year. "We couldn't come up with the necessary wins in the important games during that tough stretch in February," he said as he looked ahead to next season. "The pressure is off now. The team is playing well, but with the pressure off it is an entirely different kind of hockey altogether."

Howell had worked without a contract all season. He expected to put his name on a three-year deal before the last game of the year on April 9. "It tells me the team is going to be in business and right here in Cleveland. I would hope it's much longer than that."[29]

The general manager signed his contract between periods of the Barons' 3–2 loss to the Penguins at the Coliseum on a Sunday afternoon.

Co-owner George Gund III was asked point blank if the contract meant the Barons would still be around in three years. Gund hedged.

"I hate to be quoted as saying a certainty," he admitted. "It might not be. Saying that might come back to haunt me. Our intention is to stay here. We've demonstrated that already. I'm not going to unequivocally say it will be."[30]

Team president John Karr sounded a more positive note. "The club has not signed a three-year contract with Harry without the intention of being here three years," he said. But Gund refused to be pinned down.

"We're doing a lot of market studies now and hope to get things going for next year,"[31] he said, cautiously. Passan confidently assured his readers that the Barons would be back at the Coliseum for the 1978–79 season. But he'd be wrong. One of the market studies Gund referred to would convince him and his brother that the Barons' miserable attendance was no aberration.

A Fan Appreciation Day gathering of 7,364 turned out for what would be the final game the Cleveland Barons would ever play. Maruk scored both of Cleveland's goals, giving him 36 for the season. It established a new club record, and that record will stand for all eternity.

The Adams Division standings after the final day of the NHL's regular season:

Boston	51–18–11	113	333–218
Buffalo	44–19–17	105	287–215
Toronto	41–29–10	92	272–237
Barons	22–45–13	57	230–325

Instead of making a serious push for the playoffs, the Barons slid backward. Their 57 points were six fewer than they'd accumulated in the chaotic 1976–77 season. Their 22 victories were three less than they'd won the previous year. The fifth worst record in the NHL gave the Barons the fifth overall pick in the June draft. They wouldn't be around to use it.

14

The Survey Says...

Numbers always tell the story of a sports team's season. And all of the numbers from the Barons' 1977–78 season were downright ugly.

Their 22–45–13 record, good for 57 points and a last place finish in the Adams Division, was the fifth worst in the 18-team National Hockey League.

Their attendance of 227,209 represented a decline from 1976–77. So did the per-game average of 5,676. Both were the NHL's worst. The second worst attendance was the 347,000 fans who attended Minnesota North Stars home games. That seemingly innocuous fact would ultimately prove to be significant. Reduced ticket prices and numerous giveaways didn't attract fans to the Coliseum. Neither did the caliber of hockey the Barons played.

Of the most concern to George Gund III and his brother Gordon was their personal loss of nearly three million dollars on their hockey operation. In the same column in which he told his readers of the huge financial hit the Gund brothers had taken, Bob Schlesinger thanked them for absorbing the blow and giving the Barons a chance to establish themselves by not threatening to fold the team or move it if attendance didn't improve quickly and dramatically. The only threat regarding the Barons had come from NHL Players Association president Alan Eagleson, who repeated his oft-heard warning that hockey just wasn't working in northeastern Ohio, and the Barons were bound to be liquidated sooner or later. The Gunds wasted no time denouncing Eagleson and assuring the community that they knew it would take a substantial commitment of time and money to turn the Barons into a winner on the ice and at the box office. And they'd promised to give the community three years to respond to their efforts. The first of those three years was in the books, and the books were written in bright red ink. The community's response was, to say the least, not encouraging.

Still, no one really expected the Barons not to be open for business at the same old stand come October of 1978. Why else would they have opened a team souvenir shop in downtown Cleveland in February? Why would the Gunds have signed Harry Howell to a three-year contract? Why would they have submitted 50 preferred playing dates for the 1978–79 season to the NHL's schedule maker? Yes, the Gunds had sustained an enormous financial loss in their first season as owners of the Barons. And they were expected to swallow hard and prepare for another financial bath in 1978–79. It was their responsibility to give Cleveland's hockey fans a product they'd want to support. Then, of course, it would be the responsibility of those fans to support it.

The Gunds looked at the attendance figures after each home game and wondered just how many hockey fans there were in northeastern Ohio. Had they over-estimated the area's interest in the sport? They hired a marketing firm to find out. And the result would seal the Barons' fate.

The Barons conducted routine business through the month of May, while the teams remaining in the playoffs battled for the Stanley Cup.

Barons team president John Karr (left) at the party celebrating the return of general manager Harry Howell (center) and trainer Gerry Dean (right) from Team Canada competition in May of 1978. A few weeks later, the Barons were merged with the Minnesota North Stars and the NHL's brief stay in northeastern Ohio was over (Michael Schwartz Library, Cleveland State University).

When the club's two-year contract with WJW/850 radio to broadcast the games expired, team president John Karr said he'd put the rights up for bid. He said the Barons had no complaint with WJW, other than the fact they'd received feedback from fans about the station's weak 5,000-watt signal. Unfortunately, the only other station to express an interest in the radio rights, WBBG/1260, also broadcast at 5,000 watts. The city's two powerhouses, WWWE and WGAR, wanted no part of the Barons. WWWE was committed to the Indians and Cavaliers and had no room on its schedule for 80 hockey games. WGAR, like WWWE, broadcast at 50,000 watts. But WGAR had a music intensive pop format which it didn't care to interrupt for hockey games ... especially games hardly anyone listened to.

The fact that few people listened to Barons games hadn't dampened WJW general manager Dick Bremerkamp's desire to sign another contract to serve as the club's radio voice. He said his station lost $100,000 airing the games the past two years. Advertisers weren't lining up outside Bremerkamp's door begging to sponsor the broadcasts. Still, WJW thought the prestige of carrying a National Hockey League team's games to be worth the investment. Astonishingly, Karr was hoping to get the team more money for its radio rights than the expired contract had called for. That wasn't likely with just two bidders.

Early in May, Karr denied a rumor that the Barons would merge with the Houston Aeros of the WHA and the team would be based in Texas. The Aeros had been the class of the WHA, reaching the finals of the Avco Cup playoffs three times and winning twice. They lured the legendary "Mr. Hockey," Gordie Howe, out of retirement to play alongside his sons, Mark and Marty. The fact that a man in his 50s could put up the numbers Gordie did (369 points in 285 games with Houston) may have been a testament to the man's talent, or an indictment of the caliber of hockey played in the WHA. Or a bit of both. Aeros owner Ken Schnitzer said in April that the Aeros wouldn't return to the WHA in 1978–79, if there was a WHA to return to. Rumors were again flying that the two leagues would combine into an expanded NHL. Not all of the WHA's teams would be included. Schnitzer planned to petition the NHL for membership, and, if denied, would fold his club. He said he'd approached the Gunds about merging the Aeros and the Barons.

"I don't know of any discussions," Karr said. "If there had been any kind of serious discussions, I'm sure [the Gunds] would have mentioned them to me. It would be accurate to say it's full steam ahead for the Cleveland Barons for 1978–79."[1] Karr said he was certain that if Schnitzer had tried to initiate such a conversation, the Gunds would've told him to go soak his head.

Gordon Gund, who rarely made public comments, felt compelled to address the rumor personally. "We haven't entered into negotiations with anyone or even gotten into discussions about what kind of arrangements would be offered to move the team," he said. As to the plans he and his brother had for the upcoming season, Gordon said, "there's no way that we'd go ahead with another season unless we were prepared to make substantial improvements."[2]

In a column in the *Press* soon afterward, Schlesinger noted that a marketing survey for which the Gunds paid $25,000 had recently been completed, and the results were being studied by the owners. Plans for the 1978–79 season would be based on the findings of that survey. Schlesinger wrote that, after losing nearly three million dollars on the 1977–78 hockey season, operating the Barons for even one more year would be "a civic act of financial heroism." The word "lunacy" might well have been substituted for "heroism." And while the Gunds had more millions available to lose on the Barons, they were not lunatics.

On August 17, 1977, the Barons had traded hot-headed defenseman Len Frig to the Blues. The team, and the media, then spent the first three months of the season moaning about the fact Cleveland's defenders were too docile to compete in the NHL. In truth, Frig probably wouldn't have helped. The Blues were every bit as weak as the Barons, yet Frig wound up being sent to the minor leagues. The deal was among Howell's first, and he waited nine months for it to bear fruit. In exchange for Frig, the Barons received the negotiating rights to center Mike Eaves, who was about to start his senior year at the University of Wisconsin. When the year was over, the 21-year-old Eaves had accumulated 267 career points on 94 goals and 173 assists for the Badgers. He led the team to the 1977 NCAA hockey championship.

On May 24, the Barons signed Eaves to a three-year contract. Financial terms weren't disclosed. He said he never seriously considered signing with a WHA team. He also said he was pleased St. Louis had traded his rights to Cleveland. Eaves said that he rarely heard from the Blues while he was on their negotiating list. As soon as his rights were acquired by the Barons, he said they were in regular contact with him. The Barons hoped Eaves could do what their top three picks in the 1977 draft had proven unable to do: score goals. Mike Crombeen and Danny Chicoine, despite impressive junior league statistics, had been busts. Reg Kerr was traded to Chicago to reacquire some of the toughness the Barons had parted with when they sent Frig away.

Howell said money would not stand in the way of the Barons improving their roster for the 1978–79 season. If there was a superstar free agent who could help the club make the playoffs, he had the authority to make a competitive offer. "If there is a player available who could give us a chance to get to the playoffs, we're going to go after him."[3] But Howell added that, in his opinion, no one with such talent was on the market. And getting such a player to sign with the pitiful Barons probably would've been a Herculean task ... although money does talk, and loudly, in professional sports.

Howell's first task was to sign right wing Chuck Arnason, whose contract had expired. He responded to critics who said he should've offered Arnason an extension when he was obtained from Colorado at mid-season, when he might've been willing to sign just to have some security. Now that he'd proven his worth by scoring 21 goals in 40 games for the Barons, his price tag had increased substantially. But Howell defended his inaction by noting that Arnason had been gathering splinters on the Rockies' bench, and was likely headed for the minor leagues, when Cleveland obtained him. Signing him at that point was a gamble Howell wasn't willing to take. How would the writers have responded if Howell had given Arnason a new deal and he wound up doing no more for the Barons than he'd done for the Rockies? The fact that he was about to become a free agent may have provided Arnason with additional incentive, from which the Barons benefited.

Arnason was available to any team in the NHL or WHA. The WHA's Winnipeg Jets were expected to make him an offer, and they had an enticement the Barons couldn't match. Winnipeg was just 120 miles from his home. Arnason's agent said his client had enjoyed his brief stay in Cleveland and was willing to return for the right deal. "I feel we've made a substantial and fair offer," said Howell. "But, of course, there's been some funny numbers thrown out by the WHA. The thing is, if you're a player, where do you want to play? If it's me, I go where I know I'm going to get paid, and in the WHA that's not always a certainty."[4] The last comment, if read by any Barons players, may have made them chuckle. They'd been there and done that ... although not since the Gund brothers had taken over.

Howell didn't think he'd be able to re-sign Cleveland's other free agent, back-up goaltender Gary Edwards. He said he'd received Edwards' salary demands, and his response had been a terse "no way!"

Fred Ahern returned to the Barons in late May. Not because they wanted him, but because the Rockies didn't. Ahern had been part of the deal that brought Arnason to Cleveland, but the deal included a clause that allowed Colorado to sell Ahern's contract, which had two years remaining, back to the Barons if they decided they didn't want his services. And they didn't. Ahern scored five goals and assisted on 13 more for 18 points in 36 games for Colorado. Rockies general manager Ray

Miron said that kind of production didn't warrant paying him what his contract called for. The Barons paid slightly less than the $20,000 waiver price to return Ahern to the fold.

On the topic of the Rockies, Rich Passan noted in his Sunday, May 28 column in the *Plain Dealer* that they'd started their season ticket drive for the 1978–79 season the day after their 1977–78 season ended. That was April 4, the same day the Barons' off-season began. The NHL's other relocated franchise had fared almost as poorly at the box office as the Barons, but seemed determined to do something about it. The Barons' sales department was sitting on its hands, and Passan wanted an explanation. The Barons were the only NHL team not selling season tickets. They were the only team in any professional sport not selling season tickets. Passan also wanted to know why no one had heard "one word as to next season" from Karr, aside from his denial of the rumor that the Barons were on their way to Houston. All that was heard from the team president were pleas for patience. He reminded everyone that the Gund brothers wanted to do things right, and the process of making hockey work in northeastern Ohio shouldn't be rushed.

Sounding much like Schlesinger, his counterpart with the *Press*, Passan wrote that "George and Gordon Gund do not have a bottomless pit of cash. They cannot—and will not—take financial slaughterings, and who can blame them?" Passan also mentioned the same marketing survey that Schlesinger had written about. He said it had been two weeks since the survey was completed and presented to the Gunds. Plans for the 1978–79 season were to be based on the results of the survey. When, Passan asked, were those plans going to be put in place?

It would soon be revealed that the plans were already in place. Their secrecy was being closely guarded by the Gund brothers and Karr because they didn't include operating the Barons in Cleveland in 1978–79.

Less than a week before the NHL's summer meeting began on June 12, it was revealed that the Gunds had sounded out the management of New York's Madison Square Garden as to the possibility of playing as many as 20 Barons home games there during the 1978–79 and 1979–80 seasons. The feelers were sent out mid-way through the recently completed season. The Gunds were reported to be preparing to move the Barons into an arena across the river from New York in the New Jersey Meadowlands that would open in the fall of 1980. George Gund denied vehemently that a deal had been reached and insisted instead that the plan had been abandoned.

"We were looking at it as a possible alternative for the future if things did not work out in Cleveland," he explained. "It was a long shot and no one was serious about it. I deny categorically that a move is being contemplated. We are not going to be there. It doesn't make any sense. It would be like playing in Cleveland and Pittsburgh. This is something we are not doing."[5] Gund said the Barons would play all 40 of their home games during the upcoming season at the Coliseum.

Within 24 hours, Gund had changed his tune. The Barons weren't going to play part of their schedule in New York, but he couldn't promise that they'd play in Cleveland, either. He admitted that he'd been in negotiations with another NHL franchise about a merger. The combined clubs would not be based in Cleveland. "I can't say which people we have talked to. That would mess it up. Then we would have to fold and auction off the players. Anything said now makes it more difficult."[6] Gund said some NHL owners favored a merger, others didn't.

The team the Barons were talking with was the Minnesota North Stars. George Gund and North Stars owner Walter Bush crossed paths while in Prague, Czechoslovakia, in April attending the World Hockey Championships. Both teams were in trouble, on the ice and off. The Barons would finish 18th out of 18 teams in attendance. The North Stars would finish 17th. The idea of merging two terrible teams into one (hopefully) mediocre team came up. It was pursued and progressed rapidly. By mid–June, the Gunds and Bush were ready to present their plan to the Board of Governors.

Gund said the results of the marketing survey he and his brother had commissioned toward the end of the 1977–78 season convinced them northeastern Ohio wouldn't support an NHL franchise. "It showed only eight per cent of the Crusaders fans are coming to our games. Why is that? Is it something we've done? That's a shocking thing. Maybe it was the way we came in. We learned a lot of things, but perhaps it is too late to turn it around. Eventually, maybe people in Cleveland will want hockey, when the atmosphere is better."[7] But the Gunds had reached the conclusion that Cleveland didn't want hockey in the late 1970s. And they weren't going to try to force the NHL on a community that wasn't interested.

"If we can't do it right, it's best not to do it at all," he continued. "What incentives do we have to bring in people? The people pay the money. How can we improve the team without more dollars? It's a vicious cycle."[8]

Gund confessed that Alan Eagleson knew what he was talking about when he predicted in November of 1977 that the Barons would fold, probably during the season. "The league was ready to see us fold in December and January when we ran out of money in the original deal," he said. That deal had the Gunds putting up $2.4 million in operating capital. That money had been spent before the All-Star break. Unlike

Mel Swig, however, the Gunds didn't approach the Board of Governors to ask for financial aid. They took the money to keep the club going from their own pockets. "We told them there was no problem. We weren't going to stop in mid-season. If we're going to be in Cleveland this coming season, we're gonna be there for the year. We are not going to come up in February and March and say we can't operate. We want to be in Cleveland. We've always wanted to be in Cleveland. The problem is whether it's economically feasible. If we didn't want to be in Cleveland, we would have folded last year. I'm an eternal optimist. I still believe hockey will go in Cleveland. Maybe not right now, but in the future."[9]

The Gunds had the sympathy of other NHL owners, some of whom sat on the Board of Governors. "They think they might lose another $3.5 million again this year in Cleveland," said one unidentified governor. "Why the hell would they want to stay in business?"[10]

Coliseum owner Sandy Greenberg and president Stu Giller claimed the news about the Barons merging with another team and leaving Cleveland blind-sided them. Greenberg, as usual, wasn't talking. Giller spoke for him. "They made some requests that would give them substantial financial help, and we offered to cooperate with them," he said. "We were in negotiations. That's why the stories we now are reading are so shocking to us."[11] Giller said the Coliseum lost money on the Barons games and would actually benefit by losing those 40 dates, which could then be made available to other attractions ... attractions that would draw crowds. He pointed out that many buildings like the Coliseum thrived with just one primary tenant, which was what the Coliseum would have if the Barons departed.

On June 14, 1978, the Board of Governors approved the merger of the Cleveland Barons and Minnesota North Stars. The combined team would be known as the North Stars and play its home games in Minneapolis. All of Cleveland's players, except wing Mike Crombeen and defenseman Randy Holt, were included in the merger. Crombeen's contract was transferred to St. Louis. Holt's was transferred to Vancouver. George Gund III and his brother Gordon would own 85 percent of the North Stars once the transaction was completed. The ill-fated Oakland/Cleveland franchise, foolishly created by the NHL during its rush to expand in 1967, was officially extinct. It had drained the NHL's coffers of roughly $11 million to keep it alive when its owners couldn't.

Moving the franchise to Cleveland hadn't rescued it. The short, strange saga of the National Hockey League's Cleveland Barons was over less than two years after it began.

"We had an awful lot of people pulling for us," said Gordon Gund at the press conference announcing the first ever merger of clubs in NHL history. "We had some enthusiastic fans. Unfortunately, there weren't enough of them. We have no animosity toward anybody. I'm darn disappointed we couldn't see more results in Cleveland. It would have been a long, arduous grind to where we would have had a successful franchise in Cleveland. We're truly sorry the situation in Cleveland was such that it was impossible to continue there."[12]

As far as the players were concerned, "I think a lot of players will be hurt by this move. There won't be enough jobs to go around," said Dennis Maruk. "We had a house in mind and I'm lucky we didn't buy it. I really enjoyed it here."[13]

"When I left Cleveland after the season, I thought for sure we would be back," said Kris Manery. "Cleveland was a nice town to play in. Getting a chance to play was the main reason why I liked it in Cleveland."[14]

Said Jean Potvin, "it all came so fast. What a big development. I didn't think there was any chance there would not be a team in Cleveland next season. I liked Cleveland."[15] Like Maruk, Potvin was on the verge of purchasing a home in northeastern Ohio. The loss of the Barons made some realtors very unhappy.

The Barons souvenir shop did a brisk business the day after the team died. Any item with "Cleveland Barons" on it immediately became a collectible. On a regular day, the shop sold between $15 and $20 worth of merchandise. On June 16, more than $300 worth of Barons stuff was gobbled up by collectors, or fans who just wanted a memento of the deceased team. One of those at the wake was Marcia Slaby, who edited the team's unofficial newsletter.

"At the end of the season, we presented Mr. [Gordon] Gund with a plaque in braille thanking him for keeping the team in Cleveland," said Slaby. "Now I'm going to tell him we want our property back. We feel we were stabbed in the back."[16] Slaby would get that opportunity, because Gordon Gund made an appearance at the souvenir shop and held an impromptu press conference. He apologized for the loss of the Barons but explained again that it simply would have taken too much time and—more importantly to the Gunds—cost too much money to put the Barons on the same footing as the Indians, Browns and Cavaliers in Cleveland. Yes, the Gunds had promised to give their plan three years to succeed and given up after only one. But the survey said there just weren't enough fans in northeastern Ohio to justify having a National Hockey League franchise. Two more years of losing money wouldn't have changed that.

Marcia Slaby wasn't swayed. She didn't confront Gund, but she did talk to Karr and ask that the plaque given to the owner be returned. Karr assured her it would be.

Epilogue

With the benefit of 43 years of hindsight, it can be said that the debacle that was the Cleveland Barons of the National Hockey League could've been avoided with the expenditure of a mere $25,000.

That was the amount George Gund III and his brother Gordon spent on a survey of sports fans in northeastern Ohio to verify what two miserable seasons in the National Hockey League told them: there weren't enough hockey fans in the Cleveland market to support an NHL team. Especially not when the market was shrinking, and the team would have to compete with the established Cleveland Indians, Cleveland Browns and Cleveland Cavaliers for patronage.

If George Gund and Mel Swig, the majority owner of the California Golden Seals, had commissioned such a survey in the spring of 1976, as they looked for a new home for their hockey team, which had been ignored by the few hockey fans in the San Francisco Bay area since its creation in 1967, they could've saved themselves millions of dollars, and two years of headaches. The Golden Seals did need a new home, but the survey would've (or should've) shown them that northeastern Ohio, in spite of its beautiful new sports palace outside Cleveland, wasn't it. What good was a gorgeous building if it was nearly empty for every game?

When plans to construct a new arena for the Golden Seals in San Jose fell through, Swig vowed to move his team immediately and set his sights on either Denver or Cleveland. A lease agreement with the city of Denver, which owned McNichols Arena, couldn't be reached, leaving Cleveland as the only viable destination for the Golden Seals. The process of relocation took less than a month. Swig moved his multi-million-dollar enterprise to a city he'd never even visited and knew nothing about. Cleveland had perhaps the finest new sports arena in the country, a large population, and a history of supporting hockey. What else was there to know?

If anyone had bothered to try to slow down the runaway train that

198

the Golden Seals Express had become in June of 1976, they might have suggested conducting the type of marketing survey the Gunds commissioned two years later. The results would've given smart businessmen like Swig and Gund reason to pause.

Capacity crowds stopped swarming to the Cleveland Arena to watch hockey on Saturday nights in the mid–1960s. The Cleveland Crusaders of the World Hockey Association never averaged more than 6,900 fans per game. The Barons would have needed 11,700 fans per game to break even. Mismanagement of the Crusaders had turned off many hockey fans. The sport was in bad shape in northeastern Ohio when Swig hastily decided that moving his Golden Seals to Cleveland would be their salvation.

Someone should've suggested that Swig study the attendance statistics of the Cavaliers, who had just finished their sixth season in the National Basketball Association when he moved his team to Cleveland to compete with them for the area's winter sports dollars. The Cavaliers averaged just 3,500 fans per game in their inaugural season of 1970–71. They averaged fewer than 5,200 fans per game through their first four years. It was a wonder they survived. By the end of the 1975–76 season, victory-starved Clevelanders were storming the doors of the Coliseum to cheer their basketball team, which was on its way to the NBA's Eastern Conference finals. Those sell-out crowds got Swig's attention. But they were a long time in coming. Six years, to be exact. The Cavaliers' average attendance for 1975–76 was 12,659 per game. Swig expected the renamed Barons to draw the same size crowds in their first season in Cleveland that the Cavaliers drew in their sixth. And those crowds descended on the Coliseum only after the Cavaliers became a contender for an NBA championship. The Golden Seals/Barons, in spite of lots of brave talk about challenging for a playoff spot, were among the NHL's weakest teams.

There's no indication Swig spoke to anyone in Cleveland about the proposed move of his hockey team. Had he bothered to talk with Hal Lebovitz, the sports editor of the Cleveland *Plain Dealer* and the dean of the city's sports writers, he would've been cautioned against undue optimism. When the Gund brothers bought the team after its first disastrous season in Cleveland, Lebovitz warned them it would take at least five more years before the Barons would win the hearts of the city's sports fans as the Cavaliers finally had. Lebovitz would undoubtedly have given Swig the same sage advice, had he been asked. Cleveland's sports fans were a notoriously tough sell. Swig would have had another reason to step back and reassess his plan. But he didn't bother to ask Lebovitz, or anyone else.

Swig also didn't meet with any of Cleveland's business or political leaders to gauge the amount of interest in his hockey team. He waited until after the Golden Seals had relocated to seek local investors, and then left that responsibility up to his partner, Gund. Gund didn't find any. Had Swig determined ahead of time that there was virtually no interest on the part of Clevelanders with money to invest it in an NHL team, he most likely would've looked somewhere else. Then again, he may have felt he didn't need any additional investors, assuming the Barons drew the kind of crowds to the Coliseum that he was anticipating.

Cleveland's media cautioned Swig that the NHL brand alone wouldn't lure hockey fans to the Coliseum. Swig ignored that. The Barons did almost nothing in the way of promotion in their first season in Cleveland. The fact that the prestigious NHL had finally deigned to grace Cleveland with its presence, after numerous rejections, was supposed to be more than enough. It wasn't. Arrogance on the part of the NHL, and on the part of the lousy team it placed in Cleveland, was frequently cited by fans as a reason they failed to embrace the Barons.

Cleveland's hockey fans can't be held entirely blameless for the fiasco of their NHL experience. They seemed to take an immediate dislike to Swig, perhaps because he was an absentee owner. Clevelanders were accustomed to their sports teams being owned by Clevelanders. They'd largely ignored the Rams of the NFL, who were owned by New Yorker Dan Reeves from 1941–45. Reeves moved the Rams to Los Angeles. When New York advertising executive Art Modell bought the Browns in 1960, he immediately moved to Cleveland and became a pillar of the community … at least until 1995. And Clevelanders seemed to go out of their way to ignore the Barons, even after they were purchased by the Gund brothers, who were native Clevelanders although they no longer resided in the area. But a study of the attendance figures reveals Cleveland's fans were no harder on the Barons than they'd been on the Cavaliers at the box office. The Barons' average attendance both seasons of their existence was higher than that of the Cavaliers in any of their first four years. Not substantially higher, but higher. However, according to Bob Schlesinger, the Barons' attendance figures had to be considered within the proper context. Although they averaged 5,676 fans per game in 1977–78, Schlesinger claimed the Barons drastically reduced their ticket prices to improve crowds at the Coliseum, and often gave tickets away. He said the actual average paid attendance was closer to 3,500. That would be 1,700 below what the Cavaliers averaged in their second season, which was played at decrepit old Cleveland Arena. And the Cavaliers had the advantage of being born in Cleveland. The transplanted Barons, to most fans, never truly felt like they belonged to the city. They just showed up one summer day, told Clevelanders how lucky they were to have them, and demanded to be loved. Maybe that contributed to their quick demise.

The bottom line, as proven by the attendance figures of the Barons and Cavaliers, is that northeastern Ohio's sports fans are discriminating. They're a hard sell. And they weren't buying what the NHL was selling in the late 1970s. Swig needed to know that. He was blinded by the lure of a state-of-the-art building between Cleveland and Akron with six thousand more seats than the antiquated building in Oakland his team was playing in. Those extra seats were empty for 79 of the 80 home games the Barons played.

Swig admitted when he left town for good after unloading the Barons in June of 1977 that he didn't have good information when he made the decision to move the Golden Seals to Cleveland. He had no one to blame but himself. The information was available. A little digging would've uncovered it. If he'd followed the same procedures he'd have followed regarding any of his other businesses, the whole mess might never have happened.

Chapter Notes

Chapter 1

1. Cleveland *Plain Dealer,* March 5, 1975
2. Cleveland *Plain Dealer,* January 28, 1976

Chapter 2

1. Kiczek, Gene. *High Sticks and Hat Tricks,* p. 171
2. Cleveland *Plain Dealer,* May 26, 1976
3. *Ibid.*
4. Cleveland *Plain Dealer,* May 29, 1976
5. Cleveland *Press,* May 29, 1976
6. Cleveland *Plain Dealer,* May 29, 1976
7. Cleveland *Plain Dealer,* June 2, 1976
8. Cleveland *Plain Dealer,* June 3, 1976
9. Cleveland *Plain Dealer,* June 4, 1976
10. Cleveland *Plain Dealer,* June 5, 1976
11. Cleveland *Plain Dealer,* June 8, 1976
12. Cleveland *Press,* June 5, 1976
13. Cleveland *Plain Dealer,* June 11, 1976
14. Torry, Jack. *Endless Summers,* p. 132
15. Cleveland *Plain Dealer,* June 9, 1976
16. Cleveland *Press,* June 16, 1976
17. Cleveland *Press,* June 22, 1976
18. Cleveland *Press,* June 23, 1976
19. Cleveland *Plain Dealer,* June 22, 1976
20. Cleveland *Plain Dealer,* June 23, 1976
21. *Ibid.*
22. *Ibid.*
23. Cleveland *Plain Dealer,* June 25, 1976
24. Cleveland *Plain Dealer,* June 30, 1976
25. Cleveland *Plain Dealer,* June 29, 1976
26. *Ibid.*
27. Cleveland *Plain Dealer,* June 30, 1976
28. *Ibid.*
29. Cleveland *Press,* June 30, 1976
30. Cleveland *Press,* July 1, 1976
31. *Ibid.*
32. Cleveland *Press,* July 2, 1976
33. Cleveland *Press,* July 1, 1976
34. Cleveland *Press,* July 15, 1976
35. *Ibid.*
36. *Ibid.*

Chapter 3

1. Cleveland *Press,* July 16, 1976
2. *Ibid.*
3. Cleveland *Plain Dealer,* July 16, 1976
4. *Ibid.*
5. *Ibid.*
6. Cleveland *Press,* July 19, 1976
7. Cleveland *Plain Dealer,* July 23, 1976
8. *Ibid.*
9. *Ibid.*
10. *Ibid.*
11. Cleveland *Plain Dealer,* July 25, 1976
12. *Ibid.*
13. Cleveland *Plain Dealer,* July 29, 1976
14. *Ibid.*
15. Associated Press, July 27, 1976
16. Cleveland *Plain Dealer,* August 3, 1976

17. Cleveland *Plain Dealer*, August 4, 1976
18. Cleveland *Plain Dealer*, August 9, 1976
19. Cleveland *Press*, August 2, 1976
20. Cleveland *Plain Dealer*, August 7, 1976
21. Associated Press, August 8, 1976
22. Cleveland *Plain Dealer*, August 9, 1976
23. *Ibid.*
24. Cleveland *Press*, August 13, 1976
25. Cleveland *Press*, August 16, 1976
26. Cleveland *Press*, August 26, 1976
27. Cleveland *Press*, August 25, 1976

Chapter 4

1. Cleveland *Plain Dealer*, September 15, 1976
2. Cleveland *Plain Dealer*, September 16, 1976
3. *Ibid.*
4. *Ibid.*
5. Cleveland *Press*, September 28, 1976
6. Cleveland *Plain Dealer*, September 18, 1976
7. Cleveland *Press*, September 21, 1976
8. Cleveland *Plain Dealer*, September 22, 1976
9. Cleveland *Plain Dealer*, September 24, 1976
10. Cleveland *Plain Dealer*, September 23, 1976
11. Cleveland *Press*, September 23, 1976
12. *Ibid.*
13. Cleveland *Plain Dealer*, September 24, 1976
14. Cleveland *Plain Dealer*, September 25, 1976
15. Cleveland *Press*, September 25, 1976
16. *Ibid.*
17. *Ibid.*
18. Cleveland *Plain Dealer*, October 6, 1976
19. *Ibid.*
20. Cleveland *Plain Dealer*, October 8, 1976
21. Cleveland *Plain Dealer*, October 9, 1976
22. Cleveland *Plain Dealer*, October 8, 1976
23. Cleveland *Plain Dealer*, October 10, 1976
24. Cleveland *Plain Dealer*, October 11, 1976
25. Cleveland *Plain Dealer*, October 12, 1976
26. Cleveland *Press*, October 14, 1976
27. Cleveland *Plain Dealer*, October 14, 1976
28. Cleveland *Plain Dealer*, October 15, 1976
29. *Ibid.*
30. Cleveland *Plain Dealer*, October 16, 1976
31. Cleveland *Plain Dealer*, October 18, 1976
32. Cleveland *Plain Dealer*, October 24, 1976
33. Cleveland *Plain Dealer*, October 20, 1976
34. *Ibid.*
35. Cleveland *Plain Dealer*, October 22, 1976
36. Cleveland *Plain Dealer*, October 23, 1976
37. Cleveland *Plain Dealer*, October 25, 1976
38. Cleveland *Plain Dealer*, October 26, 1976
39. Cleveland *Plain Dealer*, October 27, 1976
40. *Ibid.*
41. Cleveland *Plain Dealer*, October 28, 1976
42. *Ibid.*
43. Cleveland *Plain Dealer*, October 30, 1976
44. Cleveland *Press*, October 29, 1976
45. Cleveland *Press*, October 21, 1976
46. Cleveland *Press*, October 28, 1976

Chapter 5

1. Cleveland *Plain Dealer*, November 1, 1976
2. Cleveland *Press*, November 2, 1976
3. Cleveland *Plain Dealer*, November 2, 1976
4. *Ibid.*
5. Cleveland *Plain Dealer*, November 3, 1976
6. Cleveland *Plain Dealer*, November 7, 1976
7. Cleveland *Press*, November 6, 1976

8. Cleveland *Plain Dealer,* November 7, 1976
9. Cleveland *Plain Dealer,* November 8, 1976
10. *Ibid.*
11. Cleveland *Plain Dealer,* November 9, 1976
12. *Ibid.*
13. Cleveland *Plain Dealer,* November 10, 1976
14. *Ibid.*
15. Cleveland *Plain Dealer,* November 12, 1976
16. Cleveland *Press,* November 15, 1976
17. *Ibid.*
18. Cleveland *Plain Dealer,* November 16, 1976
19. *Ibid.*
20. Cleveland *Press,* November 17, 1976
21. Cleveland *Plain Dealer,* November 20, 1976
22. *Ibid.*
23. Cleveland *Plain Dealer,* November 22, 1976
24. *Ibid.*
25. Cleveland *Plain Dealer,* November 24, 1976
26. Cleveland *Press,* November 25, 1976
27. Cleveland *Plain Dealer,* November 26, 1976
28. Cleveland *Plain Dealer,* November 27, 1976
29. *Ibid.*
30. Cleveland *Plain Dealer,* November 28, 1976
31. Cleveland *Plain Dealer,* November 30, 1976
32. Cleveland *Press,* December 2, 1976
33. Cleveland *Plain Dealer,* December 3, 1976
34. *Ibid.*
35. Cleveland *Press,* December 4, 1976
36. Cleveland *Plain Dealer,* December 4, 1976
37. *Ibid.*
38. Cleveland *Plain Dealer,* December 5, 1976
39. Cleveland *Press,* December 7, 1976
40. Cleveland *Plain Dealer,* December 9, 1976
41. *Ibid.*
42. Cleveland *Plain Dealer,* December 10, 1976
43. Cleveland *Plain Dealer,* December 11, 1976
44. *Ibid.*
45. *Ibid.*
46. Cleveland *Press,* December 11, 1976
47. Cleveland *Plain Dealer,* December 13, 1976
48. Cleveland *Plain Dealer,* December 12, 1976
49. Cleveland *Plain Dealer,* December 15, 1976
50. *Ibid.*
51. Cleveland *Plain Dealer,* December 17, 1976
52. Cleveland *Plain Dealer,* December 22, 1976
53. *Ibid.*
54. Cleveland *Plain Dealer,* December 23, 1976
55. *Ibid.*
56. Cleveland *Plain Dealer,* December 24, 1976
57. Cleveland *Plain Dealer,* December 25, 1976
58. Cleveland *Plain Dealer,* December 29, 1976
59. Cleveland *Press,* December 28, 1976

Chapter 6

1. Cleveland *Plain Dealer,* January 3, 1977
2. Cleveland *Plain Dealer,* January 5, 1977
3. Cleveland *Plain Dealer,* January 6, 1977
4. Cleveland *Plain Dealer,* January 8, 1977
5. Cleveland *Plain Dealer,* January 11, 1977
6. *Ibid.*
7. Cleveland *Plain Dealer,* January 12, 1977
8. *Ibid.*
9. *Ibid.*
10. *Ibid.*
11. *Ibid.*
12. Cleveland *Press,* January 11, 1977
13. Cleveland *Plain Dealer,* January 13, 1977
14. Cleveland *Press,* January 11, 1977
15. Cleveland *Plain Dealer,* January 13, 1977

16. Cleveland *Plain Dealer*, January 14, 1977
17. *Ibid.*
18. *Ibid.*
19. Cleveland *Press*, January 1, 1977
20. Cleveland *Plain Dealer*, January 16, 1977
21. Cleveland *Plain Dealer*, January 17, 1977
22. Cleveland *Plain Dealer*, January 18, 1977
23. Cleveland *Plain Dealer*, January 19, 1977
24. Cleveland *Press*, January 22, 1977
25. Cleveland *Plain Dealer*, January 20, 1977
26. Cleveland *Plain Dealer*, January 21, 1977
27. Cleveland *Plain Dealer*, January 22, 1977
28. *Ibid.*
29. Cleveland *Press*, January 24, 1977
30. Cleveland *Plain Dealer*, January 25, 1977
31. *Ibid.*
32. *Ibid.*
33. Cleveland *Plain Dealer*, January 26, 1977
34. Cleveland *Plain Dealer*, January 25, 1977
35. *Ibid.*
36. Cleveland *Plain Dealer*, January 26, 1977
37. *Ibid.*
38. *Ibid.*
39. Cleveland *Press*, January 26, 1977
40. *Ibid.*
41. Cleveland *Plain Dealer*, January 26, 1977
42. Associated Press, January 27, 1977
43. Cleveland *Plain Dealer*, January 27, 1977
44. Cleveland *Press*, January 31, 1977
45. Cleveland *Plain Dealer*, February 2, 1977
46. *Ibid.*
47. *Ibid.*
48. *Ibid.*
49. *Ibid.*
50. *Ibid.*
51. *Ibid.*
52. *Ibid.*
53. Cleveland *Plain Dealer*, February 3, 1977
54. *Ibid.*
55. *Ibid.*
56. Cleveland *Plain Dealer*, February 4, 1977
57. Cleveland *Plain Dealer*, February 5, 1977
58. Cleveland *Press*, February 7, 1977
59. *Ibid.*
60. Cleveland *Press*, February 4, 1977
61. *Ibid.*
62. *Ibid.*
63. Cleveland *Plain Dealer*, February 8, 1977
64. *Ibid.*
65. Cleveland *Plain Dealer*, February 9, 1977
66. Cleveland *Plain Dealer*, February 10, 1977
67. Cleveland *Plain Dealer*, February 12, 1977
68. Cleveland *Press*, February 12, 1977
69. Cleveland *Press*, February 14, 1977
70. *Ibid.*
71. Cleveland *Plain Dealer*, February 15, 1977
72. *Ibid.*
73. Cleveland *Press*, February 15, 1977
74. *Ibid.*
75. Cleveland *Plain Dealer*, February 16, 1977
76. *Ibid.*
77. *Ibid.*
78. *Ibid.*
79. Cleveland *Plain Dealer*, February 18, 1977
80. Cleveland *Press*, February 17, 1977
81. Cleveland *Plain Dealer*, February 17, 1977
82. Cleveland *Plain Dealer*, February 18, 1977
83. *Ibid.*
84. *Ibid.*
85. Cleveland *Plain Dealer*, February 17, 1977
86. Cleveland *Plain Dealer*, February 18, 1977
87. *Ibid.*
88. Cleveland *Plain Dealer*, February 19, 1977
89. *Ibid.*
90. Cleveland *Press*, February 17, 1977
91. Cleveland *Plain Dealer*, February 20, 1977
92. Cleveland *Plain Dealer*, February 22, 1977
93. *Ibid.*
94. Cleveland *Press*, February 21, 1977

95. Cleveland *Plain Dealer,* February 22, 1977

96. Cleveland *Press,* February 23, 1977

97. Cleveland *Plain Dealer,* February 23, 1977

98. *Ibid.*

99. *Ibid.*

100. Cleveland *Plain Dealer,* February 24, 1977

101. *Ibid.*

102. *Ibid.*

103. *Ibid.*

104. *Ibid.*

105. *Ibid.*

106. Cleveland *Press,* February 24, 1977

107. *Ibid.*

108. *Ibid.*

109. Cleveland *Plain Dealer,* February 25, 1977

110. Cleveland *Plain Dealer,* February 26, 1977

Chapter 7

1. Cleveland *Press,* March 1, 1977

2. Cleveland *Plain Dealer,* March 3, 1977

3. Cleveland *Plain Dealer,* March 2, 1977

4. Cleveland *Plain Dealer,* March 5, 1977

5. Cleveland *Plain Dealer,* March 4, 1977

6. Cleveland *Press,* March 3, 1977

7. Cleveland *Plain Dealer,* March 10, 1977

8. Cleveland *Press,* March 11, 1977

9. Cleveland *Plain Dealer,* March 14, 1977

10. Cleveland *Press,* March 12, 1977

11. Cleveland *Plain Dealer,* March 18, 1977

12. Cleveland *Plain Dealer,* March 21, 1977

13. Cleveland *Press,* March 24, 1977

14. Cleveland *Press,* March 23, 1977

15. Cleveland *Plain Dealer,* March 26, 1977

16. Cleveland *Plain Dealer,* March 28, 1977

17. Cleveland *Press,* March 30, 1977

18. Cleveland *Plain Dealer,* March 29, 1977

19. *Ibid.*

20. Cleveland *Plain Dealer,* March 31, 1977

21. *Ibid.*

22. *Ibid.*

23. *Ibid.*

24. *Ibid.*

25. Cleveland *Press,* March 31, 1977

26. Cleveland *Press,* April 4, 1977

Chapter 8

1. United Press International, April 2, 1977

2. Associated Press, April 2, 1977

3. Cleveland *Press,* April 4, 1977

4. *Ibid.*

5. Cleveland *Plain Dealer,* April 26, 1977

6. *Ibid.*

7. *Ibid.*

8. Cleveland *Plain Dealer,* April 30, 1977

9. *Ibid.*

10. Cleveland *Plain Dealer,* May 11, 1977

11. Cleveland *Plain Dealer,* May 12, 1977

12. Cleveland *Plain Dealer,* May 13, 1977

13. Cleveland *Press,* May 25, 1977

14. Cleveland *Press,* June 2, 1977

15. Cleveland *Press,* May 24, 1977

16. Cleveland *Plain Dealer,* June 4, 1977

17. Cleveland *Press,* June 6, 1977

18. Cleveland *Plain Dealer,* June 7, 1977

19. *Ibid.*

20. Cleveland *Plain Dealer,* June 8, 1977

21. Cleveland *Plain Dealer,* June 9, 1977

22. Cleveland *Plain Dealer,* June 7, 1977

23. Cleveland *Plain Dealer,* June 9, 1977

24. Cleveland *Plain Dealer,* June 10, 1977

25. *Ibid.*

26. *Ibid.*

27. *Ibid.*

28. Cleveland *Plain Dealer,* June 14, 1977

29. Cleveland *Plain Dealer,* June 15, 1977

30. *Ibid.*
31. Cleveland *Plain Dealer*, June 23, 1977
32. Cleveland *Press*, June 23, 1977
33. Cleveland *Plain Dealer*, June 24, 1977
34. Cleveland *Plain Dealer*, June 23, 1977
35. Cleveland *Press*, June 10, 1977
36. Cleveland *Plain Dealer*, June 25, 1977
37. Cleveland *Plain Dealer*, June 26, 1977
38. *Ibid.*

Chapter 9

1. Cleveland *Plain Dealer*, September 22, 1977
2. Cleveland *Plain Dealer*, September 24, 1977
3. Cleveland *Plain Dealer*, September 26, 1977
4. Cleveland *Plain Dealer*, September 23, 1977
5. Cleveland *Plain Dealer*, September 27, 1977
6. Cleveland *Plain Dealer*, September 23, 1977
7. Cleveland *Press*, September 29, 1977
8. Cleveland *Plain Dealer*, September 30, 1977
9. Cleveland *Plain Dealer*, October 1, 1977
10. Cleveland *Plain Dealer*, October 6, 1977
11. Cleveland *Plain Dealer*, October 7, 1977

Chapter 10

1. Cleveland Plain Dealer, October 12, 1977
2. *Ibid.*
3. Cleveland *Plain Dealer*, October 17, 1977
4. Cleveland *Plain Dealer*, October 20, 1977
5. Cleveland *Plain Dealer*, October 22, 1977
6. United Press International, October 21, 1977
7. Cleveland *Press*, October 24, 1977
8. Cleveland *Plain Dealer*, October 25, 1977

9. Cleveland *Plain Dealer*, October 26, 1977
10. *Ibid.*
11. Cleveland *Plain Dealer*, October 27, 1977
12. Cleveland *Plain Dealer*, October 28, 1977
13. *Ibid.*
14. Cleveland *Press*, October 29, 1977
15. Cleveland *Plain Dealer*, October 29, 1977
16. *Ibid.*
17. Cleveland *Plain Dealer*, November 1, 1977
18. Cleveland *Plain Dealer*, November 2, 1977
19. *Ibid.*
20. Cleveland *Plain Dealer*, November 3, 1977
21. Cleveland *Plain Dealer*, November 7, 1977
22. *Ibid.*
23. Cleveland *Press*, November 7, 1977
24. Cleveland *Plain Dealer*, November 8, 1977
25. Cleveland *Plain Dealer*, November 11, 1977
26. Cleveland *Press*, November 10, 1977
27. Cleveland *Plain Dealer*, November 12, 1977
28. *Ibid.*
29. *Ibid.*
30. Cleveland *Press*, November 14, 1977
31. *Ibid.*
32. Cleveland *Press*, November 16, 1977
33. Cleveland *Press*, November 17, 1977
34. Cleveland *Plain Dealer*, November 18, 1977
35. *Ibid.*
36. Cleveland *Plain Dealer*, November 21, 1977

Chapter 11

1. Cleveland *Press*, November 24, 1977
2. Cleveland *Plain Dealer*, November 24, 1977
3. Cleveland *Press*, November 24, 1977
4. Cleveland *Plain Dealer*, November 25, 1977

5. Cleveland *Press,* November 24, 1977
6. Cleveland *Plain Dealer,* November 25, 1977
7. Cleveland *Plain Dealer,* November 27, 1977
8. Cleveland *Plain Dealer,* November 28, 1977
9. Cleveland *Plain Dealer,* December 1, 1977
10. Cleveland *Plain Dealer,* December 3, 1977
11. *Ibid.*
12. Cleveland *Plain Dealer,* December 4, 1977
13. *Ibid.*
14. Cleveland *Plain Dealer,* December 5, 1977
15. Cleveland *Plain Dealer,* December 8, 1977
16. Cleveland *Press,* December 9, 1977
17. Cleveland *Plain Dealer,* December 9, 1977
18. *Ibid.*
19. Cleveland *Plain Dealer,* December 10, 1977
20. Cleveland *Plain Dealer,* December 16, 1977
21. Cleveland *Plain Dealer,* December 22, 1977
22. Cleveland *Press,* December 24, 1977
23. Cleveland *Plain Dealer,* December 26, 1977
24. Cleveland *Plain Dealer,* December 29, 1977
25. Cleveland *Press,* December 29, 1977
26. Cleveland *Plain Dealer,* December 31, 1977
27. *Ibid.*

Chapter 12

1. Cleveland *Plain Dealer,* January 2, 1978
2. Cleveland *Plain Dealer,* January 3, 1978
3. Cleveland *Plain Dealer,* January 5, 1978
4. Cleveland *Press,* January 5, 1978
5. Cleveland *Plain Dealer,* January 5, 1978
6. Cleveland *Plain Dealer,* January 9, 1978
7. Cleveland *Plain Dealer,* January 10, 1978
8. *Ibid.*
9. Cleveland *Plain Dealer,* January 11, 1978
10. Cleveland *Plain Dealer,* January 11, 1978
11. *Ibid.*
12. Cleveland *Plain Dealer,* January 12, 1978
13. Cleveland *Plain Dealer,* January 13, 1978
14. *Ibid.*
15. *Ibid.*
16. Cleveland *Plain Dealer,* January 14, 1978
17. *Ibid.*
18. Cleveland *Plain Dealer,* January 16, 1978
19. Cleveland *Plain Dealer,* January 17, 1978
20. Cleveland *Plain Dealer,* January 18, 1978
21. Cleveland *Plain Dealer,* January 19, 1978
22. Cleveland *Plain Dealer,* January 21, 1978
23. Cleveland *Press,* January 23, 1978
24. Cleveland *Plain Dealer,* January 24, 1978
25. Cleveland *Plain Dealer,* January 26, 1978
26. Cleveland *Plain Dealer,* February 1, 1978
27. Cleveland *Press,* February 2, 1978
28. Cleveland *Plain Dealer,* February 6, 1978
29. Cleveland *Plain Dealer,* February 10, 1978
30. *Ibid.*
31. Cleveland *Plain Dealer,* February 11, 1978
32. Cleveland *Plain Dealer,* February 12, 1978
33. Cleveland *Plain Dealer,* February 13, 1978
34. Cleveland *Plain Dealer,* February 16, 1978
35. *Ibid.*

Chapter 13

1. Cleveland *Plain Dealer,* February 20, 1978
2. Cleveland *Plain Dealer,* February 22, 1978

3. Cleveland *Plain Dealer*, February 25, 1978

4. Cleveland *Plain Dealer*, February 26, 1978

5. Cleveland *Plain Dealer*, February 27, 1978

6. *Ibid.*

7. *Ibid.*

8. United Press International, February 28, 1978

9. *Ibid.*

10. Cleveland *Press*, March 1, 1978

11. Cleveland *Plain Dealer*, March 3, 1978

12. Cleveland *Plain Dealer*, March 6, 1978

13. *Ibid.*

14. Cleveland *Plain Dealer*, March 7, 1978

15. *Ibid.*

16. Cleveland *Plain Dealer*, March 11, 1978

17. Cleveland *Plain Dealer*, March 13, 1978

18. Cleveland *Plain Dealer*, March 20, 1978

19. Cleveland *Plain Dealer*, March 22, 1978

20. Cleveland *Plain Dealer*, March 27, 1978

21. *Ibid.*

22. Cleveland *Plain Dealer*, March 29, 1978

23. Cleveland *Plain Dealer*, March 30, 1978

24. *Ibid.*

25. Cleveland *Plain Dealer*, March 31, 1978

26. *Ibid.*

27. Cleveland *Plain Dealer*, April 4, 1978

28. Cleveland *Plain Dealer*, April 1, 1978

29. Cleveland *Plain Dealer*, April 7, 1978

30. Cleveland *Plain Dealer*, April 10, 1978

31. *Ibid.*

Chapter 14

1. Cleveland *Plain Dealer*, May 10, 1978

2. Cleveland *Press*, May 5, 1978

3. Cleveland *Plain Dealer*, May 25, 1978

4. Cleveland *Press*, May 31, 1978

5. Cleveland *Plain Dealer*, June 9, 1978

6. Cleveland *Plain Dealer*, June 10, 1978

7. *Ibid.*

8. *Ibid.*

9. *Ibid.*

10. Cleveland *Plain Dealer*, June 12, 1978

11. Cleveland *Plain Dealer*, June 14, 1978

12. Cleveland *Plain Dealer*, June 15, 1978

13. *Ibid.*

14. *Ibid.*

15. *Ibid.*

16. Cleveland *Plain Dealer*, June 16, 1978

Bibliography

Books

Currier, Steve. *The California Golden Seals: A Tale of White Skates, Red Ink, and One of the NHL's Most Outlandish Teams.* Lincoln: University of Nebraska Press, 2017.

Kizek, Gene. *High Sticks and Hat Tricks.* Cleveland: Blue Line Publications, 1996.

Torry, Jack. *Endless Summers: The Fall and Rise of the Cleveland Indians.* South Bend, Indiana: Diamond Communications, 1995.

Newspapers

Akron *Beacon-Journal*, March 1975–June 1978

Cleveland *Plain Dealer*, March 1975–June 1978

Cleveland *Press*, March 1975–June 1978

Lake County, Ohio, *News-Herald*, March 1975–June 1978

Wire Services

Associated Press, June 1976–June 1978

United Press International, June 1976–June 1978

Index